"Notes"

A Soldier's Memoir of World War I

Clifton J. Cate
Charles C. Cate

Note for Librarians: a cataloguing record for this book that includes Dewey Decimal
Classification and US Library of Congress numbers is available from the Library and Archives
of Canada. The complete cataloguing record can be obtained from their online database at:
www.collectionscanada.ca/amicus/index-e.html
ISBN 1-4120- 5355-2

TRAFFORD

Offices in Canada, USA, Ireland and UK
This book was published *on-demand* in cooperation with Trafford Publishing. On-demand
publishing is a unique process and service of making a book available for retail sale to the
public taking advantage of on-demand manufacturing and Internet marketing. On-demand
publishing includes promotions, retail sales, manufacturing, order fulfilment, accounting and
collecting royalties on behalf of the author.

Book sales for North America and international:
Trafford Publishing, 6E–2333 Government St.,
Victoria, BC v8t 4p4 CANADA
phone 250 383 6864 (toll-free 1 888 232 4444)
fax 250 383 6804; email to orders@trafford.com
Book sales in Europe:
Trafford Publishing (uk) Ltd., Enterprise House, Wistaston Road Business Centre,
Wistaston Road, Crewe, Cheshire cw2 7rp UNITED KINGDOM
phone 01270 251 396 (local rate 0845 230 9601)
facsimile 01270 254 983; orders.uk@trafford.com
Order online at:
trafford.com/05-0250

10 9 8 7 6 5 4 3 2

FOREWORD

My father Joseph Clifton Ramsdell Cate was born to Arthur W. and Maedytha E. Cate in Dover, NH, on October 2nd, 1898 (not a year earlier, as his Canadian Attestation papers attest). Most of his early life was spent living in various New England homes in Massachusetts, southern Maine, and near the eastern Lake Winnipesaukee region centered around East Alton, New Hampshire, where distant relatives had settled a land grant acquired from England's King George III. Early on he demonstrated a desire to simplify and direct his own life by changing his name to Clifton Joseph Cate, although much of his family continued to call him "Joe". His penchant for sketching the things he saw about him, and collecting memorabilia were evident in fifth grade school papers and a collection of postcards acquired in 1908 and 1909 and carefully preserved by him in scrapbooks. It was while he was attending secondary school in Sharon, Massachusetts that events happening in Europe became known to him. After failing in an earlier attempt with a couple of adventuresome friends to "join up" he returned home to finish high school. During his 18th year, immediately after graduation, he enlisted in the U. S. Army. To his dismay, he served only three months before being discharged for medical reasons. Determined to become an active participant in the "war to end all wars," he paused only to attend the marriage of his mother Mae to Herbert White, of Belmont, Massachusetts, and then traveled by boat to Canada to join yet another army. (Mention of that wedding is of interest only in that he left behind a new family that included two young step–sisters, Elizabeth and Dorothy, of about nine and five years, respectively.) On returning to Belmont, 21 months later, he was met by the then seven-year old Dotty, who happily delivered the ex-soldier to their new home into which the family had moved while he was "in the Field" with the Canadian Expeditionary Force.

Soon after the war, he began to organize and write the journal he had kept of his service years, going through several permutations until settling on a format that fully incorporated text and illustrations. The original is a remarkable work of 280 pages, hand typed at four manuscript pages per sheet, collated into 14 folded sections, with over 40 miniature pen and ink drawings, sketches, cartoons, and maps—some in full color—plus photographs, painstakingly placed in and around the text. It was organized so that the sections could eventually be bound into a book approximately six by eight inches, although it never was. Going on eight years later, in 1927, he finally finished writing his WWI memoirs and dedicated them to that "other" step-sister, Elizabeth (known in the family as "Syd") his soon to be "P-W" (Precious-Wife)—and, my mother. The years passed and our family grew to five. Then, the crushing Depression wreaked its particular havoc, in the wake of which the almost fairy tale union that once defined Clif and Syd dissolved. Inevitably new unions formed and soon, war threatened again.

Never able to completely detach himself from the "soldier's life" Clif became active in the Massachusetts National Guard, moved up through the ranks, and received his commission as 2nd Lt. assigned to the 26th Division, Service Co., 104th Infantry, on July 13, 1933. When all units of the 26th Division were ordered into active service on January 16,1941, 1st Lt. Cate was among those who reported. Stateside duty, primarily involving the training of infantry recruits, saw him promoted to Captain–Infantry (March 18, 1941), Major–Infantry (June 4, 1942), and on June 22, 1943, to Lieutenant Colonel, Infantry, the grade he held when relieved from active duty in July, 1944.

After the war he established and operated a hardware store for several years in Shrewsbury, Massachusetts, until retiring to the Lake Winnipesaukee, New Hampshire region, which had been his family's ancestral seat for nine or ten generations. In South Effingham, NH he served as Town Clerk and was an active member of the fire and police departments until his death on September 10, 1975. The South Effingham Fire Department building, the construction of which he campaigned for tirelessly, bears a dedication in his memory in recognition of his many civic contributions. Surviving him are three daughters and a son not one of whom ever heard him speak much of his experience in the Great War, except in vague or much abbreviated terms.

It was not until after my father's death that his "Notes" and the "Kit Bag" full of his souvenirs came into my possession, and then my own life was so full of what I thought were more important things, that it was years more before I gave them their most deserved attention. I have embraced them now and marvel at the tour-de-force effort the original manuscript demanded, and can scarcely hold back my sadness knowing that the wonderment, the questions that I might have expressed and asked—want still to ask—can never be properly addressed or satisfied, victims really, of lives moving on too quickly, of children who may not even have known what questions to ask, and of fathers too burdened or too busy to listen. And, I wonder also whether I have talked enough of such things with my own sons? The story is Clif Cate's. I have included here all of his "Notes" that seem relevant, preserving his text and the arrangement of its illustrations essentially as he had them, corrected some of the typos, misspellings, added scans of appropriate surviving memorabilia and here and there (but not in all cases) made a grammatical change. For the experience this work has given me, I remain thoroughly humbled by and grateful to the author, and am pleased to finally have the opportunity to share his words with his family and friends.

The source for many of my father's statistical and historical facts was: *Europe Since Waterloo*, William Stearns Davis, The Century Company, New York,

1926. An invaluable source of text and maps allowing me to trace the movements of the 12th Battery across France and Belgium was: *Canadian Expeditionary Force 1914–1919, Official History of the Canadian Army in the First World War*, Colonel G. W. L. Nichollson, C.D., Roger Duhamel, F.R.S.C., Queen's Printer and Controller of Stationery, Ottawa, 1962. I have attempted as much as possible to verify and correctly represent the sources of all poems, sayings and quotations attributed to others by my father as they appear throughout the manuscript. Some, however (Patrique Robichaud's ballad, the night time lament of the lonely soldier on sentry duty, the song of homeward-bound Canadians, and there are others...) elude me still, but not for lack of trying.

Prior to completion of the full manuscript in its final form, an abbreviated version consisting of excerpts that contained about forty percent of the original narrative plus a small number of drawings and photographs was published in the 2002 double-edition of, *War, Literature & the Arts:* An International Journal of the Humanities. One evening a couple of months after its release, I received a telephone call from a man who responded to my "Hello!" by asking if I were Charles Cate. On hearing my guarded, "Yes", the caller identified himself as Charles Louis Bosdet III! After a moment of silence during which I processed the impact of this assertion, he volunteered apologetically that perhaps he had made a mistake and called the wrong number. I replied that no, it was indeed the correct one. Thus it was that I became acquainted with the grandson of the "oldest and wisest" of the four comrades named in my father's memoir as the "Big Four." Charles III had seen the abbreviated article and had been astonished to read of events and names, and to have seen drawings and photos of people and places his grandfather had recorded and stored in his own carefully preserved diary of *his* sojourn with the CEF during the Great War. I don't know what the odds are of such a chance meeting taking place, but the fact of it having happened could not help but have pleased my father and Charles' grandfather, "Bodie", wherever they may be...and I can't help hoping that some day, Alexander Nelson Cameron's son or daughter may yet turn up as well, and that somewhere, in the ether, all four friends meet regularly to talk of old times.

C.C.C.
May, 2003

CJC at his desk in May, 1921

TABLE OF CONTENTS

CHAPTER SUMMARIES

Chapter I. *Preliminary and Other Notes*: Introductory Wars, Balkans, Austrian-Serbian friction, Blood-bonds, Princip of Bosnia, Archduke Francis Ferdinand, the assassination, Austrian demands on Serbia.

Chapter II. *United States Army*: War, Enlistment, 1st Massachusetts Ambulance Corps, The Commonwealth Armory, Framingham, Early training, Federal inspection, Discharge, A decision, British Mission, Belmont, Canada, Fredericton.

Chapter III. *Canadian Army–in Canada*: Enlistment, C.A.M.C., West St. John, 8th F. A.C., Training, 9th O.S. Bty., Martello Hotel, Partridge Island, Drill, St. John, Chinese Labor Corps, Halifax explosion, The Grampian at sea, North Sea, Scotland, Grennnock, Clyde, Glasgow, Carlisle.

Chapter IV. *Canadian Army–British Isles, "Before France"*: Witley Camp, 12th Bty., C.G.A. (6-inch howitzers), 1st Leave of absence, Edinburgh, London, Broughty Ferry, Dundee, South Minden, Deepcut Camp, Lydd, Codford, 2nd Leave, Canterbury, Preston, Blackpool, Liverpool, Chester, North Wales, Conway, From pleasure to business at hand.

Chapter V. *Canadian Army–in France*: Le Havre, Rouen, St. Pol, Action, Vimy, Nine Elmes, Blavincourt, Arras, Dainville, Before the Somme Drive, Amiens, Death Valley, Vrely, Rose of Meharicourt, Grapes, The Long Drive, Cagnicourt, Arras-Cambrai Road, Haynecourt, Eswars, Gas, Hospital, Convalescence Camps, Armistice, Return to the 12th Bty., New faces.

Chapter VI. *Canadian Army–in Belgium*: Boussu, Mons, St. Symphorien, Brussels, 3rd Leave, Paris, "French Leave," The Rhine, Good-bye No-man's-land.

Chapter VII. *Canadian Army–in Britain, "After France"*: Southhampton, Witley again, 4th Battery, Kinmel Park Camp in Rhyl, Wales, Final leave, Ireland, Dublin, Cork, Belfast, Return to England, Burnley, Kinmel Park, Last days, R.M.S. *Mauretania*.

Chapter VIII . *Canadian Army–Home Again*: Homeward bound, Halifax, St. John, Discharge, Boston, Once more–a "civie."

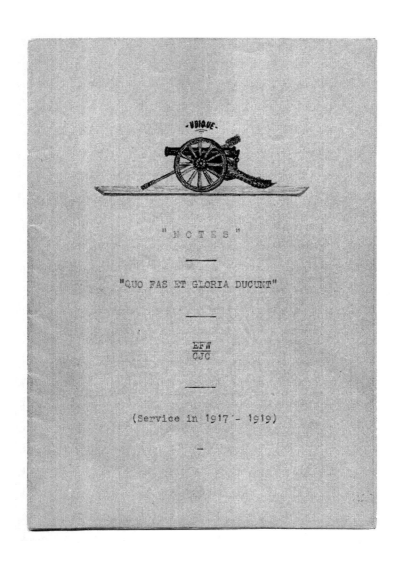

"N O T E S"

———

"QUO FAS ET GLORIA DUCUNT"

———

EFW
CJC

———

(Service in 1917 - 1919)

—

Title Page - Original Manuscript

INTRODUCTION

A Soldier's Reflections

To: Elizabeth F. White,
     Belmont, Massachusetts.

From: Clifton J. Cate,
      Ex-member of the C. E. F.

My dear "P-W":

Seventeen years ago in Dover, New Hampshire, I knew a man who had been a soldier in the Union Army during the Civil War. He was eighty years of age and looked older—certainly everything about him suggested the late winter of life. Wrinkled, withered, crippled, almost deaf and blind, unable to talk above a whisper—and even then one had to sense the thought he tried to express. Trembling, tottering, on the brink of his grave, yet he lived, for there was one spark within his life that refused to retire—or retreat. Heart, soul, and body he was a Union soldier. The thought of it brought life into his eyes, expression into his face, a semblance of strength into his body and he would show a young friend the livid scar that was caused by hot, jagged metal as a shell-splinter all but tore away his right side in battle—all of fifty years before. Then he would tell "his" story of the war as though it had just happened. It was very interesting to a twelve-year–old boy. Listening, thrilled, I wondered how anyone could remember so many things so clearly after so many years.

In 1917-18-19, I learned the manner in which war is burned into the memory of a soldier and now know how one remembers. Once a soldier––always a soldier. As I tell you "my" story of the war you listen so patiently and seem so interested I almost forget that I am talking as much to unburden myself as to please you. These typewritten sheets constitute, more-or-less, "my" story and are written because of the great advantage friend "book" has over friend "human"; the story may be turned on or off as you will.

The war had been going on for thirty-two months before the United

States entered and I enlisted. Almost another year rolled by before I saw "action." Thus you see, my part in the war was a small matter. As a soldier in the line I gave my best as did many millions of others. Out of the line I broke rules and bent regulations enough to make the good old Sergeant–Major shed tears of anguish and cry, "That damned Yankee!" His great stock of patience held out, however, and I never saw the inside of the guardhouse except as a guard on duty.

Part of my experience was not beneficial to me, but the balance of pleasure was worth the price. Though I intend to "read" about the wars of the future I am not sorry to have been a part of the last one. Much enjoyment, some hard work, has been derived from the preparing of these "Notes." I hope that my efforts to please you succeed.

As ever,
C.J.C
Belmont, January 26, 1927.

* * * * * * * * * *

Some Preliminary Thoughts:

"We hold these truths to be self-evident, that all men are created equal, that they are endowed by their Creator with certain unalienable Rights, that among these are Life, Liberty, and the pursuit of Happiness....That whenever any Form of Government becomes destructive of these ends, it is the right of the People to alter or abolish it....But when a long train of abuses and usurpations, pursuing invariably the same Object evinces a design to reduce them under absolute Despotism, it is their right, it is their duty, to throw off such Government, and to provide new Guards for their future security."
(The Declaration of Independence of the Thirteen Colonies)

July 4, 1776...April 6, 1917, a difference of 141 years in time, but the sentiments then expressed are the same. The first date led to our Revolution, the second, to our joining our former enemy in combating another people. War is a queer chemist—in '76 it allied certain of Germany's troops with those of England to crush Americans, and adds to the latter a dash of French soldiery. In 1917 it binds England, France and America together to battle to the end with Germany and still other allies. After each horrible example, the mangled remains are allowed to get together and settle their original differences over a conference table—more or less peacefully—without bloodshed.

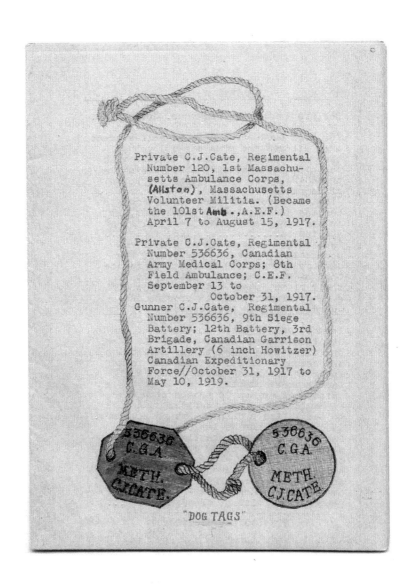

Private C.J.Cate, Regimental
Number 120, 1st Massachu-
setts Ambulance Corps,
(Allston), Massachusetts
Volunteer Militia. (Became
the 101st Amb., A.E.F.)
April 7 to August 15, 1917.

Private C.J.Cate, Regimental
Number 536636, Canadian
Army Medical Corps; 8th
Field Ambulance; C.E.F.
September 13 to
               October 31, 1917.
Gunner C.J.Cate, Regimental
Number 536636, 9th Siege
Battery; 12th Battery, 3rd
Brigade, Canadian Garrison
Artillery (6 inch Howitzer)
Canadian Expeditionary
Force//October 31, 1917 to
May 10, 1919.

"DOG TAGS"

Tours of Duty - Original Manuscript

CHAPTER I

Preliminary and Other Notes

The great struggle between Peace and War has existed since the beginning of history—and doubtless, will continue to the end. The experiences gained from the latter demand preparedness. Too great a preparedness demands a test. No one has ever found the correct balance and probably no one ever will. "There can never be another such war," has been repeated after every big war, yet greater wars have always followed.

During the hundred years that preceded the Great World War, there occurred the war between Gt. Britain and France (followed by Napoleon's exile in 1815); Greek War of Independence (1821-9); Internal strife in France (1830); Bloodshed in Italy (1848-9); Uprisings in Germany (1848-50); Austria's "iron hand" in Prussia (1850); Paris at war (1851); Crimean War (1854-6); Franco-Austrian War (1859); Disorders in Italy (1860); our own United States' Civil War (1860-5); Denmark versus Prussia and Austria (1864); Austria and Germany versus Prussia (1866); Franco-Prussian War (1870-1); Trouble in Rome (1870); Bulgarian Atrocities (1875); Turko-Russian War (1877-8); Armenian Massacres (1894-6); Graeco-Turkish War (1897); Spanish-American War (1898); Russo-Japanese War (1904-5); Turkish Uprisings (1909); Turko-Italian War (1911); 1st Balkan War (1912-3); 2nd Balkan War (1913);—and there were other wars in other parts of the world besides the United States and Europe. Sad experiences all, yet in 1914 the "powers that be" would not, or could not, prevent the greatest of all wars, into which most of the nations of the earth were drawn.

All of us have certainly felt that sullen calm just before a storm which fills us with disconcerting apprehensions. In 1912-3 the greatest peace propaganda of all time swept over the world, while Mr. Mankind settled back in his easy chair, with eyes closed, taking it all in, smiling the while in a satisfied and benevolent way. Victor Hugo had prophesied that, "In the 20th Century war will be dead, the scaffold will be dead, hatred will be dead, frontier boundaries will be dead, dogmas will be dead; man will live. He will possess something higher than all these—a great country, the whole earth, and a great hope, the whole heaven." A wonderful ideal to look forward to but we of the 20th Century are unlikely to realize it.

There were a few in early 1913 who caught a sound of distant rumbling, but it was easier to recline and dream than to investigate. The Balkan volcano sent out distinct warnings. Serbia "the small" trembled before Austria "the great," and Austria trembled before "its own guilty past." More than a few times in the history of the world, had a small nation caused the downfall of a greater nation, and Serbia had an ally in Russia. Russia, who looked longingly to Constantinople—the best road to which port was via Vienna (Austria). The Austrians had their ally as well, the mighty Germany. The disturbing rumblings increased in early 1914. Here and there a few dreamers sat up and listened. A very few, as some dark clouds appeared, commenced investigations, and made some rather startling discoveries. A tenseness pervaded the atmosphere. Then Gavrilo Princip of Bosnia was expelled from Serajevo (the Bosnian capitol). His hatred toward Austria was only too well known. He drifted to Belgrade, where he met other Slavs whose hatred for the Austrian oppressor was fanatical.

On June 28, 1914, Archduke Francis Ferdinand of Austria-Hungary arrived in Serajevo, with his wife. The living representative of a hated oppressor visiting the capitol of the oppressed! On the previous night Princip had appeared at his former home. In the morning, from the crowd watching for the Archduke, he learned of a comrade's unsuccessful attempt to assassinate the Archduke. In the afternoon his turn came. Within a few feet of his victim he fired three shots from a revolver. Almost instantly, his jugular vein severed, the Archduke Francis Ferdinand died. His wife, also hit, died a few moments later. A dangerous calm settled over Europe for a short period, then came Austria's humiliating demands upon Serbia. The deadly Balkan volcano belched forth ominous clouds laden with sparks. Low rumblings became a dreadful roar, heard over the continent. Across the channel the British leaders held secret and important conferences. In the meantime Princip and his wife had been thrown into prison where they died soon after. Daily, the hell pent up in the "devil's cauldron" gained strength. In July it burst forth. For over four years the eruption continued. When the volcano had burned itself out and a form of quiet was restored, the world counted some 8,500,000 dead amid the ruins.

When the Austrian minister Baron von Giesl presented to his Serbian counterpart, M. Patchon, the package (the Serbian Note of July 23, 1914) which, when opened, produced a figurative explosion felt all over the world, I was juggling cases of cereals and canned goods in the wholesale house of Haskell and Adams in Boston. The newspaper accounts interested me mildly for a time and then I all but forgot about "another Balkan war." Germany's declaration of war on Russia moved me little, but when German troops advanced thru Belgium and I read that France and Great Britain were in the war, my mind began to take note. Reading of Canada's first contingent overseas I saw possibilities. Canada was close to home. My age was nearly sixteen. Then my interest slumped again and I felt that Wilson would keep America out of the war and was glad.

On May 7th in 1915, a German submarine sank the mighty Lusitania with a loss of 1152 lives including 102 Americans. From the moment of reading the unpleasant news I felt that the United States should enter the war on the side of the Allies. The President could not make his notes directed towards the evolving events too drastic. Daily, growing more impatient all the time, I followed the reports from the battlefields.

In the fall of 1915 I returned to Sharon High School where I met Cann, Meister, Nelson and other boys of the upper classes who were following the war very carefully. Studies and sports were often forgotten in spirited debates––how soon the end—on whom rested the guilt of origin—what value the war––President Wilson's attitude—and hundreds of other subjects. To the question, "Ought the United States enter NOW?" there was but one voice in the negative. How little we knew the price of glory!

In the summer of '16 I found Grandfather Cate more than a little interested in the war. Blind—his information had to come through the kindness of those about him, but his intuition was rare. Our long talks have since become treasured memories. The grand old man of East Alton, N.H., told me many things, the full significance of which came to me after the war. Groping in eternal darkness he had discovered truths lost to many great men with two good eyes.

Later, in '16, Uncle Sam told me to "go on back to school where you belong" when I tried to enlist for service at the Mexican Border. That troubled me—would I be accepted to fight for America when the time came? Would I remain at home when my pals were proving their right to citizenship in France? Talk of going to Canada to enlist was common during the winter of 1916-17 while Uncle Sam was fast reaching a decision which was soon to affect the life of every American.

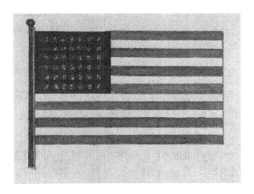

CHAPTER II.

The United States Army.

The United States declared war on Germany April 6, 1917. On the thirteenth, I tried to enlist but was told to return in a month. On May 13th, Norman Cann (who later received several decorations and won his sergeant's stripes in France) and I entered Commonwealth Armory in Allston, Massachusetts as civilians, but came out as privates (stretcher-bearers) in the First Massachusetts Ambulance Corps. "Private C. J. Cate, Regimental Number 120" sounded rather pleasant to me. I began to feel the importance of the occasion, as the following extract from a[n *earlier*] letter to Grandmother Allard indicates:

Sharon, Mass.
May 6, 1917

My darling Grandma:
   . . . This war is a terrible thing, it is just what Sherman said it was. My belief is that the harder the fighting nations go at it now, the sooner the war will end, and God will put things right again—for good.
   As expected, as the Bible says, altho not directly, this great country of ours did get into it. It is a case of war between Democracy and Aristocracy, rule without military forces, and rule with military forces. The result will be as the Bible says, a genuine Democracy, a real rule without military forces and thence without war. Therefore the quickest way for this long looked for rule to come, is for every American, in fact every ally of the democratic powers, to go into this thing, however terrable [*sic*] it sounds and is, and do his or her part by joining one of the three armies:

I	The one in khaki, who gives his life,
II	The one in overalls, who gives his labor,
III	And the one in silks, who gives his money.

In my honest opinion and belief the one to join the first is the man from eighteen (18) to thirty-five (35) who is physically fit for army life, and he should join the department where his former experiences can help him, where he is more at home.

The man for the second is every man, woman, and child who can not be a wonderful businessman, and who can do some work, in gardening, or in factory or in shipping, even tho physically they may not be O.K.

The man for the third is the businessman, and the rich man, whose money will help run the other two armies. Not one of these three armies can exist without the other, neither can this nation exist without them all, right now, and until God takes a hand.

Every home in the country will bear a share of the sorrows, but every true American will take his or her sorrow, as it comes, and not object forcibly no matter how hard it is and no matter how much it hurts, for the country's sake, their own sake, and for God's sake.

So believing all this, I joined the Marines two weeks ago, but have got transferred to the 1st Massachusetts Ambulance Corps, and will probably be called in about three or four weeks.

Hoping to see you all soon.

Love to all, Clif.

There seems to be a minor contradiction regarding the actual date of CJC's enlistment in the US. Army. I can only guess that he inquired into enlisting—or even intended to enlist sometime in late April, 1917, as stated in his letter of May 6— but was deferred (possibly the 1ˢᵗ Massachusetts Ambulance Corps was not yet fully mobilized) until actually signing up on May 13ᵗʰ. In any case, by May 20—as his letter of that date shows—he had already been in the service for about a week, although still spending his nights at home prior to being billeted in the Allston Armory. Many letters written by CJC to his Grandmother were saved by her and are presented in Chapter X, under the second "Letters" heading. CCC

Truly I did not know just what it was all about but certainly I was anxious to learn. Mother's eyes spoke volumes when I told her that I had enlisted, but she said nothing. My chief advisor, Professor Damon, objected to my enlisting so soon, but wished me a hearty "Good Luck!" My English friend Gertrude, cheered aloud, as did "Dutch" Dodge, the nurse. In the meantime, all of the old debaters had enlisted in various units.

Our training began with squad and stretcher drill at the Armory on certain nights of the week. The rest of the week being spent in our own homes. In June we took up quarters in the Armory, and were subjected, as rookies, to some rough handling from the "old-timers," as training began in earnest. Our days were filled with lectures, drill, hikes, PT (physical training), and the ever-present "physical exams" and "papers to be filled out." We all took part in the big Red Cross parade of July 4th. Nights were filled with "good times in town," "quiet times at home," "old-timer capers," discussions, and hearty slumber.

Spirits were high. A mighty army was in the making.

One day in July we packed our outfits onto trucks, and found toeholds wherever we could for ourselves, and moved out to Framingham under canvas. Camp discipline was new—and stiffer than we had anticipated—but we had to like it. Gradually we learned to awake, arise, fall-in, eat, drill, march, work, play, sleep, and live, by bugle and by numbers. We soon knew better than to fill our stomachs with tonic while on a hard march under a hot sun. Rain-trenches we found, kept our tent floors dry in spite of heavy showers. It was all right to argue with buddies of our own rank, but to question the authority of the lowest "striper"—well, that was a different sort of story. Seasoned veterans worked with us and over us—reasoned, pleaded, demanded, cajoled, threatened, cursed, fought, and explained. Somehow we were improving—becoming more like soldiers. At any rate most of us were in better health than we had ever been before. There was plenty of time "off" and we made the most of it, learning the first rudiments of how to have a home in every town, receiving friends at camp, writing letters, reading, and in a thousand ways entertaining ourselves, often at the expense of someone else. The weather was good. Appetites were good. Grub was good. We were comfortable. The "newness" had not yet worn off. Soon we were saying, "This man's army isn't so bad after all—when do we go across?". Assigned to my tent were eight men—two from high school, one from college, a teacher from Amherst, a bookkeeper, two salesmen, and a shoemaker. All but one under thirty and two under twenty. Friendships were formed quickly, some of which will last as long as the lives of those who formed them. We were a happy, healthy lot, fast getting ready, and more than willing for the great adventure.

In August the Federal Army took charge of us. We had passed many tests, physical and otherwise, taken "jabs" against typhoid and sundry diseases after standing for hours in a broiling sun. "Bring on your Federal Medicos!" we shouted in all confidence. They came, grizzled and grouchy. The line formed. Inspection and examination began. But something was wrong. Man after man came out of the long tent with his confidence shaken. My turn came. I passed the body, eye, ear, throat, and teeth tests—breathed a sigh of relief and started out of the tent. An examining officer held me back, re-examined my teeth and said, "You sure had me guessing, but it is no use old man!" "UN-FIT!" A terrible word then, as thousands can testify. My heart sank down to far below zero. All the tricks known to a fine and sympathetic Captain were tried, in vain, to "squeeze me by", and I had to face my comrades and tell them that I had failed. It WAS hell! On August 15th I left the unit to go to Belmont where my Mother lived. My discharge read, "...by reason of physical disability—no teeth upper jaw!" I doubt if there is anyone to whom I told the truth about my sudden leave from service.

August 17th I stood in the sun on the State House steps on Beacon Hill with two other "PDs" (Physical Disability). After some moments of silence I said, "Who's coming to Canada with me?" One "PD" answered, "I was good enough to go with the bunch to Mexico. Now they don't want me. Well—So long !" He walked away. The other boy came with me to the British Mission on Bromfield Street where we told the "kilties" in charge that we wanted to join the Canadian Army. Were we Canadians? No! Then we would have to buy a ticket to some Canadian town. "That lets me out", said my mate, and so it did. I made further inquiries and then, hunting up a booking-office, bought a ticket to Fredericton, New Brunswick, via boat to St. John. I waited until after Mother's wedding on September 7th to "Dad" White before leaving, however, working in the meantime for the Adams Express Company in South Station. On the 8th I left for Canada. The Customs Officer gruffly asked why I was going to Canada. I told him to join the Canadian Army. After a moment of uncertainty, he gripped my hands in his and wished me a hearty "Good bye and good luck, my lad." My first "ocean" voyage terminated at St. John. While on the way the boat had stopped for a time at Eastport, Maine, where on reflecting that there was a feasibility of my not coming back from France, I went ashore for a possible last walk on American soil. During the ride from St. John to Fredericton I shared a seat with a wounded soldier fresh from hospital in "Blighty." From him I learned much that proved of value later on. That night I slept in the Windsor hotel—still a civilian, and an American citizen.

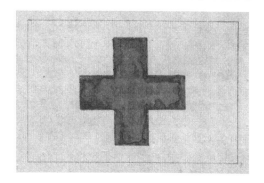

CHAPTER III.
The Canadian Army—in Canada.

Early on the morning of the 13th of September I applied at the Armory for admittance into the army. The OC (officer in charge) suggested the medical branch because of my training period with the ambulance unit at home. Examinations had been very simple, and the Canadians considered me in perfect condition. A sergeant in kilts told me that I was made for being an infantryman in a Scottish Battalion. As I considered the possibility a cool breeze blew in thru the window from off the St. John River, and I thought the sergeant's knees trembled, so I joined the Canadian Army Medical Corps...with knees covered. Temporary quarters were provided at the Queen's Park Military Hospital Barracks. In the afternoon I rode over to St. Mary with a Yankee representative of the United Drug Company, and from him learned several things about the St. John River, also something about driving Ford Coupes in Canada. My only training while in Fredericton came from a friendly old sergeant whose specialty was "First Aid Field Dressing."

On the 17th of September I was transferred to the 8th Field Ambulance Corps at West St. John (Carleton). The barracks were on the docks, and housed the 62nd Infantry re-inforcements, as well as the Ambulance and Hospital units. Here I swore allegiance to King George and the British Empire for the fifth time, was numbered 536636, ranked private, equipped, and put to serious training. Long route marches, stiff stretcher drill, lectures on first-aid, physical training, and regular guard duty about the wharf, made up my duties for several weeks. Sgt. Redfern, the first-aid instructor, had been badly wounded and gassed in action across and proved an interesting as well as instructive non-com, who knew his work and had the needed patience to put his message across to us.

New friendships were formed and from the first I found the Canadians good fellows. Off duty we spent our time in much the same manner as I had in Framingham. When I could, I hiked about the nearby country alone or with mates Swinnerton, Johnson, or Walton to Rockwood Park, Seashore Park or along the tricky St. John River. The forty-foot rise and fall of the tides in St. John's harbor gave me quite a thrill. The reversible falls, over which steamers passed in either direction when the tide was right, and which became roaring impassible rapids at other times never lost their interest for me. The camera, which "Dutch" Dodge had given me was kept busy from this time on until destroyed by shell fire in France. (Its replacement, given to me in England by Bosdet, though not quite the same, is still giving good service in 1927.) Incidentally, I found St. John a "blue law" town, especially on Sundays. It was also a  "dry" town, officially. By the first of October I began to get restless. The duties grew tiresome. There was very little talk of "going across." Thus it was that I applied for a transfer to the artillery.

On my birthday I stood before Major Whetmore at the Martello Hotel Barracks of the 9th Siege Battery—"American, eh! Why didn't you join your own army?" "I did, Sir, but was discharged." I showed him my U.S.A. discharge. "Hell!" he exploded, "Do they think you're going over there to EAT the Germans? I guess that warrants your transfer." So my rank became that of Gunner. Life at the Martello was easy for a new man but we soon moved out to Partridge Island in the harbor where training was resumed. A gunner's training was harder, but there was much of interest, and talk of "going over soon" was common. Spirits were higher, so much so that an oversensitive nature suffered. Our officers and instructors enjoyed sharpening their wits at our expense as I soon learned. During drill one morning I got badly mixed up as orders came fast, and an officer shouted, "Cate—you come damn near being 'late' don't you!" much to the amusement of my mates. One old instructor, veteran of many battles with scars aplenty, used to shout after us

Partridge Island Hospital

as a parade broke up, "Heigh There! Stop your rushing. There's only one Dublin (doubling–doubletime) an' it's in Ireland!" That was one Irishman's lone stock joke, and he displayed it frequently.

My quarters were on the second floor of the main barracks. Cots were tiered three high in blocks of six. When "lights out" was blown, shoes, pails, brushes, and often cots flew "high, wide and handsome," with frequent casualties. The top bunks were unsafe, and I had one near the center of the room. The "officer of the day" usually produced quiet, but often received a barrage as he entered the room. A foghorn on the island nearly frightened me out of my senses on the first foggy night, but like most everything else unnatural, I got used to it. On the island I received my first rifle drill, bayonet drill, and target practice. Gun drill was carried on until we showed possibilities, then we pounded away with 4.7s at targets on Red Head Point across the bay. On the island was one girl, the red-headed daughter of the lighthouse keeper, who knew more about soldiers than the troops knew themselves. On occasions we received passes to the mainland. The trip being made on the tug *Sissiboo*, of which Lt. Walker made his Patrique Robichaud say:

> "De *Sissiboo* is ver' nice ship
>   when she is by de shore,
> But near dat Isle Partridge she
>   roll, an' den she roll some more.
> You 'member how dose voyageurs go
>   sick lak little pup . . . .
> An' every tam de ship go down, de
>   inside she go up ?
> Well jus' like dat an' mebbe worse
>   de inside she is go,
> On me an' on my frien' also, dis
>   Jadus Arsenault."
> *(More of the poem, " Patrique Robichaud" appears in Chapter X)*

Ferry Pass - St. John to Partridge Island

Various clubs in St. John gave frequent dinners and dances for the boys of the Ninth which were always well attended. Incidentally, there was also another battery on the island, the 3rd Home Defense Battery of French-Canadians, whose lament will be better understood when you have heard all of "Patrique Robichaud." Now and then the *Sissiboo* would leave town with a few of us still ashore, make her last trip for the night, and leave us to get back to the island in time for roll call in the morning as best we could. A long breakwater ran out from the mainland to within a few hundred yards of the island, but the swift current of the tide made swimming out of the question. Not only the current, but the winter weather prohibited such an attempt to save ourselves from a trip before the commander, though there is on record the successful accomplishment of a very hardy few. Rowboats often helped, but seldom were they returned to the rightful owner before he reported his loss to an officer. A three-day-pass enabled me to spend Thanksgiving Day in Belmont with my family. Not long after returning to the battery a draft was drawn for overseas. My name was on the list. Those of us who were picked to go were a happy lot, the rest were truly downhearted.

> Anxious to get in the fight,
> Aching to show them our might,
> Positive that we were right,
> Holding our nerves so tight,
> Plunging ahead without sight,
> Signing off day for the night,
> Happily ignorant of plight.

This account of life on Partridge Island seems somewhat less depressing than that expressed by troops earlier in the war as was chronicled in the diary of Gunner Philip McBride who wrote, "We were placed on Partridge Island in barracks and I think it was one of the most dismal places to keep a crowd of men." (From the website www.saintjohn.nbcc.nb.ca-Heritage/3far/index) CCC.

In December we moved over to St. John on the mainland, taking up quarters in Horticultural Hall on the Exhibition Grounds. We were all ready to go across so had no further training in Canada. Our duties were to guard the docks, the powder house, the quarters, and such other sections as were likely to be the goal of spies. The winter of '17 was very severe and guard duty was a cold job. One day we were called out to line the route from a nearby railroad spur to another building on the Exhibition Grounds. We waited a long time wondering what it was all about. Then came the order to "Fix bayonets", as a long train came to a stop on the spur. "Prisoners!" we thought. Then the fun began. Not prisoners, but Chinese coolies, arriving from China via Vancouver, poured out of the cars. There were hundreds of them. Herded between our lines, they trotted along to their quarters, toting heavy bags and boxes atop their heads, laughing, gesticulating, all good natured. My post was near a patch of smooth ice. Onto it ran the Volunteers of the Chinese Labour

Corps. One after the other went down hard, got to his feet, and trotted on. There was plenty of safer surface nearby but they seemed to prefer to slide and fall. I spent much time with them in their quarters until learning that it was against orders.

As their main food was rice, a squad would leave their quarters at mess time, under guard, to bring up the great iron kettles of steaming rice from the cookhouse. Guards were needed to keep the more ambitious ones from running away to join countrymen in Canada and the States. One noon while in charge of two who were having difficulty in getting the big kettle thru the deep snow, I slipped my rifle thru the handle and gave each Chinaman an end. This made the load much easier to carry. Inside the hall things happened. Like a bunch of wild men the coolies crowded around me, making most nerve-racking noises. One pulled the bayonet from the rifle and started a wild dance waving the naked blade about him. Another had the rifle before I realized it, and he too commenced to prance around swinging the rifle wildly. In the magazine of that rifle was a clip of cartridges. The coolie began to pull the trigger and play with the bolt. I was worried, and only after showing real anger did I regain possession of the weapons. The sergeant of the guard was waiting for me outside the hall. The next five minutes were filled with words tinged with fire and smoke, and in the end I knew a thing or two about what a non-com on provocation can say to an unruly gunner.

On the night of December 6 occurred the "Halifax Disaster," when the munitions ship *Mont Blanc* collided with the *Imo*. The resulting explosions created havoc in the harbor and on shore. Fifteen hundred people lost their lives. St. John, with the rest of the country, felt the excitement. Guard was doubled and the feeling of responsibility trebled. Finally, on the 16th, we boarded the Allen liner *Grampian*, starting next morning for Halifax. After a night in Bedford Basin while the convoy formed, we steamed out onto the Atlantic. We were "going over" at last ! It sure was a grand and glorious feeling.

Canadian drafts sent overseas from 1914–1918 included 1,966 men attached to the 3rd Regiment, Canadian Garrison Artillery. CJC left for England and the War in the third draft of 1917—one among a complement of 153 men drawn from the 9th Siege Battery at Partridge Island. Unmentioned by him was that two days before their unit boarded the Grampian *one of the barracks on Partridge Island burned to the ground but by then his draft had been transferred to St. John awaiting embarkation.. CCC*

For thirteen days on a rough December Atlantic the *Grampian* pitched, and tossed, and rolled, and struggled ahead, with every available inch of space packed with men, equipment, and supplies. Conditions below decks were terrible. Under decks were covered with filth in spite of the sailors' efforts to keep them shipshape. With most of the troops confined to their closely packed bunks, nearly everyone was sick. Those of us who remained well did so by spending as much time as was possible in the open, going below only to care for the luckless sufferers and to eat. Mess time was actually a time of mess. The rolling of the ship sent dishes and food in a scramble over the tables and decks. Tables collapsed under the strain. Knives, forks, and spoons were dispensed with, for we found that the surest way to eat was to grasp firmly in our hands what food we desired, then convey it to our mouths in cannibalistic style. A very few of us were in such good health and spirits that we made many raids into the galley for delicacies meant for officers, who we knew were unable to eat. How much the *Grampian* was being thrown about we who were able to go on deck could realize by watching the *Mesinabee*, and other boats of the convoy. Waves of unbelievable size would swallow the forepart of the ships, until it looked as though they would founder, but somehow after a struggle they always pushed their bows back into sight.

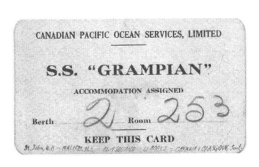

Christmas night I spent on guard duty over the storerooms, and in being thrown between the scuppers and the storeroom walls. Rumors of submarines were common, more or less founded on fact, and strict watch was kept at all times. After dark there was not an open light to be seen in the whole convoy, except the occasional signal lights. One of the best remembered sights of the war was the British destroyers coming out to meet us in the North Sea. The sleek gray speedsters swept around us cutting capers like so many lively puppies glad to welcome the master.

Thirty-seven years later this scene was eerily repeated when I, too,—as a 20-year old army enlistee—spent Christmas Eve on guard duty aboard a US troopship en route to my own overseas military sojourn, one that also took me to duty stations in three European countries. CCC

The morning of the 31st found me on deck waiting for the first glimpse of Liverpool. Very slowly the fog lifted. Gradually green hills and a little village of stone houses with red roofs came into sight. A double-decked tram crawled slowly along one street. Was this the great Liverpool? I hailed a passing dory, questioning the occupant, but it seems we did not speak the same language. Later as we made our way up the Clyde I learned that we had been anchored off Grennock in Scotland. Immediately rumor had it that our pilot boat had been sunk by torpedo, so we had put in there instead of Liverpool. From 10

A.M. until 5 P.M. the *Grampian* wallowed thru a muddy and narrow channel, arriving at last in Glasgow. All along the way we had seen ships in the making, and had been cheered by crowds who watched our progress.

At Glasgow we were rushed aboard trains without ceremony. It was difficult under the circumstances to make the acquaintance of no more than a very few of the Scottish lassies who crowded around the cars. These cars were of the European compartment type and the first of that kind that I had ever seen. At first I was bewildered by so many doors, but in time I learned to like them, for they ride smoothly and permit acquaintances to be made quickly when necessary. As the bells rang in a new year we were riding thru Carlisle at a fast clip, trying to sleep in impossible positions.

1917 was gone. More nations had been added to those already at war. Uncle Sam had been in the fighting line since October 21st when the First Division entered the Luneville Sector near Nancy. Were Cann, Dolan, Jackson, Black, and other mates of the 1st M. A. C. there too? Peace overtures there had been aplenty but the Brest-Litovsk treaty drawn up by the Germans after the collapse of Russia was reason enough that the war must go on. The Allies were gaining power, and yet the blackest days of early 1918 when Germany seemed to be crashing thru were many weeks away. As St. John's quota of reinforcements passed thru London we were all too tired to take notice of the great capital.

CHAPTER IV.

The Canadian Army—In British Isles,
"Before" France

After a run of some twelve hours from Glasgow, and long before daylight on the first day of the new 1918, several hundred very sleepy soldiers were routed out of the train at Milford, Surrey, England We detrained in a cold drizzling rain onto cobblestones slippery with mud. The outlook was none too pleasant. Just mud, and bushes, and trees dripping water. The uplook was no better. It had been raining for hours—maybe for days—and the earth had become a quagmire. After batteries were formed we "fell in," "right dressed," "counted off," "formed fours," and "by the right," moved away by sections. We marched several miles thru mud to a city of wooden huts set in, and surrounded by, more mud.

As we sloshed along, the watery surfaces of shrubbery and buildings, walls and lamp poles, metal equipment, brass buttons and faces, reflected flashes of light from occasional road-lamps. Here and there a comforting contrast appeared taking the form of slightly more cheery glimpses of the bright green leaves and red berries of holly—the one midwinter bit of color. Our destination (always "just around the next corner") was a quarantine section of the artillery area at Witley Camp. The distance marched was probably less than three miles, but seemed more like nine.

Witley Camp! With clothing and equipment heavy with moisture and our feet slipping in our shoes, we entered a barbed-wire enclosure to be assigned to wooden huts. We were issued three boards and two end-sections apiece, which, when properly assembled, were to keep us several inches off the floor when and if we slept. We brought so much mud and water into the huts that the floors became shallow lakes. The air, if there was any (and there must have been some for most of us continued to breath) was so full of moisture that the walls and ceilings absorbed to the point of saturation. Later this became most annoying in the form of steady dripping on us (or on the floor, that splashed back up into our faces). Those who knew how, or were ingenious enough to guess, put the "Five piece bunks" together and rolled into their blankets. Those who could not make the tricky little bunks work just rolled into their blankets on the floor and slept where they lay. Although tired and cold and, I repeat, wet, and a bit "touchy" as we rolled into soggy blankets, most of us were also "healthy kids" so we slept soundly in spite of it all—in this our first night in Merry Old England!

A few of us, up early next sun-up to explore our new home, were surprised to find our huts penned in by barbed wire and guarded by armed men. "What 's the bright idea?" I asked one hard looking "Jock." "We've been cooped up for two weeks. How's chances of getting out and stretching our legs?" "Sure, go right ahead and stretch where you are. You're going to stay there for ten days!" So spoke my worthy guard. He was right, for ten days passed before quarantine was officially lifted, though after six days the guard grew lax and we learned that it was possible to bribe and otherwise gain freedom for a few hours. Quarantine had been necessary however to overcome disease originating on the crowded troopships. On the ninth day we were given an examination and those who passed learned that they were in for a six-day leave of absence.

January 10th camp was broken and we were sorted according to fitness and placed with different units. A new SIX INCH HOWITZER Battery was being formed, into which went most of the old Partridge Island group, including myself. This battery was the Twelfth, and was to be my outfit from then on to the finish. No longer were we to be reinforcements without any special name or unit. We were the 12th Canadian Battery, with a definite purpose before us. With that realization came a great satisfaction. We were an "original " unit, and upon us fell the duty and honor of making its history. Our record though short, was clean. Our pride in our name, "12th Battery," was strong, and later when the old-timers dubbed us "Canada's last gift to the

Empire" we liked the idea. When put to the test we proved a worthy gift—if I may be so bold as to express my honest opinion.

Among my mates in the new battery was Clarke, a schoolteacher from northwestern Canada, and Ferney from the east. Ferney's people lived in Edinburgh, the Princess city of Scotland. When our "leaves" came thru, the three of us chose Edinburgh as our destination. Late on the tenth we received our pay and left Witley. In London we separated after setting a time and place of meeting in Edinburgh for the thirteenth. London is a great town, and the fog, of which so much is said, does not interfere with the pleasures to be found there. My next forty-eight hours were busy ones. In fact, in all the many trips made later to London I do not remember one which was not packed to the utmost with "something doing." There is so much to be seen, so much to be done, so many friends to make, that it seems almost a waste of time to sleep. The first show which I saw was "The Truth, and Nothing But The Truth" at the Savoy, after which came an excellent supper with a jolly crowd at an underground cafe on Fleet Street. My first night was spent at the American Eagle Hut where in the morning I had to steal an overcoat to replace my own stolen during the night. Some of the interesting places visited next day, and on subsequent trips to this city were: Buckingham Palace, Westminster Abbey and Cathedral, London Tower and Bridge, Madame Tussaud's Wax Works, St. Paul's, and places of lesser interest. At sundown London rapidly became the shrouded city. The mists were then more in evidence, and the city's only lights came from weak blue lamps at the "Tube" entrances. Even then the Zep's found London all too easily with their bombs. There are two ways, both interesting, of seeing part of the city. One is atop a bus and the other afoot. Of course the aviator has another way—but his way was not open to "buck gunners". The Victoria Embankment was a regular "happy hunting ground" at any time of day or night for the troops, sailors, and lonely lasses. During the evening of the twelfth, while walking thru Picadilly Circus with an Australian, we ran into a little riot between Colonials and Territorials. By the time the "bobbies" had arrived the riot had burned itself out and I was on board a train bound for Edinburgh. Once in a comfortable compartment I fell asleep and was not awakened until I was being tumbled out onto the platform in Edinburgh by a tolerant trainman.

Clarke met me at the station and in a few moments we were being carried toward High Street by a jerky cable-tram. We arrived shortly at Robinson's Temperance Hotel, located within a few minutes walk of St. Giles Cathedral, John Knox's house, Edinburgh Castle, Holy Rood Palace, Princess Gardens, Sir Walter Scott's Monument, the National Galleries, and the point of interest of which some Scots are none too proud—King Arthur's Seat.

Friend Clarke had chosen our quarters with rare judgment. After a hearty breakfast we met Ferney and his people, and a steady round of pleasures commenced. In two days we saw much of the city's more interesting sights. We had shivered at the guide's gruesome tale of how a man had been horribly murdered on that spot. We had been frightened speechless for a few moments when the time gun at the castle had boomed out the "One O'Clock" with us standing beneath it, much to the wicked glee of the old-timer who had planned the affair, and we had made some acquaintances. On both nights we witnessed fair shows with fairer companions. A trip to Glasgow was made on the fifteenth.

On the following day Clarke invited me to come with him to Broughty Ferry where we were the guests of the hospitable grandparents of some of my mate's pupils in Canada. In the afternoon the old grandfather drove us to a Dundee Hotel for a welcome dinner. It was not until the good old Scot told us "confidentially" that the hotel manager was a German, and possibly a spy, that Clarke and I realized what a rare lot of excellent Scottish hospitality we had been enjoying. This thrifty old Scot was a shrewd business man. His comfortable home, a few moments ride in the bus from Broughty Ferry, was situated on his own land. His own sheep roamed his pasture lands, adding their wool to that brought in by neighbors to his mill. His decisions settled matters one way or the other in the economic and political questions that arose in the vicinity of his home. For nearly twenty years he had gone to Dundee at ten o'clock in the morning on the day of the week that my mate and I had chosen to call, to do the shopping for the coming week and to attend to certain business matters. Even the Great War had not interfered with this custom. When Clarke and I arrived he was just about to leave the house. There was no doubt but what two young soldiers could find plenty to do until he returned. He explained his leaving and offered apologies, but could not break a custom of so many years standing. Certainly not! Then his wife, who was ill and confined to her bed at the time, called to him from another room. There was a great tenderness in the Scot's voice as he answered, and a quality of gentleness seldom seen, in the manner in which he smoothed her pillow on going to the side of the bed. No word passed his wife's lips, but her eyes were talking. For several moments I watched the play of expressions on the two pleasant faces. Then he nodded in acquiescence. What a wealth of understanding existed between those two fine old lovers, for he did not go to town at ten o'clock, nor at eleven, or twelve, but waited until late afternoon when he went with Clarke and me to the hotel to dine. At just the right moment the old man ushered us out of the private dining room and led the way to his car. A few moments later my friend and I were aboard the Edinburgh train, having thanked our host for his many kindnesses and his invitation to come again. Clarke slumbered all the way back to the Princess City, while I discoursed at great length to all who cared to listen, on the merits of Scotsmen in general.

On the 17th we were joined by Ferney for a trip to the Firth of Forth, where we could see British and American naval boats moving about their various duties, and where Ferney told us some facts about the great bridge. The following day was spent on a most enjoyable trip to Aberdeen. In the evening Ferney and Clarke returned to the battery after trying in vain to take me with them. One more day of perfect pleasure in company with a lassie of whom I say little but think much, and then I went back to work. Incidentally, I had to go "on the carpet" before my commander for overstaying my leave.

For a time the Twelfth remained at Witley, drilling hard all day, from five in the morning until five at night. In the evenings the boys were willing, as a rule, to rest, though now and then we attended a show, or walked to some nearby village to spend a little money if we could find any. Then we moved to South Minden Camp in Deepcut, Hampshire, not far from Aldershot, which has been a training ground for British soldiers for many years. Here for some weeks we worked at preparing ourselves for battle. It was in Deepcut that we received our first night training. Day and night we maneuvered, with and without our howitzers. We learned to dig gun-positions, trenches and dugouts, and to understand orders given in rapid-fire manner, and what is more, we learned to execute orders. At this time I was on the Signal Staff. My training was therefore with the large and small flags, flappers, buzzer, Don-4 Telephone (the D-4 type of field telephone), heliograph, and other means of communication. We learned the Morse and Semaphore codes, how to receive and send code messages, how to decipher the Playfair Code (providing we had the key), how to find "breaks" in the wires and how to repair them, what was expected of "dispatch runners," as well as a great assortment of other things necessary to our proper development for the line.

At Deepcut we learned also, how to put on our gas-masks in three seconds, and many were the "supposedly" dead men after a "timed" trial. To teach us the difference between the gasses used in battle we were forced to walk in single file thru a hut, sealed except at entrance and exit, and charged with various of the temporarily dangerous gasses. In we went poorly concealing much nervousness. Out we came (some of us with help from attendants wearing masks, as we wore none), coughing, spitting, sweating, crying, laughing, or otherwise, according to each man's individuality. Brass buttons, watch cases, knives, coins, and any other metallic surfaces about our persons were turned black. Even gold crowns turned color in the mouths of the owners. The gas usually used for this trial was called "pineapple" or "tear" gas, and for a few moments a very small dose could render a man absolutely helpless, though its effect was not permanently harmful. The 12th Battery began to look like a fighting unit, with its days of training fast slipping by, and its "baptism of fire in action" not far off. The weather at Deepcut was a delightful change from that of Witley. Perfect days and nights, with just rain enough to temper them.

Toward the end of our stay there was much free time. Thru the camp ran a canal, so old that it radiated romance. Not far off was a WAAC (Woman's Aid Auxiliary Corps) Camp, and lonesome soldiers found a cure in the girls from the other camp. Bicycles could be hired for an hour, a day, or any length of time for a few shillings in any of the nearby towns. It was chiefly by cycling that I enjoyed my time. There were many good friends and good times in many places: Woking, Farnborough, Farnham, Aldershot, Bagshot, Sandhurst, and a host of towns within a short ride from our camp, and those of us who rode out around the county boasted, and not without some justification, of a "home" in every town. There was a girl in a grocery shop in Frimley Green that sent my heart a-fluttering every time I went there. She was MY girl. No doubt about it. Until one night when I called "out of turn!" But, all in all. military life was wonderful! What was all this fuss about a War? What War? Where?

It was here at Deepcut that the "BIG 4" was formed when Cameron (Cam), Bosdet (Mex), Fisher (Dreamer), and Cate (Yank or Cankee), shook hands and bound themselves together according to the old formula, "One for all, and all for one." In training, on leave, in action, the Big 4 stuck together and many were its common joys and pains. It really wasn't so big, but as a combination dedicated to the welfare of its individual members the group was unbeatable.

There was Charles Louis Bosdet (*below, right*), born of English parentage December 19, 1887 at Arichat, Nova Scotia. In 1911 he completed a special mine engineering course at Colby College in Maine, from which he found his way into Mexico where he followed the mining industry until he heard the "call to arms" and traveled all the way to the "10th Battery" at Halifax, Nova Scotia to enlist as gunner with the regimental number 2100833. At Witley he transferred to the 12th where he found this Yankee. His service with the 12th came to an abrupt end in September (16th) 1918 when he "got a Blighty" in the form of a smashed knee. Much later, after a series of hospitals he rejoined the two remaining members of the "Big 4" at Rhyl and returned to Canada with them. Dubbed by some as "the smiling Mex" because of his rare good humor and naturally pleasing smile, he

was a true friend, uncannily lucky at games of chance, and is yet I presume, as of old, by far the wisest member of the "Big 4".

Alexander Nelson Cameron, 2100743, was also born in Nova Scotia, on February 18, 1896, of Scottish-English parentage and he too enlisted in the 10th battery at Halifax in 1917. "Cam" was (still is, I hope) the most perfect specimen of healthy youth, physically, mentally, and morally, in the 12th, to which he was transferred at Witley Camp. He alone of the "Big 4" went thru it all without any visible scratch. In 1922 after graduating from a special course (won thru his efforts with a Canadian Insurance Company) at Carnegie Institute he visited with me for several wonderful days in Belmont.

Harry M. Fisher—a college professor—was another 10th battery man, transferring to the 12th at Witley where our old outfit was formed. His strength was in a well-developed brain, his weakness a Canadian sweetheart—and his nickname (if you will) "Dreamer." Until the Eswars episode which sent me out of the war for a short period he also served continuously with the 12th and the "Big 4", and because of that episode he too went out of the war for all time. I have never seen him since that night in a dry ditch on the outskirts of Eswars.

The spirit of the "Big 4" lives—its members are separated by thousands of miles, but someday we'll all get together again—to serve one another on and on thru eternity—with perhaps some younger editions of ourselves to help.

Attesting to the hazardous duty of the WW-I artilleryman is the attrition rate of members of the two crews making up the 12th Battery's "A" sub-section. Of the 14 members present on June 1st, four were lost before August 8. After the 2nd Somme offensive, only four of the original crewmates were left in the Battery to begin the occupation of Belgium—to be joined later by a fifth (my father) who returned to his outfit in December, 1918. Only one member (Cameron) remained unscathed. Of the "Big-4", three were wounded, one fatally. CCC

The last days at Deepcut were more than pleasant—but there WAS a war—and one night we moved out on short notice. At the end of Dunge Ness Point in Kent, is Lydd, and just across the Strait of Dover is Boulogne in France. It was to the camp at Lydd that we moved from Deepcut. Here the huts were of metal, and it was well that they were, for at Lydd the gunners got their first actual target practice with the shiny new six-inch howitzers. The rivalry between gun crews, the jarring of the guns as they blasted away at fixed or moving targets, the nearness of France, and a none too jolly relationship between ourselves and several English Territorial units in the camp, sobered the 12th. The business at hand became the chief interest, and in spite of many trips out of town on foot or by cycle, faces wore a more serious aspect.

Hastings, Eastbourne, Foldstone, Dover, Ashford, and the flying school at New Romney, were the more frequently visited places. At the latter many of us took our first ride in a balloon or aeroplane. This "air-school" was American, and their baseball team provided worthy competition for our own, which came very near being the best in the vicinity.

Out on the range, one day, a thousand men were picking up brass and copper scraps left by the exploded shells. These scraps were piled near the narrow-gauge railroad that lay across the range, sometimes in a straight line, though often thrown criss-cross by shellfire. Later this valuable metal would find its way back into the munitions plants to be used over again in fuses and bands. Many unexploded shells, or "duds", lay about, and when found were left unmolested. Their location was marked by placing sticks upright in the shale nearby with a rag tied to the upper end to attract the attention of the Royal Engineers, whose duty it was to care for these dangerous explosives. Over our heads the blue sky was dotted here and there with fleecy white clouds. The sun sent its warmth into our hearts and the beauty of the day was manifested by much song and fooling. For several miles about us the earth was covered with loose pebbles or shale. In the direction of camp there were patches of coarse grass, and beyond them, sand and more grass. Not far away was the sea—restless and mysterious as ever—cloaked in all the splendor of a perfect day. To our right stood a small stone building enclosing the laboratory in which many secret experiments were carried on with highly explosive materials. Here Lyddite had been developed. Suddenly—a roar! Many of us were knocked to the shale. When we were all again on our feet, one British Marine lay still. Someone had "fooled" with a "dud". This was the first of the many deaths to shellburst that we were to see. The work went on—but many pairs of eyes watched the little flatcar as it rolled slowly back to camp with "somebody's boy."

One morning on "parade" we received a lecture from Major Robinson, a seasoned old veteran who had already lost an eye in France while an Infantry officer. The substance of what he said was that—our period of training was over—our instructors had done their best to prepare us for the test which was soon too come—we had "almost" developed into soldiers—we had all the appearances of a fighting unit—we would conduct ourselves accordingly— meanwhile we were to be granted an eight day leave—we were entitled to a good time but must remember that we were Canadians—on expiration of our leave we would meet at Codforn in Wiltshire—that was all. During his talk I thought of Lieutenant Inches, one of our officers on Partridge Island who had said much the same thing several months before, and who, when the time came for us to leave Canada was held behind as an instructor. I thought how much it would have meant to him to have been with us, for when the order for him to stay behind was read, his disappointment had been tremendous.

This passage is particularly poignant as much later, at Camp Rucker, Alabama, during the Second World War, Lt. Col. Clifton J Cate, then Commanding Officer of one of the last segregated, essentially all Black army combat forces to train as a unit (938th Air Base Security Battalion.) was forced to oversee the disbandment of his command after more than six months of intensive training. To watch members of his command being "absorbed" piecemeal into other units as part of the military's desegregation effort while he was left behind, and to know'"his" 938th would never be given the opportunity to distinguish itself (as did the 12th Canadian Battery) was a bitter disappointment, perhaps contributing to his decision to leave the service as soon as the opportunity presented itself. CCC

Spring had come while we were in training in England, and nature had already come to life. For the last leave "before France" Bosdet and I joined lots, and shutting our eyes placed a finger apiece on a large map in the battery office. Half way between where our finger tips touched the map was Preston in Lancashire. Thus Preston became our "official" destination. Unofficially it was our intention to go where our fancy suggested. Much depended on chance and on the girls. "Old-timers" looked quizzically at a leave marked "Preston" and passed us to trains going elsewhere. Canterbury, where Bosdet's uncle, Charles Fixot, managed a hut of the Church Army, became our first stop. A rare fellow was that uncle, and a most excellent judge of good steaks and wine. A remarkable old town, that Canterbury, with its grim old walls and gates, and beautiful historic cathedral. We visited also the cathedral cloisters and Bell Harry Tower, and that "old-time-first" steam locomotive resting proudly on its stand near the locomotive factory. After Canterbury came London, then Birmingham, then Manchester the great mill city, followed by Stockport where we saw how airplanes were made, and then—Preston. As Bosdet and I stepped from our compartment, two girls stepped in. Instantly we decided NOT to stop over in Preston.

Just as the train started I assisted a lady with a dog and a heavy bag into our compartment. The fates were kind that day, for that lady was Mrs. Fannie Thompson of Number 11 Baker Street, Burnley, in whom I found a good friend. It is to her that I owe my thanks for what few notes, snapshots, postcards and souvenirs, survived the war to remain in my possession. When possible I sent to her what few things I wanted preserved—she did her part well. At Blackpool we left the train, and while Bosdet escorted the girls to their home I carried Mrs. Thompson's bag to the home of her mother. It was just such homes as this, that made my stay in the British Isles one long series of pleasant memories.

There were many pleasant hikes about the famous seashore town of Blackpool. On the second day Bosdet and I started out to meet the two girls whose acquaintances we had made on the train coming from Preston, but in some manner we were separated. Bosdet eventually found himself in St. Ames. I reached Fleetwood. Later we met under the tower in Blackpool, and after swapping stories, shook hands. We had both enjoyed the day. Time went fast and our leave was all too short, so we left Blackpool to go to Liverpool. From the tops of trams we looked over the city, agreeing that most of the fine buildings were sadly in need of a sand-bath. We rode along the docks on the elevated train—got into a scrap in St. George's Square—found English "bobbies" not immune to argument—and finally were carried to Birkenhead by ferry. Here we visited the observatory, walked thru the park running into another scrap, which decided for us that the mist from the Mersey was unhealthy. Then we arrived in the city of Chester—one that I can never forget. In this old town that was begun in the year 48, we roamed about for many hours. Here we forgot the war, the Mersey, etc. as we walked along the old walls, climbed into the Water Tower and King Charles Tower, visited God's Providence House, Hawarden Castle, the cathedral, and Eaton Hall, marveled at "The Row" on Watergate Street and its quaint old buildings, climbed over the ruins of St. John's Church, Museum Tower, and the Roman Bath. We wound up our visit with a long walk around the city, which ended on Dee bridge over the River Dee. (There were no "scraps" in Chester.)

Chester was only the beginning of a period of "enchantment." At the station we had boarded a train bound for Holyhead, and as it rolled smoothly along the coast of northern Wales we found ourselves in a country so beautiful that I find myself at a loss for adjectives suitable for properly describing it. At Conway *(Conwy)*, no longer able to sit still, we left the train. This charming old castle town became our headquarters, with a place to eat and sleep, when we grudgingly took the time, at the home of Mrs. Johnson (Number 3 Newbury Terrace) snug up against the castle wall. Many hours were spent in exploring the castle, "Built in 1284 for Edward I, by Henry of Eaton, designer of Carnarvon Castle, famous during the Civil War, finally granted to the Earl of Conway by Charles II," so our fourteen-year-old guide told us in an almost un-intelligible English. From a tower above Queen Eleanor's Chapel, I picked a primrose, a beautiful yellow flower, which I sent that night to my Mother in Belmont. Clinging to the ancient town wall, facing the Conway River, is the smallest house in Great Britain. In its two tiny rooms, one over the other, lived an old couple who contrived to get a living out of visitors. As we roamed about town we found in an old churchyard a grave bearing the well known inscription, "We are seven."

> "And where are they? I pray you tell."
> She answered, "Seven are we
> And two of us at Conway dwell,
> And two are gone to sea.
> Two of us in the Churchyard lie
> My sister and my brother,
> And in the churchyard cottage, I
> Dwell near them with my mother."

From William Wordsworth's "We Are Seven", written in 1798, reflecting on his conversation with the child speaker during a chance meeting in 1793 near Goodrich Castle at Vale of Clwyd. Years later, Wordsworth returned but was unable to find any trace of either child or mother. The gravesite still lies in the yard of St. Mary's Church, portions of which were once part of the Cistercian Abbey of Aberconwy. CCC

Nearby, we toured Plas Mawr, an imposing building that we learned once sheltered Queen Elizabeth. Oh! There was much of interest to see in that old town. Conway is a fishing town, and the river, too, provided us with much pleasure.

As pretty and as charming as the town in which she lived was Gladys Evans—a Conway sweetheart. Bosdet and I argued long over who she was going to save her best smiles for. I reminded him of his sweetheart in Canterbury, but he came back with, "How about yours in the States?" I won out. She had a chum, however, who did her best to console Bosdet. The four of us enjoyed some wonderful times together that April of 1918. Almost exactly a year later I retuned to find dear Gladys about to be married to a "before the war" sweetheart. Good!

With these two girls Bosdet and I spent many enjoyable evening hours along the river banks, on the river, and in climbing about the hills which are a part of the town. Bicycles again came into use and many wonderful trips resulted, with and without our guides, to places with unpronounceable names: Deganwy, Llandudno (pronounced Klandidnoo) with its cable-tram to the summit of Great Ormes Head, and Happy Valley, Marine Drive, the wonderful beach and bay. Then on to Llandrilloyn, Rhos, Colwyn Bay, Dwggyfylchi, Penmaenmawr, Llanfairfechan, Aber, Bangor, Penryhn Castle, Bethesda, Carnarvon and its castle, Llanbiris, Snowdon, which is Britain's highest peak (3560 feet above sea level), Capel-Curig, Llanwrst, and Bettws-y-coed, where Bosdet and I met two other Welsh girls who seemed pleased to guide us to Swallow and Machno Falls, after which hike we were served a fine lunch at the Oakfield...(I tell you, Syd, New England nearly lost one of her most loyal sons among those enchanted hills of northern Wales.)

Over in France the Hun was advancing all along the line. His guns were playing havoc particularly with the British near Cambrai. Lives were being sacrificed on all sides to hold the line until re-enforcements could arrive. It dawned upon Bosdet and me one evening as we witnessed a wonderful sunset from a hill back of the castle with Gladys and her chum, that our leaves must be up. We checked up on the dates, and the next train carried us away from Wales and into Crewe. Here two Red Cross girls serving buns and coffee held our attention just long enough for us to miss one train. At Birmingham we met two old friends and went out of our way a little to visit Bristol with them. Then on to Bath, and Salisbury. We arrived late in the evening, proceeding at once to get into trouble with two "MPs" (Military Police). Strong arms, and later strong legs, saved us from arrest. At the "New Crown Inn" we found food and shelter for the night. Early next morning—out in Salisbury Plain, the gathering place for British and other soldiers for years—and by ten o'clock we were in Codford, several days "AWOL" (absent without leave).

Of course we went on the inevitable "carpet" before Colonel Beeman of the Third Brigade, to which the Twelfth was attached. With the Colonel was our own Major Robinson and our Captain, Colin McKay. The charge read, "...conduct unbecoming a good soldier...and absent without leave," among other things. The "Mex" had an idea, and said, "If we tell them the truth, they won't believe us, but if we tell 'em a 'good one' he (the Colonel) may 'let us down light'." I agreed with Bosdet. Then he said, "We'll both tell the same yarn—and STICK to it." Before we could rehearse our parts the Sergeant-Major called Bosdet into the "presence". As he came out a few moments later he winked. I went in. As I passed thru the doorway my hat was snatched from my head. (A soldier without his hat is "undressed") As I stood at attention, facing the three officers, the "charge" was read. Thru my mind ran a host of thoughts, chiefly concerned with what Bosdet had told them. I thought of a dozen possible explanations, any one of which might have formed the nucleus for my mate's story. Which should I pick to tell? How soon after I commenced would I be able to read upon those stern faces what

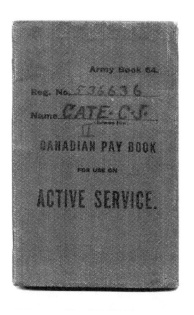

Bosdet had said? Then the Colonel said, "Gunner Cate, what have you to say in answer to these charges?" I answered at once, "I was with Bosdet, Sir." The Colonel grunted, stroked his chin with his hand, pressed his lips firmly together, and looked at me, and thru me, from under his wrinkled brow. Then he said, after several moments, "Do you think it adds anything to the color of the cloth to go off and get drunk and come back days after your leave has expired?" So that had been Bosdet's idea. The "old man" looked angry. For some moments his gaze, burning directly into my eyes, called forth all of my nerve to keep from looking away out of the line of fire. I could not suppress a smile as I said, "No, Sir." Then the old man's eyes were turned to look at my Major and Captain. Robinson was grim, but McKay's lips twisted into a smile, which was followed by a chorus of smiles from all three officers. "Thirty days R.W." (Royal Warrant, or stoppage of pay*), snapped the Colonel. That was all. Outside, Bosdet was waiting, and as I walked up to him he smiled and said, "A few days Royal Warrant! Was it worth it?" I answered, "Yes, old 'wise one'." (*Note: This pay was given to us at time of discharge.)

Although related later somewhat lightheartedly, that this episode concerned Gnr. Cate (at least in so far as it might jeopardize his reputation back home), is evidenced by the little confession expressed in one of many letters to his grandmother. CCC

#536636   C.G.A.
#12 Canadian S. Bty.
B.E.F., France
22nd May, 1918

My darling Grandmother:
  For once I have four full hours when I am sure of being undisturbed—just the chance for a word with you—eh?

  In my letter to Mildred not long ago I told her of my fine rest leave in Northern Wales and a few English places. She has no doubt told you all about it so I won't repeat it.

  Whether I told her about getting "admonished and two days'[*Tch!*] pay stopped" or not I do not remember--this the colonel gave me as a punishment for staying away two days overtime – it was well worth the trouble to me for one can not see Wales in a day. However since I know how anxious you are to have me keep a clean crime-sheet I will say for the benefit of us both that that little extra vacation is not considered bad enough to dirty my sheet—which so far has never been touched. Further to give you an idea of my physical condition, may as well add that my name has never appeared on the hospital or sick list. Never was better—the worst thing I have had being a cold which I lost way back on Partridge Island in Canada...

  Codford in Wiltshire, one of the small villages on Salisbury Plain, consisted mostly of plaster or clapboard homes with straw thatched roofs. There were one or two fair estates, boasting of stone houses, and a very few brick buildings, with tile roofing. Most of the shops were cheap affairs, as were common in all troop-infested towns. The several churches monopolized the structural beauty of the town. Here the Australians had a large camp and hospital. Several big hills shut the village in on one side. The rest of the place looked out over the plain. Though the River Avon was not far off, the only stream here was the Ford, which ambled lazily thru the town. To this place, which without the excess of troops, would have been serene indeed, came the 3rd Brigade for a short rest before going to France.

Our camp was comfortable, food was good, duties were very light, the weather was perfect, and our time was spent for the most parts in sports. Long hikes over the hills rewarded the hikers with sound sleep when they turned in for the night. One bright day I watched a plane come sailing, apparently, out of the sun. It circled over the camp and headed off over the big hill. All at once a wing flashed in the sunlight and collapsed against the body of the craft. The plane came tumbling to earth like a giant wounded bird. As it crashed, rebounded from the gentle slope of the hill, and settled back a complete wreck amid the shower of turf and dirt, the hillside swarmed with men running from every direction. When I reached the spot, its two occupants were being removed from the fuselage. In a few hours they had gone on the long flight. The story was that the pilot, a major of the "RAF" (Royal Air Force), was giving a New Zealand Infantry Captain his first (and last) air ride, as part of the latter's birthday celebration.

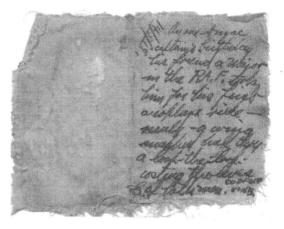

Patch cut from crashed aeroplane's wing

At Codford our equipment was inspected and put in completeness for service at the front. Though life was easy there, we all knew that the orders for our move to a channel port were in the brigade office. On one fine morning we paraded in marching order, and preceded by the "Aussie" band, marched to the railroad where we were assigned to first class compartments for a ride thru malt and hop fields to Southampton. In short order we were aboard a transport, steaming out by the Isle of Wight into the English Channel. Ahead of us: France, the Line, and the Hun.

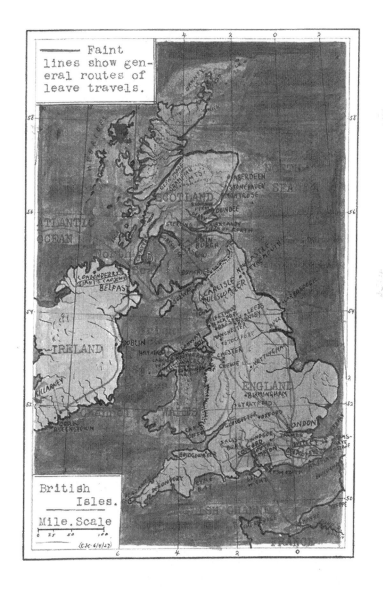

Map of the British Isles

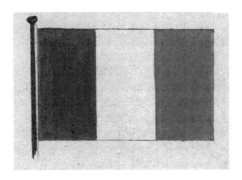

CHAPTER V
The Canadian Army—in France

With Britain and "playdays" behind us, and France and "workdays" (and nights!) ahead of us, the channel transport was not long in covering the hundred and twenty-five miles from Southampton to Le Havre, at the mouth of the Seine. As we trotted over the gangplank onto French soil, a few dockworkers, soldiers and sailors gave us a welcome. Deep within our secret thoughts was the realization that our coming was tardy, so the little welcome cheer helped to put our consciences at ease. Thru dingy streets leading away from the gaunt old warehouses, we marched to Rest Camp Number One, carrying all our personal equipment. Assigned to tents, we began looking around the camp, finding that it was but slightly different from the camps across the channel. The camp next to our own was occupied by American "doughboys," and with them we compared notes until mess time.

After a meal of bread, cheese, jam, and tea, the "Big 4" proceeded into the town to try out their French. We soon discovered that Bosdet was best suited to be official interpreter, though Fisher was not too bad. Cameron and I knew before half an hour had passed that we had to learn a new language. We looked about town until dark, visiting L'Eglise Notre Dame because a civilian in the Grand Place had told us that it was the finest sight in Le Havre. In an estaminet we sat for an hour or more, drinking wine and trying to converse with the other patrons. About nine o'clock we left to escort two quickly made friends to their homes in the finer section of the town. This we found to be a rather arduous performance, as the route lay over a steep hill and all four of us had imbibed freely. The matter was taken care of, however, and we returned to camp, to find the tents considerably overcrowded. By placing our feet at the tent pole (the tents were round Bell tents) and then falling in the general direction of the crack between two other sleepers we managed to squeeze into place for a few hours' sleep.

Our next move was into the little boxcars, the markings of which, "40 Hommes ou 8 Chevaux," have found their way into practically every story of the war. Then a long, tedious and bumpy ride into the interior. All along the first day's route ran French youngsters crying, "Bully Beef—Biscuits!" (Actually, the cry went something like this: "Boooolleeee Beeeef—Beeskeeeeet", in wavering, "singsong" tones.) Because we had not yet learned what a shortage of rations meant we answered their cries with showers of hardtack, bread, jam, cheese, and tins of corned beef ("tinned Willy," "Bully Beef," "canned cow") and machonikee (I never knew how to spell it, but we pronounced it "mak-on-i-kee," a vegetable stew of no known character!) Later we learned to greatly respect the cook who could serve corned beef in countless more or less camouflaged ways, twenty-one times a week, and still live to tell about it.

Now and then as our boxcars crawled over their tortuous route, a detail of men on the leading cars would hop to some wine-laden car coming from the opposite direction, and by the time the end of our train was passing the last cars of the other train, a keg of "vin-rouge" would be resting bottom-up in one of our cars. A few kegs of wine were as "drops in the bucket" to a trainload of men, but on several occasions we "annexed" casks, and then the fun would begin.

"40 HOMMES OU 8 CHEVAUX" means forty men or eight horses. The boxcars on French railroads were toy affairs, and forty men per car meant that most of them stood on their feet (or some other fellow's feet) for the duration of the ride. Usually, in cool weather, in the center of the car, burned a brazier, which so filled the atmosphere with soot, smoke, and gas, that breathing was all but impossible. On many of the cars, at one end, was a small ell or tower, the top of which extended anywhere from one to three feet above the top of the car proper. To get away from the uncomfortable atmosphere inside the car, many of us rode in these towers or on the car roofs. This practice was all right in fair weather or when our route did not lie thru some of the many low tunnels. Often the clearance of the latter was less than six inches on all sides, so that casualties were common occurrences.

At Rouen we disembarked and marched to a rest-camp for food, a much needed cleaning, and a night's rest. Next morning Gunner Stratton and I visited the city across the river. In a few hours we had "seen" the place, spending some time in the cathedral which had often been a target for German shells. Starting back for camp, we climbed into a lorry going, as we supposed, in our direction, but which actually carried us some six miles out of our way. When we did get back, we saw the battery lined up waiting for us, and in less time to tell about it the Sergeant-Major exhibited the finest soldier's vocabulary I had listened to up to that date. Before leaving Rouen, Johnny Kyle annexed a small tiger kitten, which for days afterward clung to his blanket roll on the march, and kept close to him when in position, supplying us with much laughter at its crazy antics.

St. Pol followed Rouen. Here the guns were unloaded from the flatcars which had brought them from Le Havre, and fastened to "FWDons" (Four-wheel-drive-trucks). Supplies and ammunition were also transferred to lorries. Then we found room wherever we could and the caravan started for "up the  line". Every kilo covered brought further evidence of the struggle that had been going on for over three years––razed homes, blasted trees and posts, fields turned topsy-turvy—and then we came to an area of absolute ruin. Just before dark we reached a small group of corrugated metal huts, covered with sandbags and "elephant tin" (curved sections of corrugated metal) where we found shelter for the night. Bunks on the "hen wire springs" were quickly prepared, and we soon fell asleep.

Our awakening came not naturally, nor with the morning, but at about midnight, to find our scalps strangely bristling, our spines all aquiver, and in our mouths a strange "stingy" taste. The night was crowded with awe–inspiring sounds: whines, whirs, growls, crashes, shrieks, and just plain bangs; the whole exhibition accentuated by many weird flashes of light. This was Jerry's "Welcome–in" party. We were getting our "baptism." A few of us just stared––wondering, while others ran about bewildered, and some 'just naturally' disappeared, to be rounded up later covered with mud and dirt. On leaving my bunk I had run out to a little mound apart from the huts. There I stood, and watched, and listened, too fascinated to run or duck. My emotions during that first few minutes (if I registered any) are not on record. There were no casualties. As a matter of fact, as the "old-timers" explained, those shells were on their way to Mt. St. Eloi and vicinity, and none were likely to land nearer than a thousand yards. Then the "OTs" ordered us back into our bunks. All of us obeyed—some of us slept.

Thru a section of France already made famous by Canadians—Vimy Ridge,
Thelus Wood, Plank Road, Suicide
Corner, and other names full of meaning–
–the 12th moved, and at Nine Elms went
into position. I was back with the "Big 4"
on the guns, or to be more explicit, with
Number One or "A" gun, as Number Two
of a crew. My duties included handling
the breach, raising the gun into firing
position or lowering it to be loaded, and
firing the gun. This place on the crew I
held until "gassed" at Eswars October 13th,
leaving only for short periods of
reconnaissance duty as an assistant to Lt.
Bacon.

"TO CANADIAN ARTILLERY-MEN. VIMY "

*Note: In fact, although they too are inconsistent, CJC's medical records obtained
from the National Archives of Canada indicate the gassing incident occurred at
Eswars, most likely on the 11th of October, which gives some indication of how
unsettling such events tend to be. CCC*

Our first firing was done under ideal conditions, with fair weather, and
no answering fire from enemy batteries. Except that we were firing from a
"pit," we might have been back in Lydd, firing at a hidden target, so unexciting
it all seemed. With our brains busy interpreting orders, and our hands at
work executing them, we grew accustomed to conditions quickly. Firing
hundred-pound shells at German troops, gun positions, trenches, machine
gun nests, posts of observation, and all manner of targets, became "all in the
day's work"—just as we soon
learned to take the noise of our
own guns, the sudden "opening
up" of a nearby battery, the
whining and exploding of Hun
shells, gas, the sight of
wounded and dead men and
animals, filth, cooties, and air
raids as routine in the line—
along with all the rest that goes
with the ghastly senselessness
of "civilized" warfare.

"Nine Elms", Early 1918 - An uncanny spot!

Gun crews were "on duty" twenty-four hours, and "off" the same length
of time before going back. During the "off" period, they kept busy "while
resting", by digging dugouts, "humping" shells and ammunition, and doing all
the other work that could be found by sharp-eyed officers. Of course, there

was great rivalry between different men, for the position of honor in the outfits, which gave one credit for being able to "duck" the Sergeant-Major most often. I believe that Bosdet and I were tied for first place. For a while Bosdet and I spent much of our "off" time in prospecting the vicinity for souvenirs and sights, finding a lot of both. Out alone one morning, I had roamed some distance from the position when an "inquisitive" shell buried me alive in an old trench. This spoiled my taste for exploring, so Bosdet and I went to work on a two-man dugout that was to be a work of art. Incidentally, one of our officers who had heard of my "hunting" proclivities warned me that the last fellow who had strayed away from his battery was still "out there."

"ENTRANCE TO THE FIRST "BIG 4" DUG-OUT. BUILT BY BOSDET AND CATE, BUT LOST AS SOON AS COMPLETED."

This also helped to keep me near home. The dugout WAS a work of art, but the effort was wasted, for on the day following its completion the battery moved away from that vicinity.

The Nine Elms position cost the battery very little in casualties, though other batteries near us seemed to suffer. While there, reserve positions were prepared back of the lines in the event of a forced retreat, but were never used except as an excuse to get away from the battery for a few hours in an estaminet not far from Aubigny.

Leaving Nine Elms, the Battery went into Arras. In this town the positions were changed from time to time. Sometimes a position would be subjected

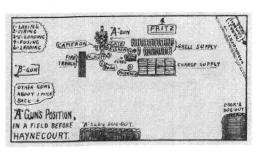

to shells from Heinie's guns continuously, while at others we enjoyed days without receiving a shell in our direction. The Dainville "orchard" position of "A" gun was such for almost a week. From this emplacement we were firing mostly gas, and at night the gunners were often forced to don masks to protect themselves against "leaky" shells. Almost every time we fired during the first night, we were showered with apple blossoms and little apples from the trees overhead.

In the Dainville part of Arras were many civilians, going about their

41

business paying but little heed to shells and gas. Usually they quartered themselves in cellars, though a few lived in the floors above, reserving their cellars for bombardments. All civilians were, of course, supplied with gas masks.

A-Sub's quarters were in the cellar of a brick house, about five minutes' walk from the gun. On real "quiet" nights we used to sleep on the first floor, but were always ready for a dash cellar-ward. After a few hours work, Cameron and I succeeded in connecting the water pipes in the basement to the main line in the street, and until a "mean" Hun gunner placed a shell in our backyard we enjoyed running water. Before the arrival of this same shell I had played at gardening in the area back of the house, with results that were pleasing. "Homelife" became so "homelike" in Dainville, that on several occasions we built a fire in the fireplace on the first floor, but this practice was discontinued forever after an air raid on one memorable night.

One afternoon as I climbed a brick wall near our quarters, I was delightfully surprised to see a large strawberry patch laden with perfect fruit. As I proceeded to sample the berries, however, I learned that they were the valued property of a civilian neighbor, who with his wife and eighteen year old daughter occupied the cellar which lay at the edge of the patch. His daughter was an excellent violinist, in spite of her blindness caused, so she said, by gas. Possibly the smoked glasses which she wore were but a camouflage made necessary on "general principles" to discourage further inquiry.

For the trooper who cared little for sleep, or who could not be worried by "harassing fire", machine guns or long range snipers, there was much to be seen about Arras. The "Big 4" accomplished much exploring. There was a college building which had not been emptied entirely of supplies and

instruments, where we spent many hours of reading and experimenting in the laboratory. The ruined convent buildings, shattered and scattered homes, desolate parks, deserted squares—all were duly "inspected," sometimes nearly at the cost of our lives when an unexpected high-explosive shell found a

La Grande Place, Arras

place to bury its nose near us sending showers of debris over and around our positions.

The two sights that never failed to bring forth harsh remarks about Fritz were the wrecked dwellings, and the Arras Cathedral. The latter was but an irregular mound of gray dust, with here and there a section of a wall poking its few remaining feet of raggedness up above the rest. A few statues there were, still standing upright, but pitted and cracked by the shell splinters. Beneath the surface were many subterranean corridors and chambers. In several of these were great piles of irregular gray blocks, and on most of the blocks were written the names and addresses of soldiers—many thousands of them in all.

Quite often it happened that Military Police or officers from various infantry units would challenge our privilege of "looking around," and in the end, order us to "Get back to your battery, damned pronto!" Of course we would use, if any, the standard alibi, "We are looking for a canteen, Sir." Eventually we moved out of the Arras section and into "rest" camp.

The vicinity of Blavincourt was quiet, boasting of fair-sized groves, fruit orchards, vegetable gardens, fields crisscrossed by hedges and dotted with farms and villages of no particular note. Our camp of wooden huts and bell tents was situated on the edge of a little forest near Blavincourt. On the other edge of the forest was Beaufort and beyond Beaufort was Avant-le-Comte, Tincques (where the Canadians celebrated Dominion Day), and Harbarque. Here our only danger lay in air raids which occurred at rare intervals, and in disease, which was more common. Pneumonia took our first life. Influenza followed, reducing the active force of the battery by about one-third, as evidenced on one dull morning during a "GOC's" (General Officer Commanding's) inspection. As far as I know there were no fatalities. Segregation followed by prompt medical treatment saved the day. The fact that we were out of the line and able to rest properly helped also.

About this time, the great generalissimo, Ferdinand Foch (Commander-in-Chief of all allied Armies since April 3, 1918), was putting the final touches onto his masterpiece "to be." As soon as the Flu was overcome, we were put thru a vigorous training period of a new type of howitzer action. Soon we were able to drop into position, fire a few rounds, limber up and move forward, go into position again, fire more rapidly than before, and on again. The use of pits was dropped. Thus we became true field pieces. This new method was to prove extremely effective as well as more likely to result in a greater casualty list.

The creeping barrage was a innovative artillery tactic developed by the French during the battle of Verdun. It employed a strategy in which infantry marched directly behind solid artillery fire that had been moved to the front, leaping 100 meters at a time, thereby ensuring that attacking troops and covering shellfire reached the enemy lines almost simultaneously, theoretically trapping the defenders while still in their bunkers. Having aggressively mobile artillery units was a refinement that afforded even greater support flexibility. CCC

Canadians under canvas in Blavincourt

Between drills and fatigues (Oh, the "SM" (Sergeant-Major) often caught the "Big 4" napping at Blavincourt and gave us plenty to do), the "Big 4" found (stolen) time for frequent banquets at the expense, by the way, of the civilians. Bosdet was chief chicken collector, Cameron was a wonder at picking green-stuffs, and Fisher made a reliable sentry while I coaxed milk from suspicious cows. Bosdet and I were the reconnaissance committee and knew the location and condition of every garden, orchard, and hen yard for miles around. Out on the march we checked up on conditions, and just at the right time, under cover of darkness, were back to collect. Once in a while we were caught by civilians who knew that martial laws forbade our actions. Penalties were severe. On these occasions we developed unsuspected qualities of diplomacy, departing as a rule, with good will existing on all sides. Once, Bosdet, high up in a large cherry tree in the daytime, looked down to see several officers seat themselves beneath the tree to play cards. For a long time he remained quiet, while I lay hidden in a blackberry patch less than twenty-five feet away. Officers would be difficult to deal with. At best, our "SM" (Sergeant-Major Candy) would be asked if he had nothing for two such willing workers to do. A question that the Honorable Mister Candy would surely be pleased to answer with deadly effect. Then—Bosdet fell asleep—and out of the tree! I forgot the thousands of thorns that were biting into my flesh. To say that the officers were astounded, would be putting it mildly. They were dumfounded, speechless...but Oh! the awakening! Bosdet was not hurt in his fall and hardly had he hit the ground when he was on his feet, saluting, smiling, and still holding tight to a ration bag filled with cherries. D I P L O M A C Y !! If Bosdet had held Bethmann-Hollweg's position in July 1914, there would have been no war, and I might never have seen my mate sell a Major, a Captain, and two other officers an idea contrary to every law of the service.

Charles Louis Bosdet was quiet, unassuming, with just the suspicion of a smile playing about the corners of his eyes and lips. In the stiffest action his expression seldom changed. Good nature radiated from him at all times, excepting perhaps the one or two rare occasions when he felt that someone had "put a raw one over". Once when the "SM" had caught me for wood fatigue, I told him where to find Bosdet. The joke amused me and so far as could be seen Bosdet did not object to helping ME. After an hour of hard work we started from the grove near the cookhouse with a heavy green log on our shoulders. I carried the forward end while Bosdet brought up the rear. At the cookhouse I warned Bosdet and let my end drop to the ground. My good fellow-laborer's end caught in his tunic and before he could free himself my end hit the ground—hard! Bosdet was thrown on his back, and for a moment lay still. Then he bounded to his feet and came at me as though shot out of a gun. The "smile" was gone from his face as he said, "Yank, if I thought you did that on purpose, I'd..." And then, the smile returned.

One fine afternoon, I was perched in a low tree dropping luscious cherries into the haversack held open below me by Bosdet, when the French owner of the tree saw us. In the mad scramble to beat him to the wall I lost my pipe though I didn't know it at the time. Halfway back to camp I noticed my loss and, as that particular pipe was a good one, I went back alone to recover it. The same Frenchman caught me hunting around under the tree, and with the wrong end of an antique shotgun at my spine I was in no mood to argue. I tried hard to explain but apparently was getting nowhere, when suddenly the old man laughed. He had "got the idea" and evidently considered the whole thing a good joke. After a joint hunt, it was he who found my pipe. Arm-in-arm we walked into his house, never flinching under a heavy barrage of words from his irate wife. Volley after volley she fired at my host. A wordy bombardment that only he could understand. He fed me and drank with me, in spite of the still fuming woman of the house. Before I left the good couple, peace reigned in the home, for as is the custom, a crowd of relatives and neighbors had been called in to celebrate—nothing in particular.

On the day before our departure for the line, the "Big 4" had made all plans for a final grand banquet. In the dead of the night before, Bosdet's clever hands had picked two fine birds off a full roost without causing a single squawk to be uttered. Cameron had harvested fresh potatoes, beans, and other vegetables. Fisher had stood guard while I milked a peaceful cow whose kind eyes had spoken the thanks she felt for the relief I gave her. With all in readiness in the woods back of camp, Bosdet, Cameron, and I left Fisher to

45

stand guard while we answered the bugle's call of "payday." Getting our few francs we stopped at the canteen to purchase a few "Huntley and Palmer" biscuits and a can of peaches, then hurried back to the feast. As we approached the spot chosen for the spread, we were met by a faint scent of scorched food! What dread thoughts entered our minds! What devil of perversity had caused the disaster which met our gaze as we reached Fisher, the Dreamer? Seated on the ground, head in hands, was the noble gunner. Before him the banquet––spread to the ants and lesser insects! A few scorched remnants of chicken clung to the rim of the overturned petrol tin that had been our stove. The terrors of battle in all its hellishness we could bear, but never this! And yet, no one knows until called upon to learn, what terrible agony the human frame can endure, and still continue to function! We did not crucify Fisher, for the poor devil was in love, and the agony which gnawed away at his own soul was sufficient punishment.

A second trip into the line near Arras was not like the first. "A" gun was somewhere in the vicinity of the famous Daisy-O-Pip (Daisy Observation Post), where the earth had been soaking up the blood of thousands of Canadian, Australian, New Zealand, English, French, and German youths at intervals for nearly four years. A desolate region indeed. A hill, sparsely covered with withered tree stumps and tangled barbed wire, a section of filthy trench, a

cemetery where even the dead had been torn from their slumbers to peel in the sun and bleach in the rain; a veritable "no-man's-land"—and another storm was brewing.

It was while on a trip with a ration detail from this position that I first saw the "White City," a level waste of grayish-white color, where once a prosperous village had stood. The army existed in this section, under cover, because it had to, but aside from the rats and vermin there was no other life. Always included with the word "army" was the horse and the mule, eternally suffering in silence and always true to the trust placed upon them. From one position to another we moved, with conditions steadily growing worse, the German shellfire more deadly, with the 12th sending its contributions with the rest to the dressing stations—"walking cases" when they had the strength, ambulance cases otherwise—and at the dressing stations an endless line of mutilated humanity, painfully moving "down the line" to Base Hospitals and "Blighty." Hun bombing planes were getting more reckless, making life on earth hell, and life "in the earth" almost as bad.

One night, as I lay in a hole in the wall of a trench, I heard the faint crying of a cat. "I've got 'em now all right," I thought, and so I investigated. There, on the parapet was a kitten. How she got there I do not know, unless some of the fresh troops had just brought her in. Until the gas killed her a few days later, I found much pleasure in her company.

Mention of this incident appears in the following letter: CCC

Dearest Grandma:

While I was out on my rest the last time, I sat in this same little cozy hole in the wall of the trench and wrote home. While writing, a kitten walking across the wire jumped into the trench and we two speedily became acquainted. I was just thinking of her and where she went when I had to go back up the line—and behold—ye kitten's mind must have been thinking of me for here she is, returned to my hole now that I am back—guess she is hungry, and my stomach says time for lunch too— so good-bye & love to you both. Clifton

About this time Bosdet left the battery to take a special course of instruction at the "mining and sapping" school down the line. Roaming was, of course, impossible. The instant my relief reached my gun I was instantly ready to rest, and thus spent most of my "off duty" time "under ground." "This business of War is getting worse all the time," suggested one of the gunners one night. Nobody laughed at this. Even the old-timers held their customary "wisecracks", saying only that the worst was yet to come. And, so it was, as planning for the final Somme drive was already well underway!

The '18 Somme Drive

On July 19th, we were in Blavincourt for a short rest. A few days later we were back in the line sandwiched in between Flanders and Picardy pounding away with everything our guns could fire. Vague rumors were in the air. Things were happening all along the line. "They say"—that Heinie has just failed to make good a great drive on the Marne—that the "Frogs" and the "Yanks" are pushing him back all along the line—that thousands of prisoners have been taken—and a hundred other things. In the Artois Region (our own sector) we knew that things WERE happening. Our guns were seldom, if ever, cool. Positions were moved forward often, firing elevations were getting higher, the "wounded" lines grew heavier, prisoners aplenty were in our hands, and Jerry's artillery was becoming "uncanny" in the way it found our positions.

47

Then came a sudden move away from Arras, a fast night ride, a day in Reubaumpre (?), another night ride, bouncing over rough roads at top speed: Amiens, the Somme, and into position in a valley near Villers-Brettoneux. (The valley has been called "Bloody Valley," "Dead Man's Valley," as well as several other names. Just what its proper name is I do not know.) The 12th was not alone. Apparently endless columns of Infantry, Cavalry, Artillery, Tank Corps, Red Cross Sections, ammunitions and stores, and all manner of battle array were pouring into that sector with us, under cover of a heavy mist and camouflaged highways.

The Great Spirit seemingly could no longer stand the horrible crime that was being committed by the most "civilized" nations of the earth. A "victor" was chosen, and all that was left for him to do was drive, d r i v e , DRIVE! In mud, knee deep, Right Section struggled to get its two guns into position. The whole battery tugged and grunted and perspired for hours. Center and Left sections performed under even worse conditions, accomplishing great feats of engineering skill to place "C," "D," "E" and "F" guns in their proper places. In a cold drizzle we "humped" shells and charges until near each gun were piles of "canned death" for German consumption. Then when all was in readiness we were ordered to get some rest. Cold, wet, dirty, nearly exhausted, we rolled into our wet blankets wherever we happened to be, and slept the sleep that only the weary soldier knows.

On the following morning I went with a detail after "ammo", and before dark, every available space was filled with shells, charges, fuses, tubes, and supplies. During the day I had seen more men and guns, as well as more of every other device of modern warfare, that I had dreamed was in France. Over our heads the air force was unusually busy. As we went to rest on the night of August 7th there was a feeling of great expectancy throughout the battery. General Haig, working with Marshal Foch, was ready for the last Somme drive.

The following passage from the British Official History describes one of the precautions taken by the Allied Command leading up to the impending offensive: "...Since it was impossible to conceal the preparations for the attack from the troops who were to take part, further security instructions were ordered posted in every individual's service and pay book. Under the emphatic heading 'KEEP YOUR MOUTH SHUT!' these cautioned against loose talk before the offensive and directed that anyone

having the ill fortune to be taken prisoner should supply no information beyond rank and name..." CJC's "...sudden move away from Arras", was part of activities that began on July 30th with movement of the main body of the Canadian Corps to an area southwest of Amiens, with all travel made at night. Troops were told they were going to the Ypres Front to repel a suspected German attack. The Battle of Amiens began early on August 8th, and over the next three and a half days the 12th Battery advanced, apparently in support of the 4th, 5th, and 6th Infantry Brigades of the 2nd Canadian Division, almost nine miles (as the crow flies) through Villers Bretonneux, Wiencourt, Vrely, Rosieres en Santerre, and on to a forward position at Meharicourt. There they dug in and remained for the next seven days. CCC]

Long before daybreak on the eighth we were "standing by." Each passing moment added to the tremendous strain of "waiting" for the "zero" hour. We tried to hide our emotions under cover of unnecessary odd jobs about the guns. Number Four, testing his sights for the tenth time, Number Two polishing the mushroom head of the breach, "blowing" the vent, testing over and again the swing of the breach mechanism, the lift of the "quick release," cleaning tubes, while the rest of the crew re-wiped shells, inspected the trail and the spade, the brakes, cartridge boxes, fuse boxes, and cases of the silk-wrapped charges. With every man nerved to the utmost, we received, at last, our second set of orders. The act of carrying them into effect overcame the greater part of the waiting strain, in fact, no gun crew was ever more calm, more certain, more deliberate than "A" crew as they swung the gun into line, loaded, placed it into firing position, and reported, "A" gun ready, Sir." Upon receipt of elevation, the elevating gears whined a tune as they were spun just over the mark, and then back to "Take up the lash," and then...C R A S H !! ...the gun shot back along its carriage, its mouth belching fire, and out over the rim of dead man's valley hissed a hundred pounds of trouble for Fritz. At that very instant, "ALL HELL BROKE LOOSE"! The darkness of the night became a glare of lightning-like, red, yellow, and white flashes. The earth shook as from an earthquake. Breathing suddenly became difficult as our nerves grew numb from the terrific concussion caused by the crashing, roaring, blasting, air-splitting din about us. Thousands of guns were firing from wherever room for one could be found, on a front twenty miles long. Thousands of tons of high explosive and gas were being thrown into the German trenches, gun positions, and routes over which his reserves must march. How any of the troops in that part of the German line ever escaped that terrible bombardment is a miracle. Yet, some of them lived to retreat or to be made prisoners later. (The ex-German soldier, with whom I talked the other day in Boston, was one of those who lived, but when I asked him to describe what it was like at the bad end of that early morning barrage, he simply shook his head and bit his lower lip.)

The Hun was taking a dose of his own medicine, and he did NOT like it. Right behind the barrage, as our elevations were raised, crawled the tanks and the infantry—faded khaki and blue colored lines—the shock troops first, and then the "mopping-up" units. At first there was some strong resistance by a few brave troops, but the spirit of the majority was crushed. During that preliminary bombardment, that merciless shelling that followed them as they retreated, the Huns learned to know their master. Our infantry went forward over the havoc created by our guns, slowly at first, and then as they met little resistance, more rapidly. They were not to be denied their absolute victory. In the two days that followed, the line of advance widened to forty miles. Thirty thousand prisoners were taken, most of them without offering any trouble. The few brave men who stood their ground for Germany during that advance were not taken prisoners. Ludendorff's 41st Division "absolutely refused to fight", and when such a condition exists in any man's army, things begin to look black indeed.

Soon after daybreak on that memorable August eighth, the 12th moved forward thru Villers-Brettoneux, where we realized for the first time something of the telling effect of our shells of the night before. As far as eye could see, complete devastation. Not a thing left upright. Homes, trees, poles, wires, railways, wagons, trucks, guns of every description, ammunition, and men, scrambled together into one immense "dump." The bodies of men and horses were strewn all about, mangled in every possible manner. How many men were buried in that "mess" no one will ever know. Many khaki and blue-covered forms were being put beneath the ground as quickly and carefully as possible. As we jolted along, over the blasted excuse for a roadway, we watched thousands of German prisoners at work clearing a passageway for advancing troops. Among those gray-clad troops, with pale and weary visages, were many young boys, and men well over the middle age. Very plainly they showed how sick of any manner of war they were, and it was evident that as prisoners, for the first time in a long while, they now felt certain of food, rest, and a fair degree of safety from further shell fire.

Short halts to fire a few rounds were followed by a continuous forward movement. Everywhere the dead, and streams of wounded. Those who were able to walk helping those who had not found room in ambulances, but who were more seriously hurt. There were both wounded and dead of our own and of German troops. Every mound held its silent machine gun and its complement of dead gunners. Officers had been no luckier than men of lower ranks. Large and small groups of disarmed Huns were finding their way back down the line unaided and unguarded. They needed no watching for they had had more than enough of fighting. We passed thru Wiencourt and on to Caix, where we stopped for a night. Here we were under scattered German fire of no particular danger. Our own range grew greater and greater, until the enemy retreat carried it beyond our reach with howitzers. In Caix many walls were left standing, and here and there were four walls and a roof. Throughout the village we found mute evidence that the German occupants had not dreamed of leaving so soon, if ever. It was more than evident that they had had no time to prepare for so vigorous an assault. Depleted Canadian equipment was speedily reinforced from former German supply stores. From Hun canteens we obtained cigars, cigarettes, tobacco, and beer. Right Section quartered itself at the base of a towering sand cliff, the face of which was burrowed with hundreds of small dug-outs connected by cleverly arranged tunnels, dry and well ventilated. Each hole contained trophies for exploring gunners, and now and then we found Huns, who after being wounded, had crawled back into their shelters to die, or who had been caught hiding there by the "moppers up."

As the sun went down, displaying a wonderful galaxy of colors, a column of cavalry advanced by our camp. When the moon had advanced high into the heavens, the end of that column had not yet come into sight. The "plop, plop, plopping" of the horses' hooves, the rattle of bits and chains, the clanking of sabers against the creaking saddles, the silence of the riders in that seemingly endless column, made one of the most impressive experiences of my period of service. That night the battery enjoyed a much needed sleep. But not the battery as it had been a few days earlier, for more than a few of the boys had been left behind.

The next day we moved forward at the "double". Our guns had fired at their extreme range the night before, therefore much ground had to be covered before we were again within easy range. The scenes of the previous days were renewed with somewhat of an increase in our own dead and wounded. The Hun's back was against the wall, and his gunfire was more deadly. No army, no matter how great, can advance too far ahead of its supply base, without sustaining prohibitive losses, and many an apparently certain victory has been turned into a disastrous defeat because its fighting units had moved ahead too fast for the slower moving supply bases. The "brains" of this advance knew and did not forget this fact. Disabled tanks and lorries of our own were common. At a captured narrow-gauge railhead we found thousands of rounds of German ammunition, guns, wagons, and several engines with their cars on the narrow-gauge rails. Here firing was  resumed by the other crew of "A-sub", thus giving me the opportunity to roam around a little. Also, my first balloon ascension in France was made not far from this position, and was thoroughly enjoyed until the mobile winch had hauled in the cable, and I found that both the observer and I were in for trouble. I was not "supposed" to do such things, and he was not "supposed" to permit me to do them. Air fighting was on the increase, with both sides making good their right to the name of "Hero." As I roamed I used my camera, and some of the "shots" made that day are with me now. Several of us, who had roamed, were left behind when the battery moved forward again. We became separated after night had fallen, so I rolled into a shell hole to sleep until daybreak. On awaking, my nostrils were besieged with a terrible odor. On moving my head I discovered the cause in the body of a German officer, dead for at least forty-eight hours. Such is not a pleasant bedfellow! By nine o'clock I had located my battery which soon pulled into Vrely. With the advancing of two guns into a hidden position between Rosieres and Meharicourt under cover of darkness the 12th reached the limit of its advance on this drive.

At Vrely there were many periods of very stiff action, with enemy fire heavy and deadly. While the ground forces blasted away at one another, the air forces did their part to make life on earth and in the air more than miserable. "Dog fights" between numbers of our own and enemy planes occurred daily, always with losses to both sides, but with the better average steadily growing for our own fliers. Enemy armored planes carrying their photographers often flew so low and so slowly over our positions that on several occasions we were able to hit them with stones thrown from the ground. At such times our antiaircraft guns could not, with safety to our own men in the vicinity, fire at these planes, though the machine guns sent steady streams of lead and "chaser" bullets against their sides and bottom

Eyes of the Artillery

while many of us lay on our backs with captured German rifles trying to catch the pilot with his own lead. Either we were poor riflemen or he was too well protected to worry, for always he took his time, made his pictures of our positions, and escaped back to his own lines before one of our planes could catch him. For variety he would sometimes answer our fire, which on several occasions left him the winner of the engagement. Gun positions in the village were shifted from time to time as Jerry's artillery found us, thanks to the good efforts of his photographers. Our quarters were underground and when off duty there was but little roaming done. Vrely was an uncanny town. Shells seem to fall without warning at just the wrong time in just the wrong places. Men were with us at one meal, and gone forever at the next. I was glad to be attached to the crews of the guns in the "forward" position beyond Rosieres, which for some time were kept silent. When they did go into action it was with a vengeance, and many were the busy hours out there, several miles from the main battery, while the territory between us was continuously under fire and thus practically impassable. In spite of the condition just mentioned, it was necessary for us to rely for food on messengers from Vrely, and though they were often late we knew that as soon as was possible our rations would arrive. Here duty on the Right Section guns was for twenty-four hour stretches, with a twenty-four hour stay with the main battery between each stretch. These last days in this section were busy ones, though no further advances were made. Bosdet had come back to the battery wearing a new insignia for his effort at the mining school.

Sometime in the latter half of August, the French came in to relieve us, filling Vrely Square after dark with a host of men, horses, and battle paraphernalia. Someone was careless enough to display a tiny light which was seen by German observers in their bombing planes so high above us that we had not heard their motors. Immediately there came the unique whistling sound of falling bombs, followed by the dread C-R-U-M-P! C-R-U-M-P! as they detonated in the square and vicinity. Some thirty men were lost, including several of our own. Our good Major lost a leg, and Captain Colin McKay, a rare "OC", became our chief officer. The events of that night were sickening––too much so for me to attempt a description here—and out of them came a Medal Militaire for Bombardier Brown, a medical orderly of the 12th. On the following morning, Canadian and French joined in funeral services, punctuated

Vrely Churchyard - September, 1918

by frequent shell bursts, in the little church yard. (The following story I will not vouch for as true, though it is quite likely that some such thing did occur.) The French detail sent to the churchyard to prepare the graves for their dead, found most of the space there occupied by German graves. Rankling under the unhappy loss of the night before, they tore open many of the graves, and throwing the dead Boche into an old dry well nearby, applied petrol and then a torch to the lot. (You have the story as it was told to me. Such things seem far more horrible in times of peace to those who have never been drawn into the real active fighting area of war, but to those who "know," far worse things have often happened.)

With us at Vrely, as everywhere else, was the Canadian "YMCA." To its personnel, mostly wounded men from the front unable to stand more active service all honor is due. (Particularly so because as "Y" secretary in any advanced position, their plight was no less dangerous than any other)

Canadian "Y" and lineup at Vrely

One afternoon while on duty at the "forward" position I found to my horror, that there was not a cigarette, a "chew," nor tobacco of any kind among the two crews. Such a sad condition was a most serious one with us, as "fags" were as necessary as "ammo." At the time a man could be spared to find a "Y" and replenish the supply, so I volunteered for the honor and started for the rear. Finding my path blocked by heavy enemy fire I retraced my steps and headed for Meharicourt, where I had heard that the infantry had established a "Y." Two kilos over shell pitted ground spread with tangled barbed wire were covered after much ducking of shell splinters and machine gun fire. In the town an infantryman directed me to the dugout where I purchased a good supply of "fags," plug tobacco, and sweet chocolate at a reasonable price. (Cigarettes were 1 franc, plugs 2 for 1, and chocolate was 2 bars for 1 franc.) On the return I skirted the area where Hun machine guns had so nearly found me a target not long before, and in so doing had to climb over a mound of debris. At the top of the mound was one straggling rosebush bearing a single rose in full bloom. Less than a foot away was the outstretched arm and hand of an all but buried German private. Seemingly his last thought had been to pluck the rose, though of course, such had not been the case. At first sight however, the view held an uncanny appearance. I still have that rose of Meharicourt (which is in Picardy) as a treasured souvenir. As a result of the thoughts that were set going in my mind on the occasion mentioned above, I "waxed poetic," as the boys called it, and for a long time after that day, a certain old song kept running thru my mind. It was "Roses of Picardy," a story of roses, and longing, and of love.

> She is watching by the poplars,
> Colinette with the sea blue eyes,

She is watching and longing and waiting
  Where the long white roadway lies.
And a song stirs in the silence,
  As the winds in the boughs above.
She listens and starts and trembles,
  Tis the first little song of love:–
"Roses are shining in Picardy,
  In the hush of the silver dew,
Roses are flow'ring in Picardy,
  But there's never a rose like you!
And the roses will die with the summer time,
  And our roads may be far apart,
But there's one rose that dies not in Picardy!
  Tis the rose that I keep in my heart!"

Lyrics: Fred E. Weatherly, Music: Haydn Wood,
Chappell-Harms Inc, NY - 1916

Taking my cue from that song, I composed my own tragic and comic versions of what took place that day in homage to the Rose of Picardy.

A Rose of Picardy

There's a song that fills the heart with warmth,
The mind with reverie,
'Tis a song of love and lovers,
And of roses grown in Picardy.

There's another song less known perhaps
And of somewhat dissimilar theme
That also speaks of a rose that grew
Nearby a Picardian stream.

Here's a petal from that latter rose
Found where romance, ageless, thrived.
In a land where Cupid with arrows and bows
Many terrible wars survived.

'Tis part of a rose that I found one day
In Meharicourt in early September,
'Neath a smiling sun in a clear blue sky.
How well, indeed, I remember.

55

The Great War surrounded me
Disgorging its hell and its sorrow,
Its whine of bullets, and roaring of shells.
Warm life today—cold death tomorrow.

Alas! Poor war-torn Meharicourt !
Smoking mounds of twisted debris,
Trenches, dug-outs—now a Canadian fort,
Protected by our Infantry.

At the top of one heap that once was a home,
In full bloom grew a lone untouched rose.
Near it, together, and forever asleep,
Lay two of my German foes.

Half buried they were, in the dust and dirt,
Bodies crushed, their souls long flown.
In their sleep they smiled, forgetting the day,
Unmoved by the wind's low moan.

One lay with his hand stretched toward the rose,
As though his final wish had been
To find in its petals some word from the land,
That never again would he ken.

Standing there, I thought of the ache
His folks would feel when full sure
That the boy whose being they so carefully wrought,
Was now but one price of the War.

Then, a shell bursting near knocked me down,
And my hand touched that of the Hun!
Gripping it tight! My emotions exploded!
Laugh! If you think it was fun.

I jumped to my feet and hurried away,
Plucking the rose as I left,
'Twas the one thing of beauty in that desolate street,
Of all other beauties bereft.

Thus ends the story, such as it was
Of the last rose of Picardy, somewhere in France,
Its sweet scent has gone, but in my memory yet,
Burns clearly that sad "day of chance."

Gnr. C. J Cate - #536636
Canadian Expeditionary Force
Vrely, France, 1918

The vignette of the Rose of Meharicourt is enhanced by events that resulted in the rose petals' disappearance and ultimate reappearance some time later. The following journal entry relayed in a letter by CJC explains: 20/3/19 – On the 3ʳᵈ of October after a 5'9 had terminated a swift journey in the dug-out on which I was sitting, I naturally went "down the line" (It would have been more natural, under the

circumstances, had I disappeared altogether.) En route all of my personal belongings were lost, and however much it may surprise you to know it, that which I missed the most—tho among my losses were several things which represented very dear friends at home—was my rose of Meharicourt. And now after nearly an elapse of six months—back comes these two petals and a bit of fern—it hurts to have lost so much of the beauty—but it is a great satisfaction not to have lost the whole. St. Symphorien, Belgium, '19. CC

In a lighter tone, CJC describes the importance of, and the hazards of seeking– –at almost any risk—those all important 'smokes." CCC

1970 - Granddad Tells a Tale

-I-

Listen my lad—and I'll tell you a tale,
Of a time when more faces than mine grew pale.
'Twas down on the Somme—that last little stunt,
The beginning of which began Fritz's last grunt.
Our guns were silent for the time, you see,
But not so old Boche, who was busy 's could be.
My mates were all weary—and shaky as me,
And it wasn't the shells—from them we were free.
That which we needed was just o'er the wire,
But between us and it was Jerry's hot fire.

All day we had watched for a bit of a slump,
But the sun began sinking with him still on the jump.
So our hopes went down—we'd all done our best,
Though 'twas plain that the night would send us all "West,"

-II-

"I say! I've a hunch! On the right of that slope!
I'm off to it boys—'tis our one and last hope!"
And away goes the speaker, a man of two score,
With a home in God's country—and kiddies four.
Yet here in this Hell with so much at stake
He risks losing them all for his gun crew's sake.
Dan's running—ducking—and now's by the slope,
Full half past the wire is our one and last hope.
And now! He is through it! And over clear ground
He's beating the splinters, bound after bound.
Good God! What's that! Beside him a thud!
That shell has got him. No!...NO! It's a DUD!
Now then the smoke blots him clean out o'sight
But our hero has WON the first half of his fight.

-III-

"Well—it's over I guess, for our hope isn't back.
With the night closed in, blacker than black,
And now—hear you that?" "ACTION ! S.O.S.!"
We've no heart for such, of strength we have less,
Yet somewhere off there in this black inky night,
With our lads in the outposts, Jerry's starting a fight.
The quick-release sticks! My breach—damn, she's stiff!
My tubes are all wet! That's GAS! Get that whiff!
Good Lord, what's next..."Here's your lanyard old man",
And into the gun-pit—thank Heaven—jumps Dan!
And—with him the F A G S! Away goes the gloom,
As away go our shells bringing Kultur its doom.

Finis—(Gi' me a light!)
Rosieres Forward,
(Vrely) September, 1918.

When the 12th left Vrely for "down the line" and a rest, there were many
new faces with her, for the Somme drive, like every other great success, had

58

been heavily paid for. The British had captured thousands of prisoners, with more thousands of dollars worth of supplies, ammunition, and guns (on several occasions I enjoyed the extreme pleasure of turning captured German guns upon the Hun and blasting him out of his shelters with his own shells), as well as a great zone of territory which had been German for four years.

Back over the route by which we had come into Vrely rolled the 3rd Brigade, with every kilo covered bringing us nearer to the final grand drive, though few of us realized just "how final" that drive was to be. When the noise of battle had become but a distant rumble, the column halted on the south bank of the Somme, near Longeau. Everywhere about us a wealth of restful country atmosphere—stately trees, green fields and hedges, wild flowers in blossom, singing birds, and thru it all the quiet Somme flowing slowly along its route to the sea. The war "seemed" far away, but close inspection brought forth blasted tree stumps, barbed wire entanglements, trenches, and machine gun emplacements, for we were not far from Amiens. Nature's brave attempt at hiding those gruesome scars called for fertile land, and that luxurious green received its nourishment from a soil saturated with the blood of warriors not so long ago. Along the south bank of the river crowded the troops, washing clothes, cleaning equipment, and enjoying much needed baths. With my wash spread out to dry, I left the column with the "Big 4" to explore the opposite bank of the river. On and on we rambled over rolling hills and thru sweet scented valleys. All along the way finding blackberries and raspberries growing luxuriously. Perfectly ripened and our own for the taking. We came upon a gully thru which ran a railroad, crossed over it, and saw Longeau Station far down the stretch of shining rails. Gaining the tip of one incline we came upon a large plain, on which were gathered hundreds—perhaps thousands— of captured German guns. There were machine guns, field pieces, howitzers, lights, heavies, mortars, the famous "whiz-bang," the anti-aircraft guns, the deadly 5.9 and many more. They were silent there, but what death-dealing missiles had belched forth from those yawning muzzles! What price the prize! How many of the aching hearts in America, Canada, Australia, New Zealand, British Isles, South Africa, India, France, Belgium, Germany, and God alone knows where else, could trace the cause of the ache to those very guns! Seeing them we shuddered! It is not wise, sometimes, to think. We went on, and in a little while came upon a great camp. Here, living in a city of canvas, were brother Colonials, who had come from far off Australia. They were having a rodeo, and as we watched we saw feats of horsemanship, such as no Wild West Show had ever shown us at home.

The sun was still above the horizon when we arrived back at the long column of "FWDons", guns, and supply lorries. Three of the "Big 4" voted to rest, but I had not seen enough, for my appetite to "see" was always great. Far to the south I could see the top of a glass dome above the trees, upon which the sun was painting all the colors of the rainbow. Toward it I walked—over hills, thru vales, climbing fences, charging hedges, now and then losing sight of my objective. Plunging thru one hedge I found myself in a large fruit orchard, all marked off into squares with neat cinder paths forming the boundaries. There was an abundance of apples, berries, currants, and grapes. Evidence of a brave attempt at "up-keep" in spite of the great labor shortage were plenty. As I slowly followed the path that seemed to be leading me toward the center of the orchard, the war seemed far away. But an occasional rumble persisted in reminding that the Hun was still active. Once when I left the path, to save a few steps, I dropped suddenly into a pit hidden by grapevines. This had been part of the original defense lines constructed by the French in 1914-15. A few steps further, and I reached my goal, which proved to be a fine hothouse. Two long wings extended in opposite directions from a central house, on top of which was an immense glass dome. Entering thru a tiny side door I was alone with countless vines overloaded with wonderful grapes. I ate grapes until my appetite was satisfied, and then I ate more, against the next appetite. Then, picking as many big bunches as I could carry, I found my way back to the column. Here many busy mouths quickly disposed of my offering. "Just a teaser, Cate," they cried. "Where did you get 'em?" Unwisely I told them, and as the sun sank out of sight a raiding party entered the hothouse on the hill. That they too satisfied an appetite of long standing I had little doubt as the column moved on later that night, for "grapes" was the main topic of conversation.

We had been resting at Blavincourt for about three days when a special parade was called, and a charge of "grape stealing" and "property damaging" was read to us. A fine of some 1800 francs was paid out of our canteen fund and the next day we moved on. Undoubtedly the sudden cutting short of our stay at Blavincourt had much in common with the raid at Longeau. The satisfaction obtained by the rightfully angered owner of the hothouse, however, was no greater than that of our own. A part of the branch and stem that once held the finest and most expensive bunch of grapes that I have ever seen, is now among my few souvenirs.

Back to the business of teaching the Hun that no one nation can enforce its own idea of rule upon the world. The 12th was entering upon its last drive, its longest and costliest drive, which was to end with the declaring of an armistice, with the battery not far from Mons, about ninety miles away. Into old territory we went. Arras—and on to Cagnicourt, pounding away at the Boche day and night. Forward, slowly but surely, with Jerry hotly contesting every inch gained. On the second day of September the British artillery alone fired 943,857 shells, and yet the German defense held. Ludendorff and the Great General Staff were plotting desperately. The tide was about to turn. It was FRITZ who now fought defensive warfare.

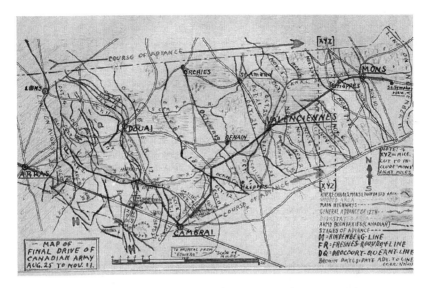

Map of final drive of the Canadian Army - Aug. 25 to Nov. 11

Actually, the towns of Blecourt and Eswars are located West of the Canal de l'Escaut, with Blecourt approximately on a line between Epinoy and Eswars. CCC

A study of the map of that final drive will show that the line or "front", ran from a point some twelve miles north of Arras, south to Arras, and beyond that city about five miles. Extending in a south-easterly direction from Arras for twenty miles, with a depth of from two to eight miles, lay the "Hindenburg" Line. From Lens (ten miles north of Arras) in a southerly direction to join with the Hindenburg Line lay the Fresnes-Rouvroy Line. Beyond these two powerful defense lines was the Drocourt-Queant Line. Thus for a depth of fifteen miles along the whole front the Germans held positions which were all but impregnable. An underground and surface trench system, complicated beyond belief, bristling with rifles, machine guns, and trench-mortars, below which were reenforced concrete dugouts packed with manpower. Everywhere were concrete "pill-boxes" or forts manned by hand-picked troops. Before, in, thru, and around it all was the barbed wire. Back of it all was the artillery with every sort of gun. As though this was not enough, the enemy had also on his side miles of marshy land, mostly under water, the Scarpe river, the Trinquis, the Etaing, the Sensee, and the canals (Sensee, Escaut, and Du Nord) all fortified to perfection. It was a simple matter to flood the whole area in the event of retreat. Forty years of trained thought applied to the possibilities here, and four years of extensive labor putting the thought into actuality produced fortifications being constantly improved and better organized, until it was little wonder that the enemy considered his defenses in this position too much for a war-sick army to force.

61

The tremendous job of overcoming the Hun in his favorite stronghold was given to the British First Army of which the Canadian Divisions were a part. General Sir Henry S. Horne, K.C.B., K.C.M.G. (and some other things), who had commanded many of the same men in this army on the retreat from Mons in 1914, was our Commander on the return to Mons. Our job consisted of overcoming the Hindenburg, Fresnes-Rouvroy, and Drocourt-Queant lines, the fortified Canal du Nord, Bourlon, and capturing Cambrai with its high ground to the north which was the key position. This done, it was up to us to "carry on" to Berlin! Foch's system of creating the impression of an attack in one place while launching a series of small attacks at rapid intervals, at different points along the line, thus harassing and wearing down the enemy, was renewed. The main attack had started on August 26 at 3 A.M. without artillery preparation. By the time the 12th had reached Cagnicourt, some 9,000 prisoners, with hundreds of guns, and much material had been taken. A big gap had appeared in Heinie's plans, and he not only did not like it, but showed that he did not by fighting desperately all the time. At times it seemed as though the 12th would soon have all new faces, for his fire was hotter than anything we had seen. No one was excused. A 9'2 was no safer than a six-inch howitzer. On one occasion as I ran thru a courtyard in which were two 9'2s firing from behind a brick wall, the Boche dropped a single shell so close that the burst killed fourteen and wounded the remaining seven of the men on duty there. It was about this time that the "Big 4" lost its first member, as Bosdet went down the line with a shattered knee.

The 12th moved on, Once again the long lines of wounded men streamed by us, the dead lying everywhere, the wrecked tanks, lorries, guns, and all the rest. Grave digging resulted in such heavy strafing from our "friend" across the way that we were forced to be content with throwing a few shovelfuls of turf over bodies. Horses and mules were dragged to shell holes and old trenches, tipped in, and thinly covered with dirt. The variety of ill scents was surprising in its strength. As on the Amiens drive, there were continuous battles in the air. Sometimes there were so many planes involved that it was impossible to tell which side shot down the greater number. The danger from falling pieces of shells from our own antiaircraft was on the increase. Yet, very calmly did the observation balloons make their daily trips above, long lines of them, seemingly indifferent to enemy airmen. To see one German plane destroy several balloons in one attack and make a safe getaway was getting common. There was one hardy Hun who came regularly for several days at tea-time. From a height so great that we could neither see nor hear him, he would dive with a dead motor, and our first intimation of his arrival was the "rat-a-tat-tat" of his machine gun. Then would come the roar of his motor as he swept up and away from his first victim, and on after the next. His aim was deadly accurate, as the burning tracer bullets proved. As flaming streaks reached the gasbags, there followed a puff of smoke, and the balloon would rise suddenly, jerking at its cable, then bursting into flames. Bag, basket, and cable, shot earthward, leaving behind a trail of smoke and sparks, and one or more observers hanging limp in their parachutes. Often when the observer hit the ground he was found well filled with "MG" bullets. The particular Hun mentioned above met his end one afternoon when a death-charge placed in a decoy balloon caught him unawares. At night, huge searchlights sent their beams skyward to locate enemy planes. When their dazzling shafts of light caught a flyer in their converging paths it went hard with the plane and its occupants. At such times we were treated to an exhibition of "stunt" flying which baffles description. Failing to extricate his plane from such an unhealthy situation, the pilot would dive directly down the path of one light, with his machine gun firing at top-speed, in the hope of putting that particular light out of action. Very often Fritz lost the fight, and a long tail of flames and sparks marked his fall.

Still, the 12th carried on. Along the Arras–Cambrai road we moved, stopping now and then to go into position in a field or grove. The guns were seldom cool, and Jerry's fire was seldom quiet. Occasionally, Sgt.–Maj. Candy put German prisoners to work "humping" shells and ammunition thru the nearly always present mud, while dirty gunners rested weary and aching muscles. If the promise of soup accompanied the "SM"'s request for assistance, the prisoners were willing enough, excepting German officers who were either too proud or too well aware of the fact that the procedure was a little irregular. Haphazard remarks addressed to the "PWs" about their K a i s e r , Hindenburg, and other highlyplaced Germans known to us, brought a chorus of guttural

63

"boos" and a fervent demonstration of "nose-thumbing". It was quite evident that these were not the gray-clad troops who crossed the Belgium border in 1914. One night we rolled into blankets in a little wood for sleep. Shells were dropping much too close, but we were too exhausted to worry. My side rested upon a hard and rough surface, and in the morning I found a spot there, bigger than the palm of my hand, that was black and blue and tender. On investigating I found that I had been lying on an unexploded Hun "potato masher" (hand grenade) all night!

On the first of October the Canadian Artillery fired seven thousand tons of shells. It was a busy day for the 12th. Moving forward to a position on the plains before Haynecourt, "A" and "B" guns were driven past their point of departure from the main road, and after questioning several runners met on the highway, discovered they were very much lost. The "Big 4" less Bosdet, rode in the first lorry, and until shaken awake by an abrupt halt, were sleeping peacefully. An unexpected reply was given to our officer's request for directions which, as near as we could find out, was to the effect that we would reach the German lines in about eight minutes, if we kept on as we were headed. Our informer could not guarantee that our reception among the Hun would be particularly pleasant. In fact, he was surprised that we had not already drawn fire. In the act of turning about, the drone of German bombing planes reached us. This, added to the proximity of German machine gunners who no doubt were enjoying our predicament, did not raise our spirits any. Suddenly all was as light as day. The flyers had dropped flares, and we were in plain view. We scattered from the lorries which were loaded with shells and ammunition, and very liable to create quite a racket if hit by bombs. I fell flat on my face in the shallow gutter by the roadside, and there awaited the first bomb—the others I never expected to hear. Someone said something about, "Good-bye France—Hello Satan!" And then came the dread whistle of descending trouble. Cr-r-ump! Cr-r-ump! Crump! Crump! The air was split with the shock of the exploding bombs. The stench which always follows after heavy explosions stung our nostrils. Steel flew in all directions. Then the flares went out, and the planes flew on, evidently too sure that we were wiped out to stop to look. Three minutes later we were hitting a wild course for "down the line" without having suffered a single casualty. In a short while we had located our position and were placing our guns. (What a celebration for one's birthday—October 2nd!)

Later in the day I was sent back to our last position with a message to bring up the rest of the battery. On the return to "A" gun I came across a young German officer, stretched out on his back, with a bullet hole thru his head. The corner of a black-bordered envelope protruded from his tunic pocket. This I took, wondering what the folks at home were writing to their soldiers of the Rhineland. Here is the letter.

September 22, 1918

My dear Fritz,

Only a week ago, I would have written your birthday letter in a different way. Today, everything within me is dead and destroyed, I am waiting for more bad news.

When I received your letter in which you spoke about spending a vacation together, I was sad. I don't know what will happen now, but I'm prepared for the worst. For your birthday, I wish you the best with all my heart. May all the dreams you have today come true. Above all, I wish for you that your luck will continue and that you will withstand all perils safely and soundly.

This is the third letter I have started to write, two I have already torn and thrown into the waste paper basket. It's not easy for me to find the right tone to express myself, because I don't know what will become of us. I don't want to write you about myself and my love, you should make your decisions free of any influence. Impatiently, I am awaiting your answer. Until then I don't want to write as much, it does not help anyway. After all you know how I feel. For my poor mother's sake I must keep my head up and show courage. I'd rather lie down and neither hear nor see anything anymore. We need someone who would take everything into his hands and who, over all, is good with finances. My uncle is no help at all. On the contrary, he leaves everything to me.

The times in Brussels were all too beautiful, and I remember them in a bittersweet way. Maybe we could have celebrated your birthday together? Now, you are celebrating it all alone, who knows where? Is there a chance for any time off? I don't know yet what I will do now. I have asked for extra vacation and must return to Brussels after that. Maybe then [I] must come home for good. It depends on how things will develop. It is terribly hard for me to find the right tone in my letters. So dearly I would want to pour out my heart to you, like in earlier times, and yet I cannot do it. After all, I don't know yet what I am to you.

So, dear Fritz, accept again my warmest wishes.

Sincerely yours,
Gretel

Translation provided by Astrid Muender & Sophia Bienek-Cate, West Virginia University.

(This boy was a lieutenant in the 8th Battery, 21st Field Artillery Regiment. Probably a part of the 12th German Division—origin Upper Silesia—6th Army Corps). In 1918 the 12th Division was commanded by General Lequis. In

1914-15 this was a part of the German Crown Prince's 5th Army Command. The division saw service in Russia (1916-17), Italy (late 1917) and against the

French and English on many fronts. Had the Lieutenant lived another week he would have gone out of the line with his battery on October 6th and might have been alive today—but what are "might-have-beens" in battle? He gave his life. CJC)

At noon on the 3rd of October, with the battle noises quieter than usual, I sat on the raised edge of "A" crew's dugout bathing my feet. A few yards to my right the rest of the boys were getting their noon rations. One lad (Graham, I think)had just passed in front of me carrying a bucket of tea and a "hunk" of bread in one hand, and balancing a pan of soup and a cover on which a boiled potato and some queer looking mush had been placed, in the other. The whine of a shell reached our ears—but of course, as every old-timer knows, the "ones you hear never hit you." This, however, was one exception to that rule. An instant of the whining, which became a roar, and then....

As the roaring sound in my ears became more defined, I knew that someone was moaning. Then I knew that there were many different groanings and moanings. Suddenly I realized that I, too, was groaning. So I ceased. Opening my eyes I saw, as in a dream, the familiar surroundings of our position, with the ground strewn with bodies, some moving a little, others still. The blackness again. I returned to consciousness , and immediately felt that my back was on fire. That I was about to die, I had no doubt. Placing my hand at my back, I felt but a slippery surface (never realizing that my tunic, shirt, and undershirt had been ripped away), and then my convictions that the war was over for me were strengthened when I saw my hand covered with blood. Again I looked about—some of the bodies were now on hands and knees. One only was upright, and that belonged to Graham, who stood astride one mate who would never move again. Graham's left hand and arm hung limp, but his right hand still held an empty and battered mess-tin. His face wore a most bewildered look as his eyes gazed upon the rest of us. Over against a gun wheel, one of the boys had been propped by Fisher or Cameron, and was being given first aid treatment. Then I crawled on hands and knees into our old dugout—not aware of the fact that I was crawling thru a space where a few moments before had been some three feet of sandbags and several thicknesses of elephant iron. Then darkness for the third time.

When I finally regained my senses, one of our officers was trying to do something to my back. He asked me how I felt, and I told him that I was fine. Then he informed me that my back had been stripped of clothing as well as some flesh. After a rest, I walked to a field dressing station with Bombardier Budd, in whose breast was a tiny red hole. At the dressing station, two orderlies picked a neat pile of steel and gravel from my back, painted most of me with iodine, gave me an inoculation, and tying me up, ordered me to lie down to await an ambulance. For some time I slept. On awakening I saw that the sun was low in the west and remembered that I had had nothing to eat since morning. Beside me was a 12th non-com, who said as soon as he saw me awake, that if it was "jake-a-loo" with me, he for one was ready to return to the battery. I asked him about the dressing on his neck, but he seemed to think that it was nothing serious, so we started back to the guns. Almost back, Cameron, white faced and much out of breath, met us, and commenced cursing me roundly. "Why did you go away without letting me know about it? They told me that you were killed. Damn you, I've a mind to give you a good licking!" But I never got the "licking" and Cam was not as angry with me as he appeared. At the battery we ate, and as we ate I learned what the 12th had suffered from that one lone 5.9 that had entered so suddenly into our dugout. Several days later our Medical Officer removed more steel from various parts of my anatomy. Luckily these tiny splinters had not entered very deep.

It was from this same position that I first entered upon a new type of work, as a runner with Lt. Bacon on reconnaissance duty. The change was a desirable one. On this first trip, there were three of us, including the lieutenant. We hiked forward thru several fields, skirted a village, and then took to a long communication trench which led us out onto a slightly sunken road. Here on the enemy's side of the road were infantry, lying face down, with rifles handy, keeping a close watch ahead. On the other side of the road were small dugouts in which more infantry were sleeping. Here and there was a man busy with needle and thread, or with cleaning rags. The lieutenant talked a few moments with an officer in private's uniform, who closed his conversation by pointing off over a field and saying, "...and keep down." The other gunner was left behind, to be ready to send a message over the wire, in the event that Lt. Bacon thought it necessary. As we advanced out of hearing distance from the road, and reached the wire, the lieutenant began to walk nearly doubled up. This did not strike me as being as pleasant an outing as I had anticipated, for unquestionably I knew that we were being watched by German snipers. There was ample proof of the fact. A sharp command from the officer to "duck" was followed by a sudden burst of "pip-squeeks." Fritz was beginning to wonder just how far we intended to come. My first wishes were for a deep, cool dugout, but as no splinters found us, my courage increased, and I found the experience good fun. It was a relief to reach the protection of a trench which ran along in the general direction of our destination (wherever that might be). This we followed for some time, halting every few minutes, while Bacon looked at the face of some dead Canadian. There were many of them, slouched into every conceivable position. Rounding a curve in the trench we came to an abrupt stop, to find this last outpost manned by a single machine gun and its crew. Bacon talked with the non-com in charge, who showed a very decided distrust of anyone so plainly crazy as to go further in bright daylight. With a crisp, "Follow me, gunner!", Bacon climbed over the parapet, and started to run toward the not far distant roadway. I followed—fast! At the edge of the road we dropped—none too soon, for lead was flying close. About this time I decided to ask where we were going. Bacon obliged me with the information that we were headed for a crumbling brick house on the other side of the road some hundred yards away. We crept along our side of the road to a position opposite the house, and then taking a deep breath, made a dive for the other side. We made it all right, but with hot lead uncomfortably close. From a position behind the dusty brick wall on the second floor, we looked out toward the German lines, and I, at least, was surprised to see that we were within easy calling distance of many troops. The lieutenant was busy making notes. I watched our friend the enemy, seeing many things which interested me. Now and then I pointed out something to my companion, who sometimes examined what I had noticed more closely, then made more notes.

That day I learned that in many respects, all soldiers of all armies are alike. The most noticeable item of all was the fact that without doubt the army opposite was preparing to retire, under protest. Long after dark we made the return to the 12th, with no more excitement other than a few bullets and shells, none of which injured us. I have never mentioned before, that one queer sound of war, is that made by the shells of both armies as they pass overhead, going upon their business of destruction in opposite directions.

About the sixth of October, "A" and "B" guns again moved forward. This time to a position on the outskirts of Haynecourt. As the time drew near for us to open fire the OIC became worried about ammunition, which should have reached the position about the time we did. Lt. Palmer asked Sgt. Troop for a runner. Troop asked Number One of "A" crew (Cameron), and he in turn looked at me. As a gunner I had no one to "pass the buck" on to, and so was "it." My job was to locate the "ammo" train wherever it might be, and direct it to our position, in other words, "Get to that 'ammo' gunner, and get it up here—Snap!" No directions. No suggestions. I remembered having read somewhere something about a "Message to Garcia," and felt slightly important for a very few moments. Darkness, strange country, and weird sounds, soon knocked the "importance" out of me, and I placed my whole thoughts on the route I had chosen. At a crossroads I decided my turn, by remembering which way I had been thrown when our lorry had skidded around the corner for a rutted banking on the left, as on the trip up our lorry had been in trouble getting from a field into the road. I found the spot on my right. Here I met a battalion of Territorials coming in, and at a curve in the road, the Hun caught them with shrapnel, raising havoc. Those who could, carried on, those others just helped each other as best they could. Locating the road over which we had passed thru the field, I commenced to run, for the shrapnel and light shells were close. In the dark I ran onto a dead horse, whose rear legs were stretched out across my path. In falling I lost my helmet and received a mouth full of dirt, then ran on, coughing, spitting, swearing, sweating, and ducking. This "Message to Garcia" stuff makes fine reading, and right there it stops. Of course the train was eventually reached, a message hurriedly delivered to Lt. Bacon in charge, and the trip back to the guns commenced. Back over the route by which I had come I directed the driver of the first lorry. Always on the watch for trouble, I was surprised when after covering more that half the distance, nothing had "dropped" within a mile of us. Just before reaching the crossroads a few shells landed on our right, and our driver was hit. Beyond the turn, all was quiet, but a sting in the air told of many shells which had burst there not long before. Just as we reached our destination Fritz found us with everything he had. Shells, fuses, and charges were dumped out of the lorries into one big heap. With the motors out of the way, Right Section "opened up" and for several hours fought an artillery duel with Fritz. Despite a severe shelling I do not believe we lost a single man that wild night.

"A Message to Garcia" refers to a then much quoted piece written by Elbert Hubbard in 1899 extolling the virtues of Lt. Andrew S. Rowan who, responding to the need of President McKinley to get an urgent message to the Cuban Insurgent General Calixto Garcia, in order to enlist his aid in overthrowing the Spanish occupation forces there, unhesitatingly and without concern for his own safety, underwent a particularly arduous and dangerous journey alone across Spanish held Cuba to successfully fulfill his mission. The pamphlet by Hubbard was written as a best example of how one should respond when given any task. It was so well received by the public that over 40 million copies were printed, to be distributed and read to soldiers and civilian employees alike all over the world. From my father's point of view, the telling of the tale was considerably simpler than the execution of the deed. CCC

Behind the remains of an old wall all six guns of the 12th were pulled into position for the great effort to straighten the line before Cambrai. The famous Hindenburg, and southern Drocourt-Queant lines, and Canal du Nord fortifications had crumbled as the Canadians advanced nearly twenty miles between August 25th and October 2, south of the Sensee River. The double defense systems to the north of the river were still German. The loop thus formed left us in position with German fire reaching us from every point of the compass between southeast and northwest via north. It was indeed an unhealthy sector. The enemy clung desperately to all he had, using in his struggle every device known to modern war-science to hold back a determined army. On the 8th the 12th fired steadily all day and night. About midnight Jerry placed a shell in our "ammo" dump, setting it afire. The blaze was a big one, and a hot one, and drew fire heavier than ever for the remainder of the night. A salvo of two shells falling between "E" and "F" guns wiped both crews off the battery strength. Men were taken from the other guns to keep Left Section in action, and the battery "carried on" as though nothing had happened. Twenty minutes of tying up wounded, and moving dead, were all that was necessary to satisfy any normal man that civilization had not yet reached a point to boast about. Cambrai was in flames, but the red glow which lit up the sky for many miles, was no greater than the red stain of blood which soaked into the fields of Flanders during that drive. The Canadians entered Cambrai at 1:30 AM on October 9th.

The "L o o p" - Somme Drive, 1918

Black line from Lens to Cambrai shows the "loop." Red lines show the defense positions of the Germans. The position of the 12th battery on October 8th (*) is shown.

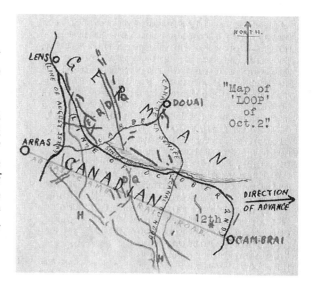

The battery moved to Epinoy, then on to Blecourt, and from there Right Section headed for an advanced position at Eswars. En route the Hun caught us in the light of mid-afternoon in an open field. We must have presented a perfect target for he let us have everything that could be shot from a gun. The leading lorry was hit and stalled, and the whole party stopped. We scattered for shelter, through a hail of steel which hissed and screeched, and sent dust and dirt flying. The field was dotted with little one-man "rat holes" no more than eighteen inches deep, and shell holes of various dimensions. Into these we threw ourselves, often onto the dead bodies of Heinies. From one hole to another we ducked, as our hunches demanded, usually just in time to escape being blown skyward with the shelter just vacated. It was a hectic game of tag, which must have harassed our guardian angels aplenty. After some minutes, with fire increasing, two of the boys jumped into a lorry apiece and we moved on. Before us a deadly curtain of high explosives blocked our entrance onto a little village, but behind—and on both sides—things were as bad, so we kept going. Into the village over the wreck of a road we bounced, with shells churning the ground until it seemed boiling. The din was terrific. Dust and smoke hid the sun. Splintered steel, rocks, pieces of wood, and a lot of most everything filled the air. The canvas, as well as the wood work on the lorries, was ripped to pieces, but the motors continued to function. Out of the village—on to our selected position, and not a man lost! (Talk about the "luck of the navy!")

With "A" and ""B" guns in position, the crews went to work digging their fire trenches (emergency "covers") ten feet long by two feet deep. "A" crew dug down about two, only to find the hole flooding with water. Abandoning the trench, we found a dry ditch about fifteen yards ahead of the gun, and into it we dropped for some sleep before ordered to "Action." One man was left on watch for SOS signals from the trenches ahead, and for gas. At twelve o'clock McNutt woke me for the next two hour stretch. As I rolled out of my blanket, he rolled in, mumbling something about some neighboring batteries opening up during the last hour, and that probably I would get an SOS soon.

Standing erect, the upper half of my body was above the top of the ditch, and although it was too dark to see my comrades less than five feet away, I knew that there was nothing before me to prevent my seeing the expected SOS. Several batteries of eighteen pounders were firing at intervals not far off. Occasional bursts of machine gun or rifle fire added their quotas of disturbance to the night. Now and then Jerry dropped a few shells in the vicinity, and his planes sent down a few bombs. All over the sector there was evidence of life. Now and then Heinie would send up his "onion-strings" in the hope of bringing down one of our planes in flames, and the long rows of white balls of fire would sail crazily through the air until burnt out. Very lights, flares, and varicolored signals flashed up from time to time. Single lights, and lights on strings—white, green, yellow, red, or blue—but the signal for which I watched was three balls of fire in a vertical line—red over red over red. Seconds after sighting it my gun would be surrounded by action—seconds more, and our shells would be hissing on to prearranged targets. But no such signal came during my watch. The time dragged on, the war-sounds continued, the rumble of distant guns, a more defined boom of nearer artillery, the crack of rifles—sometimes almost dying out, and then increasing to a steady rattle, every now and then the sudden uneven "rat-a-tat-tat-tata" of machine guns, the crash of shells landing (some near, some far) and their various warnings as they tore thru the air, the even purr of our planes and the uneven whine—increasing to a roar as they passed overhead—of the Hun planes, followed by the "K-R-R-UMP! KRUMP!" of their bombs after they had whistled their way to earth, and finally, the dull "pouf" of our anti-aircraft shells as they exploded far up along the powerful beams of light from the searchlights. Many noises. But none of particular interest to the man on watch, yet he listened intently for one particular sound, as he watched for the SOS. The sound created by a certain shell exploding with less force than the others. The dread gas shell. The night was a bit chilly, and the man on watch turned his coat collar higher about his neck. It was also a bit lonely as he hummed a song of the British Tommy:

"Night Lites"

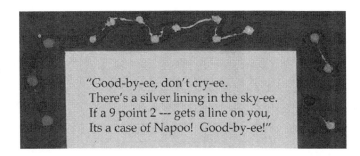

"Good-by-ee, don't cry-ee.
There's a silver lining in the sky-ee.
If a 9 point 2 --- gets a line on you,
Its a case of Napoo! Good-by-ee!"

Suddenly—A red–yellow glare! A choking sensation! A gasped warning true to habit, well drilled, of: "GAS! GAS! GA_!" Then...!!

Short flashes of consciousness left me with some knowledge of what happened after that first sudden shock: Being carried on a stretcher—a night a million years long in the skeleton of some old building with the wind and shell splinters whistling thru it—an awakening to hear faint voices—a hazy suspicion of a sunny morning—a miserable ambulance ride—an overcrowded dressing station—another ride—a field hospital where someone did several things to me—more riding—a restless night at a (#22 Canadian) clearing station—a ride in a much crowded, badly heated box car full of groans, prayers, and curses—more handling—more riding—more night—and a sleep that must have lasted for many hours, for when I awoke I felt myself between clean bedclothes, and these on a real bed (hospital cot).

Note: During the last few months of the war, gas (first used by Germany on April 22, 1915 at the 2nd Battle of Ypres) was nearly always present in quantity more or less severe, making it necessary to wear masks for hours at a time while hard at work on the guns, either moving or firing. A most uncomfortable though necessary condition. The shell mentioned above, detonated on the edge of the ditch directly in front of me, without warning. CJC

Just what occurred in the next few days I do not know. It was the 10th of October when I left the 12th Battery at Eswars, and at least the 16th before I knew for a certainty just what "it was all about." Doctors and nurses worked at their best at #4 General Hospital at Camieres, and their charges recovered because of that fact, or died, but not for want of attention. For some time the wonderful quiet of the ward disturbed me more than it rested me, for it was difficult to realize that for me, there was to be no more of shells, gas, mud, bugs, bombs, filth, action, or in fact, much of anything until the

"MO"s decided that I was once more fit for active duty in the line.

In another letter home following the gassing at Eswars the author's treatment of his injuries was typically lighthearted—although subsequent transfers to two additional convalescent camps while many of his fellow casualties were being returned to duty kept him "in hospital" until discharged on November 15, whereupon he bounced back and forth between convalescent camps until finally, in December, yielding to the overwhelming need to rejoin his comrades, instead of transferring home, he found his way back to the 12th, then stationed in Belgium. CCC

October 16, 1918
No. 4 General Hospital,
B.E.F., France

Dearest Grandma—

Above all do not be frightened because my heading includes a hospital. True I did not come here by choice, but since I am here, and am out of bed again and running around as usual in my hospital suit of blue, am getting the best rest I have had for months. Reason for my winding up at the base is due to a very light touch of gas—one of Fritz's weapons of war which without breaking any bones sure breaks a fellow's heart for awhile. However under care of the finest of Briton's [*sic*] doctors and nurses a fellow is soon out of bed and ready for business. And speaking of beds— can you imagine the comfort of a soft, clean, white bed after months of hard, dirty and scarcely white bunks found "up the line?" No madam, instead of worrying about my state of health—just assure yourself that the comforts derived from being here are almost worth the discomfort endured at first..

The country about here is very different from any I have met with in France since en route to our first position. The hospital is pretty well surrounded with big hills—have not climbed them yet, but if they keep me here a day or two longer I'll know what is on the other side by seeing it from the top. As is my walks have been only along the different walks and roads near my own ward—from the top of any of these hills I should be able to get a fine view.

Yesterday while finishing a letter to Mother one of my mates who came down the line with me but who got separated at the C.C.G., walked up and I learned that we have been in the same ward all the time. Our luck is poor there tho—for mate goes off to Blighty while I remain (so far as I know) at the Base.

Speaking of meeting mates—old timers—yesterday was my big day. During a walk to the Church Army Hut I met a fellow in Yankee uniform who looked natural—he seemed to think I looked familiar as well, and before we had spoken we knew each other—he was a member of the 1st Mass. Amb. Corps in Boston, and we were side numbers on the same ambulance at Framingham. A good chat resulted.

All manner of British troops are in this ward—thus plenty of life and humor to pass away the time. Furthermore, breakfast is up and my appetite is as lively as ever—both you and Aunt Mary know the meaning of that. So love to the both of you and regards to folks interested.

Write soon, Clifton

There did not seem to be much left for me to worry about, so I got busy worrying about "A" gun, the rest of the "Big 4," my pack of souvenirs left behind, and the condition of my ward mates. Most of them were worse off by far than myself, for in some hour of the night, a Canadian flag or the Union Jack, was sure to be draped over the bed of more than one broken soldier. For several days I felt sure that I was going to be blind, but the worries turned to other things when my sight proved to be as fine as ever. A man with a slight ankle wound and a moderate dose of gas should keep in rather good spirits when he sees on all sides men without arms, legs, or with artificial bones in their bodies, laughing and joking, and even smiling when in pain. Once, "Dutchy" Dodge, a nurse "back in the States" had said, "I am glad that you are going over to do constructive work." I failed in my original purpose (that is, to attempt to relieve pain rather than to inflict it) when I left the Medical Corps for the Artillery, but "Dutch" would have given anything she had to have been in some hospital in France, had it not been for a leaky heart valve.

To prompt and proper treatment my system responded as it should. I soon sat up—stood up—walked. Then I received mail from home that was more than welcome. It seems that Mother had been notified that her son had been "killed in action", but an efficient Red Cross Service soon assured her of the true state of affairs. My first day out-of-doors was blessed with a blue sky and a warm sun. I felt so good that I ran after a football which came rolling by me, kicked from a nearby field. That little bit of exertion sent me back to bed for a few days. Then my interest turned to a certain nurse and her dog

"Dinkems", with the result that I regained my lost strength all too rapidly, and was slated to go to #6 Convalescent Camp at Etaples. The following day, which was about the ninth of November, I was transferred to #12 Camp in Auberque, on the heights near Wimereux and the sea. Here I remained until fit for travel, when I was to be shipped back to Etaples en route for "Blighty." "Blighty," by the way, is England.

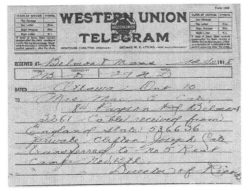

Toward the end of his convalescence a touch of weariness or melancholia seeps into CJC's correspondence... or perhaps he is just eager to get on with things. CCC

S Company, #12 Convalescent Camp
B.E.F. France. 8/11/18 [Nov. 8, 1918]

Dearest Grandma:

Have not heard from Berwick for a long time—is everyone well as usual? Even Mildred has deserted me or else has not received my letters of Sept 15th and October 17th. However I can forgive her all if you will just drop a few lines now.

The weather here has been of the dampest—plenty of mud and other accessories to weeks of rain. Today however dawned with a frost covering everything in the open—our tent flap crackled and snapped in fine style when we hopped out of our warm blankets at reveille. The sun got to work early and all bids fair to be dry and fine by night. It is so clear now that we can see for miles out on the Atlantic from our camp on a coast hill. The smacks and steamers seem to forget that there is a war on—they with the calm manner which the few farmers about here are hauling in their turnips or preparing the ground for next spring produce such a peaceful appearance that the spirit of the troops is high. Not only that but the chalk cliffs of Dover across the channel are very plain today—hundreds of lads whose homes are in Blighty are cheered by that sight, tho the camp spirit here is of the best—all the rain in France can't quench their feeling.

The proper amount of physical training and the afternoon hikes are making us more fit for the line than we were when we came down. Good food and plenty of sleep are also great factors in the freshness of our health. These things with regular passes to town and the numerous manners of recreation are making me feel better than ever—so much so that the doctor will soon decide that my wounds are completely healed and away on the job I'll go, and ready for anything too since a better rest and change I have not had for months.

Naturally in the hospital I made acquaintances which came in handy when we reached our convalescent camp. Now all of them have returned to duty but me—however I have the companionship of several other Canadians so we are well away.

Wish I could spend this Thanksgiving with you—however next year either that or Xmas day will be spent at #16 Bell St.

Since this letter will be the nearest to Xmas of any, accept my love and best wishes for a Merry one now. [*running out of ink, he continues in pencil*] (Ink gone!) Of course this includes Aunt Mary—her hens and your kittens!! Regards to Shoreys and other friends interested.

Love, Clifton

From time to time I got reports from the Battery, either by official communication posted on the bulletin boards, letters from old mates, or other casualties. There seemed to be no doubt that the drive toward Belgium was still going on, and that the Canadians with the British, French, and American troops were surely tying up the Hun. Following the occupation of Cambrai on October 9th, Douai had fallen on the 17th, and then Ypres, Lille, and Ostend were also won. The old city of Valenciennes fell into our hands after much severe fighting thus ensuring, from the first of November, a rapid advance to the Franco-Belge frontier. Countless stories of the great work of the Canadians came to my ears, as they overcame all obstacles—flooded areas—bridgeless streams—"booby traps"—relentless rifle fire—holding together their means of communication by a superhuman effort as they advanced mile after mile over ruined country, much of it under water and practically impassable. We had suffered heavy losses, of course, but the enemy had suffered more. They staged many strong counterattacks, gaining back a little ground only to lose it forever shortly after. One report showed that in one small section of the battlefield near Aulnoy, over 800 Germans were killed by artillery fire alone (most of this wrought by forty-two six-inch howitzers, including those of the 12th). Thousands of prisoners were in our hands. At the end of October the Canadian Corps alone was feeding and caring for over 75,000 liberated French civilians, whose homes (whole towns as well as the surrounding countryside) had been wantonly destroyed by the retreating Hun. The wild manifestations of the civilians' joy at our successes were becoming more and more pronounced, often causing much embarrassment to troops who were surrounded and clung to, even while in the act of ousting enemy soldiers and while under heavy shellfire of high explosives and gas. After Valenciennes the enemy's withdrawal became more rapid, and on the 3rd, 4th, and 5th of November, our mates took Sebourg, Angreau, Roisin, St. Waast, and crossed the Belgian frontier. On the 6th, Quievrechain was captured after stiff fighting, and progress was made along the Conde Canal. Floods and bad roads were causing more hindrance than the German army, but by the 9th, Tertre, Boussu, Jemappe, and Maubeuge were in our grip. German flags were being torn from their standards daily, to be replaced by the Union Jack and the Tri-colors of France or Belgium. On the 10th, at Le Verrerie Chateau, were some of the same troops harassing a beaten enemy, that suffered from that same enemy's hands in August, 1914 at the same place. On the 11th Mons was in the charge of Canadians, and as the 11th Canadian Corps Headquarters was established in the Grande Place, Sir Douglas Haig's last communique was sent out: "Canadian troops of the First Army have captured Mons." By eleven o'clock in the morning our line had been pushed to a point seven kilometers east of Mons. In two months the Canadians had won three great battles: Amiens, Arras, and Cambrai. They had captured over 28,000 prisoners, 501 guns, 3,000 machine guns, much needed supplies, 69 towns and villages, 175 square miles of territory, and defeated decisively 47 German Divisions. In other words, Britain's North American Dominion, had proved quite a help to the Mother Country. A long looked for message was finally received at Headquarters, which read, "HOSTILITIES CEASE AT 11:00 HOURS, NOV. 11, STAND FAST ON LINE REACHED AT THAT HOUR." An answering message of recognition read: "Warning order re-cessation of hostilities received. Thanks."

(Foch's original message to his generals was: "Hostilities will cease on the whole front on November 11, at eleven o'clock. The Allied troops will not, until further orders, go beyond the line reached at that hour." CJC)

The morning of November 11th, found our tents at #12 Convalescent Camp stuffy with dampness. Outside, the sun was hidden by a cold drizzle. Most of us poked our heads out of the tents to turn back with a mean "grouch" well underway. Call to breakfast failed to excite interest. Persistent rumors of an armistice evoked no response. About eleven in the morning a few gathered near the canteen to hear the Armistice Order read by the Camp Commandant, and to hear prayers offered by the Chaplain. I heard no cheering, and saw no signs of great joy. When one man shouted, "Great God, Boys! It's all over! Don't you get it?——" There was no answer. Some of the boys returned to their games. Some went back to the canteen for their beer and light lunch. Here and there were gathered little groups discussing the possibility of truth in the report with slight interest. The whole world was going crazy with joy—up in the line the boys had started a cheer that had grown to a deafening roar—but here at "Con. Camp" the thing failed to go "so big." It mattered "ALL," and yet "not at all." The stupendous meaning of that order did not get "home" because as more than one fellow expressed it, "Aw Hell! In what latrine did they start that rumor?" Gradually, however, as the hours passed, I noticed a new expression coming over the faces about me, and by the time we received word that we were free for twenty-four hours, to go and do as we pleased, we knew that "something" had happened. There was much grumbling at the luck that had kept us out of the line at the finish, and I for one, would have given much to be with the 12th at that moment.

At dusk as I walked into the sea town of Boulogne along with the crowd from surrounding camps, I was startled at the sight of open lights. A new condition—for there would be no air raid that night. The "MPs" (which means Military Police, and some other things) had suddenly and mysteriously disappeared, and it was just as well, for on the hike from camp I had overheard many sinister threats cast in their direction, as well as some reference to a certain incident earlier in the war which occurred at Etaples, and in which some British MPs and some wounded "Jocks" had played a prominent part. In the town, all was wildest confusion, representing celebration. The civilians had gone wild, and they were joined in impromptu parades by uniformed "Frogs," "Limeys," "Jocks," "Canucks," "Aussies," Anzacs," "Southies," "Yanks," sailors, nurses, "WAACs" and all manner of servicemen and girls. Even the dogs yelped with the shouting humanity. Men, women, wine, song, all joined in one great jubilee. The "time" was "NOW"—what of the regrets of an unknown "tomorrow?" Thru the noisy mobs, I pushed my way to the best restaurant in town, previously "For Officers Only," held up every few steps by some man or maid to receive my allotment of hugs and kisses. At the restaurant things were happening. The big plate glass windows in front had been smashed to bits. The "For Officers Only" sign had been trampled under foot. A battle royal was in progress between those inside, mostly officers and their female companions, and those outside, mostly privates and civilians of both sexes. With the attackers I threw my weight—fighting, kicking, pounding, and laughing against the others. Slowly, we fought our way into the room. The month of ease had softened me, and just before I "passed out of the picture," I saw an Australian Major and a private of a Canadian-Scottish Battalion, pounding each other heartily on their respective jaws, grinning broadly all the while. Coming back to my senses inside the restaurant I found my head resting in one ma'mselle's lap, while another was pouring champagne in the general direction of my mouth. Sitting up, I received a cheer, for no good reason at all, except that the fair maid with the champagne improved her aim with invigorating liquid. On a nearby table danced a bright eyed girl, who was suddenly carried away in the arms of the Australian officer of previous mention. Up onto the table jumped a "doughboy" waving an American flag. Under his leadership was sung every national anthem known to the universe, actually including "The Watch on the Rhine." I decided to wait until quiet was restored and then enjoy the balance of the evening with my lady of the champagne. But there was no quiet that night—which of course did not prevent my enjoying myself.

At daybreak of the 12th, I was plodding toward camp in a heavy rain. My veins seemed ready to burst. My whole body burned with a fever. My brain was not functioning as I knew it should, though it did tell me that I should have taken the advice of my friend of the night before and remained in town another night. The close of my "armistice account" will be retold as my London Regiment friend told it to me at a later date: "About 4 AM you came stumbling into our tent and asked if the boys were all back. Two were still missing so we started out to find them. It was raining harder than ever when we reached the first estaminet on the road to Boulogne. To offset your fever we decided on cognac, and so went to the cafe entrance. Here we found a big "Jock" arguing with the proprietress who wanted to close up. The "Jock" objected. She attempted to push him thru the door, and he grabbed a bottle and took aim for the big mirror behind the bar. You jumped for him, and pulled the bottle out of his hand. Just then another "Jock" bounced a bottle off your head and you "flopped." I was carrying you away when both "Jocks" jumped on me—and that's all I remember." As it happened, the same two mates for whom we had started a search, located us, and brought us both back to camp. It was several days before normal routine was restored, and all hands accounted for.

Once again the long hike over hills along the shore of the Channel, and the "dates" with nurses from Wimereux against "Rules and Regulations." Across the channel, on clear days, the chalk cliffs of Dover were plainly visible, and my London friend told me many stories of his life "just over there", often mentioning a certain girl near Tovey Place, Kentish Town. There were more trips to Boulogne—when room could be found aboard the trams overcrowded with "WAACs" and their "Tommies." In camp there was little for me to do but enjoy myself as best I might with lacrosse, or other sports. The "Crown and Anchor" games, "500," "cribbage," and the old standby, "poker," passed away many hours of the nights. In spite of all I might find to do, time began to drag, and though I was subject to fainting spells at every slight overexertion, my condition was much improved.

For weeks I had been homesick for the 12th. Where was it? What was it doing? How about the boys of Right Section? Was the "Big 4" still represented in "A" gun's crew? Fisher had been in the ditch with me on the night of October 10th, and Cameron had not been far away—what of them? The few letters received from men of the 3rd Brigade had not mentioned either Cameron or the "Dreamer". On November 15th I was moved to #7 Ration Depot at Boulogne; on the 17th, to the South Camp at Etaples, on the 26th to Marenla (CCRC–4thDiv), and on the 5th December to Aubin St. Vaast (CCRC–2ndDiv). Not very long after reaching Aubin St. Vaast, a party was to be sent on to "Blighty" by way of Etaples. I was in that party.

Etaples was quite a railroad center, and a little information quietly gathered showed me in which direction the trains bound for Arras went. Next I deserted the party to which I had been attached, and stowed away on a train going "up the line." Arras was easily reached, and I went on toward Cambrai without stopping to look up old friends. At Cambrai I could learn nothing of the whereabouts of the Battery, but found plenty of "MPs" willing to arrest me on general principles. The trek to Valenciennes was a long, slow, hard battle. Of food I found aplenty—but transportation was scarce, and I was not feeling as healthy as when I left. I spent some time in this old town trying to gain some word of the 12th, but to no avail. Eventually, I decided to go on to Mons, in Belgium, where I felt certain that there would be someone to direct a weary traveler. Then my luck asserted itself. As I trudged along a muddy road, a lorry passed me, and on the wide panel at the driver's seat I saw painted a six-inch shell, upon which was a big Figure 3. A 3rd Brigade Canadian Artillery ration lorry I guessed, and the 12th was part of the 3rd. As fast as heavy feet could carry me I ran shouting after the lorry, but it soon passed out of hearing. Uncertain whether to laugh or cry, I stalked grimly along. My feet and legs were carrying twice their own weight of mud. My every muscle ached. But I had gained one thing, and that the knowledge that our ration lorries came to Valenceinnes for their supplies and mail. About an hour later I again saw the same lorry, parked outside a ration depot. I charged toward it, and there before me was Bombardier Holmes, ration orderly of the 12th. Confronting him I spoke (I wanted to embrace and kiss him!). For an instant he stared at me, then said, "Cate! Well I'll be damned! I thought you were..." But it matters not what he thought. Far more important was the fact that he found room for me in the back of the lorry, and as we rattled and bounced along toward the Belgium border he told me much about the Battery.

Ghoulish Nightmares

CHAPTER VI

The Canadian Army—In Belgium,
And a Trip To Germany.

In an old convent in Boussu, I located the battery, and into a room on the second floor, marked "RX" I hurried to greet my old mates. Inside the room I soon became convinced that the "RX" marking was wrong, for the six faces about me were not the old familiar faces I had expected to find. Then...the reassuring voice of Cameron, as he bounded into the room. Preliminary greetings over, we visited the other rooms on a hunt for old friends. A general exchange of experiences followed, and I learned that the 12th had played its part well in the great advance, although losses had been heavy. This fact explained the many new faces. Fisher had "gone down" with me, and reports had it that he had been sent home to Canada, to die there from the effects of gas and wounds. No word had come from Bosdet. Several of those wounded since the commencement of the "Somme do" had found their way back "home" as I had. The 12th was still ready for instant action at a word from higher up.

It was not long before the "SM" sent for me. Reporting to him, I was greeted with, "Gunner, you are not on battery strength. I have had no orders to place you there. Where have you come from? What are you doing here?" Momentarily cheered and strengthened by Cameron and other old mates, the SM's wordy barrage brought back the feeling of exhaustion that had come over me in Valenciennes. The SM was an "old-timer," and presented a hard boiled front, but his heart was in the right place, as subsequent action proved. While I went to bed to sleep off a fever, he took my case before Major McKay, and by morning of the next day I was once again official #2 of Cameron's crew on "A" gun.

The fatigues about quarters and guard duty at the gun park were play, but

I was surprised to learn that at an early hour every day the brigade must have a dress parade, also that "Rules and Regulations" demanded that the brass on the guns, carriages, and caissons be polished daily. This state of affairs was the cause of much grumbling among the boys. An ordinary parade at a more reasonable hour, and thorough gun cleaning every week, would leave the troops in a much more satisfactory mood. The right to a less strict discipline seemed due to us after many months of severe action. Several of the original members of the 12th spoke of a change to their non-coms and found the latter in accord with their ideas, but the officers were inclined to remind us that "orders are orders." Thus it came about that first one battery, and later the whole brigade, struck to obtain their point. There were threats of arrest for insubordination and refusing duty, but in the end a wise Colonel Beeman made several satisfactory changes.

Boussu was an ordinary Belgium town, of somber aspect, made more so by weary-faced civilians and dreary weather. The Hun had left little of value behind that the townsfolk could gain a living from. Most of the nearby coal mines were flooded, and what few factories might once have existed were then in ruins. The winter season prevented farming. Food was scarce. Daily the bread and soup lines at our kitchens grew longer, and the government communals became greatly overtaxed as civilians crowded back into the district so lately occupied by Fritz. Wearing apparel for all except a few of the "wiser" ma'mselles was a combination of old rags and parts of clothing once worn by Belgian, French, British, Canadian, American, and German troops. The Army Medical Corps worked hard to keep down disease, aided by the efforts of many thrifty housewives with their well worn scrub brushes. Amusements were severely plain. Of course, the small estaminets did a good business with their poorly varied stocks of wines and beers, and their "entertainers." The latter were not the clever, thoughtfully costumed, highly decorated "chic" dolls of Bruxelles and Paris cabarets. With few exceptions they were strong, overdeveloped girls, from fourteen to forty, with plain features emphasized by plainer covering, and, as often as not, shod with "bottines de bois." They were, nevertheless, far less dangerous playmates than their better appearing "sisters of the trade" in the cities.

In spite of all their many hardships, the civilians' hospitality seemed unlimited. Every family had its quota of soldier-friends and visitors, made as welcome as possible. If, in the back of a "civie's" mind was the thought of profit gained thru attention offered, no censor of the fact is admissible, for troops are human beings after all, and to each individual comes first the satisfying of his own personal desires. The truthfully complete story of each soldier-and civilian-life during the war will never be known, and it is better so. The thousands of personal and historical accounts, censored and selected as they are, are sufficient to an imaginative mind. War, at best, is rotten, yet through it all runs a certain indiscernible atmosphere which leaves something missing from every ex-soldier's peacetime life.

Nearly every Belgian youngster made it his proud duty to "adopt" some one of us as his own particular Canadian. One cold and rainy night on guard duty at the gun park, the rain had so soaked my greatcoat that its weight had become burdensome. My cap lay limp upon my head, sending little streams of water down my neck and over my face. My shoes having slopped thru the mud and water along the beat, were soaked thru and heavy. The rifle, its breach protected under my armpit, sent a steady stream of water off its down-pointed muzzle onto my puttees. The canvas-covered guns lay in shadowy rows in the park like many sleeping monsters (which they really were). It was one miserable night. I stopped at the end of my beat to wait for my relief just before two o'clock. A brother sentry splashed and slouched over his route spitting vehemently at every puddle reflecting a bit of light. I dropped the rifle butt to the ground, and rested my weight on my hands, crossed over its muzzle. My thoughts were not of the gun park, Boussu, or Belgium, but of "home". No particular place...just a combination of Sharon, Mass, Berwick, Maine, and East Alton, New Hampshire.

Very faintly at first, and then more distinctly I heard a timid voice. I suddenly realized where I was, and saw before me, a small, scantily clad boy of about fourteen (though he looked much less) looking up into my face. His hands rested lightly upon my own. "Bon soir, Monsieur. Le nuit est mal." "Right you are, Sonny. But why are you out so late on such a night?" He told me that he had been watching me for over an hour, waiting for the time when he knew that my relief was due, so that he could invite me to his home for cafe. "Votre mere–et votre pere?" I asked. "It is all right," I gathered from his native tongue, "You are expected. My father works at the mine. My mama keeps the coffee hot." "And who else?", I asked. "Olga, ma soeur—" but I interrupted him with, "No. No. Mon ami. Je suis trop fatigue. Un autre nuit, peut-etre." Too many sisters had sent out older or younger brothers with similar invitations, and quite often the results had not been benefiting to good health. My new found friend divined my thoughts and his expression showed plainly his disappointment. He spoke again, his eagerness to make sure that my mind translated his language as he intended, causing him to tremble slightly. "Mais, mon Canadien! Vous no comprendez. It is not for *that* I invite you. La petite Olga—she is younger than I!" In the end, I agreed to accompany him to his home, and he disappeared into the shadows until I was relieved from my post.

Although officially attached to the guard, and not supposed to leave the guardhouse except on duty, I received permission from the corporal to be absent for an hour. Meeting the young man whose invitation I had accepted, we started for his home which I had thought was within a few steps of the park.

For some distance we walked thru the rain. Up alleys, down roads, thru a small field, skirting some deserted factory. I began to wonder just what sort of a home this fellow lived in, and also where it was. After about twenty minutes of fast walking we reached a long, low, whitewashed building. From a shaded window in the end nearest, shone a dull yellow light. Opening a door, the young man called, "Mama! Le Canadien!" Stooping low so as to miss the low doorframe, I followed my guide, and stepping down over one or two stone slabs found myself in a small room. The ceiling and walls were whitewashed, and the floor was of red brick. Two curtained windows I noticed, and two doors, one to the street, and the other (as I learned later) into a tiny bedchamber and another chamber a bit larger. A few old and cheap pictures, a religious illustration, a statue of Mary, and the inevitable Cross, graced the walls and the mantel over the small open-grate stove. An old sideboard, a closet, a table, several chairs, a few cooking utensils by the stove, and a few dishes on the table, made up the rest of the furnishings.

As my young friend hung up my cap and coat on a chair, his mother poured the coffee and produced some dark bread, a saucer containing what looked like lard, and a dish of hard brown lumps. I found that the 'lard' was somewhat sweet and meant for the bread, and that the lumps were also sweet and for the coffee. The boy told me to call him Jean, and that his full name was, Jean Baptiste St. Pierre. My name became "Charles," in spite of all my attempts to make him say "Clif." The moments passed. Jean and I had munched the last of the bread, drunk our coffee, and I was about to refill my pipe as the chamber door opened slowly. "Olga!" said the mother quickly, as a tousle-haired girl of eight or nine slipped thru the opening and dashed into the shelter of her mother's dress. There she remained, peeking out from time to time. Conversation was slow. The mother's eyes were ever on the boy, whose gaze never left my face except to study my uniform. My hour was up, and after a hurried promise to return the first time I was free I returned to the guardhouse. There were many visits made to Jean's home, and to the homes of several of his relatives. An evening at the home of any, meant an evening filled with many new faces, many old faces, wine, lunch (in which I saw much evidence of our own canteen and kitchen), laughter, music, dancing, and a bit of all around good cheer and friendliness. Often I slept at Jean's home in the tiny chamber off the kitchen-dining-living room. From these visits I learned much about the stay of the Hun, his arrival in 1914, and his leaving not so long before. Jean's cousin, Georgia, who cared for the small store "up the street," provided me with the companionship which helped my stay in Boussu.

(Note: A letter to Jean, sent in care of his father, Monsieur Demonstier Nicolas, #36 Rue Montanbon, Boussu-Bois, Belgium, was never heard from nor was it returned to me. So it seems that my friend of Boussu had left his old home after I reached America. CJC)

Chateau entrance, Mons, Belgium

From Boussu, I made many trips to nearby towns to poor "moovies," dances, and other more or less futile attempts at amusement. Hornu, Jemappes, and even Mons, failed to excite much comment. The troops were, to say it in the army way, "sweating about leave to Bruxelles and Paris."

Shortly before Christmas, the brigade moved to St. Symphorien, about seven kilos beyond Mons on the road to Chalroi. "A" subsection was billeted in a two-family brick house on the outer edge of the town in the direction of Germany. The crossroads at this spot was where the leading patrols of the German and British armies met in 1914. The civilian occupants of the house were a middle-aged couple, who looked more German than anything else, and often acted very much as though they were German. This red brick two-family house was not very large, and though I never investigated, I do not think it had either a second story or cellar. The floors were red tile, the walls were barren, and the ceilings dirty. The crew was divided into three parts, each finding a section of the floor in the two larger rooms for blankets, kits, and sleep. Cameron and I commandeered a small room for ourselves. Where the two civilians slept is more than I can remember. Each of the larger rooms boasted of an open-grate stove of ancient manufacture. Water was out in the well in the yard, and none too clean. The rest of the battery was spread over the town in this same vicinity, with the cookhouse and quartermaster housed in an old factory. Baths were to be had in the little mining town of Havre, some six kilos away, and to them we went about twice a week.

The town was a cluster of dirty brick, wood, and plaster buildings, intersected by mud or slimy cobbled streets, with neither a decent building nor a pretty face to relieve the strain. The civilians were more than "fed up" on war and occupation, and though they tried at times to be hospitable, their efforts lacked both strength and conviction. Certain actions at

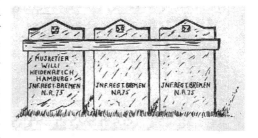

times, from a few of them, indicated sorrow at the Hun's departure. Even the wines and beers in the several miniature estaminets lacked all punch. About the only thing in or near the place of interest was a soldiers' cemetery not far from "A" sub's quarters, built by the com-

bined efforts of civilian and prisoner labor under German supervision in 1914 and 1915. On its main shaft was inscribed the legend, "DEUTSCHEN UND ENGLICHEN SOLDATEN." Here slept many young men from over the Channel and over the Rhine. The German graves were marked by marble slabs, many of which had all but returned to dust from neglect. The British graves were large circles in which many occupied one grave, and around which had been planted evergreen trees, for the most part in flourishing condition in the winter of 1918. On one big grave the legend on the wooden monument read, "46 ENGLISH SOLDIERS of the ROYAL MIDDLESEX REGIMENT," mute testimony to the loyalty and sacrifice of England's "Contemptibles."

Most of us spent a great deal of our time in Mons, where the buildings

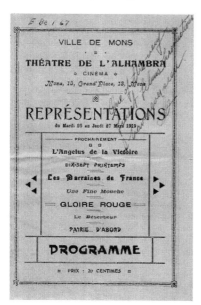

were more respectable, and where there were several good estaminets and cafes, one good cabaret, and a good movie house, the "Theatre De L'Alhambre." At this cinema house I saw an excellent picture, "Vendemiaire." Here too, was where the "3rd Brigade Concert Party" first performed, which produced much first-rate entertainment, enjoyed by troops and civilians alike, before starting on a tour that ended with them in Canada. Every soldier located a "home" somewhere in the vicinity, and some more than one. Also, inevitably, from the doorway at #8 Rue de "Something-or-other," as well as several other places, could almost always be seen a long line of waiting soldiers, many of whom would be seen later, lined up for a different (though related) purpose involving physical inspections—"Nighttime Line-ups" leading to special treatment followed by a trip down to base hospital.

As the time drew near when leaves were to be granted there arose a wild search for money. A shady practice developed. Civilians were found to be in possession of everything from an army toothbrush to a motor lorry, claiming that they had purchased all in good faith from soldiers and officers. Everywhere there suddenly developed a shortage of blankets, clothing, and articles of equipment. A kit inspection would have met with failure! Cameron and I collected some cash by way of a few "sales", but chiefly thru poker and "the old board" (Crown and Anchor). Dice rattled and rolled continuously. It was then that I more than missed the best "go-getter" in the army—Bosdet, who could always be relied upon to produce needed cash. On the other hand, life in St. Symphorien took on a new aspect, for at least, we had Paris and Bruxelles to talk about. On Christmas night I was on guard duty at the gun park, thus missing the Christmas dinner with the boys. One old reliable, Cameron, came out and relieved me so that I could get in "on the finish." To the eternal honor of QMS Bailey, and the chefs, Young and Sharpe, I want it known that our Christmas dinner of 1918 was a rare success.

CHRISTMAS SUPPER 1918

* * * * * * Soup * * * * * * *

* Turkey * * * * * * * * * *
* * * * * Roast Pork * * * * * *
* * * * * * * * * Roast Beef *

* * Creamed Potatoes & Gravies * *

* Carrots Cabbage Turnip Beets *

* * * * * * * * * * * * * *
Dressing Catsup Pickles
* * * * * * * * * * * * * *
* Plum Pudding & Cream Sauce *

* * * * * Mince Pie * * * * *

* * * Apples * * * * Oranges * * *

* * * * * * * * * * * * * *
* * * * * * * * * * * * * *

* * * * * Concerts * * * * * *

*In a history of the Canadian army in the First World War, Canadian Expedition-
ary Force 1914 - 1919, the official version of Christmas, 1918 reads: "The Canadians' occupation role in Germany lasted well into the New Year. A timely snowfall
on the night of 24 December enabled all units to celebrate the white Christmas to
which so many were accustomed at home. The traditional turkey and accompanying luxuries might be missing (they arrived later), but resourceful messing officers
ably backed by expert battalion cooks saw to it that all enjoyed a Christmas dinner
worthy of the name." Truly, in the 12th's case those heroic efforts were well appreciated. In yet another letter home, Gnr. Cate commemorated the occasion to his family. CCC*

Reg #536636 C.G.A.
B.E.F. France
X'mas Day

Dearest Grandma:
      The Christmas that we all expected to be so unlike X'mas has so far
proved out to be somewhat like X'mas after all. The first snow of the year
in this part of Belgium fell during the night—and this morning dawned
unusually bright and snappy, with patches of snow here and there over the
houses and fields. And even now at mid-afternoon there is some snow
left. After breakfast my section met in one of the billets and received
cigars, tobacco and candy from our section commander, and his wife in
Canada. Of course there are no parades today—and in spite of any reason
there may be for our not enjoying X'mas as usual—that reason is being
brushed aside for the spirit of Christmas has invaded the place in a most
earnest way. A mate and I had made arrangements to spend the afternoon
and evening with some civilian friends in Hornu, but as it happened my
mate was hit for guard duty. As a result I have taken his place since it is
quite important that he should keep his engagement whereas it makes
little difference to me. This evening our battery will have its X'mas dinner in a very good hall in town—and it is to be some dinner too. Roast
turkey and all the fixings, vegetables of all the necessary kinds, puddings–
–good things to drink—we shall be well off indeed. There won't be any
pumpkin pie such as I used to get, and hope to get yet before very long at
#16 Bell St., but there are numerous substitutes. One of the best things of
all is the fact that the War is over!—and that we know, in so far as it is
possible, where our next X'mas is to be spent.
      We are no longer quartered at Boussu, but have changed for billets
which are more quiet and which are not uncomfortable. Our particular
hostess is very kind—forever trying to make us more comfortable. Much
of our washing she does for the sake of the help it is to us. Last night she
cooked some ruffles—in other words queer looking things tasting much

like our own griddle cakes—those with syrup (which we made ourselves) went very well indeed. On the whole we are quite well off.

My turn for the beat comes in about five minutes so will finish up with love for you and Aunt Mary, and regards for the Shoreys and others who may ask for me. We may well feel thankful that there is such a short while between now and the time when I shall give you my love in person. Write soon. Clifton

A perhaps more poignant remembrance of Christmas day is revealed in the memoir narrative. CCC

On the 24th Jean had trudged all the way from Boussu to Mons to find me, for I had promised to be with his family for Christmas. All thru the afternoon and evening he had hunted about the little city for me or for someone who knew me, all in vain. Back to his home he went early Christmas morning— perhaps I would not forget—but when the family and the relatives had gathered at the table to honor an ordinary buck gunner of the line, I did not show up. Guard duty held me fast, and there was no way of notifying my friends. With them at the New Year supper, I had to do a lot of explaining before some of them believed that I had not found a better home. Jean and Olga trusted, Georgia was willing to, and the others managed to forgive as best they could. To me it was evident that all had dug deep into the meager supply of cash to prepare the "great" Christmas celebration to which I had failed to come.

* * * * * * * * * * * *

The last half of 1918 had spelled "absolute failure" to German militarism. The German navy had never been able to crawl out from under the rust of inaction. The U-Boat policy had been a bitter disappointment. Ludendorff's "great fifth offensive" of July, in which 650,000 troops were to advance once and for all time thru the Allied lines, never really got under way before the wise Foch had labeled it "FAILURE." The Belgians, supposedly "done," had broken thru from the Yser. The British and the Colonials had raised havoc in Flanders and Picardy. The French had left the once Hun-possessed Aisne and Champagne far behind in their advances. The Americans had not only won the Meuse Valley, but had gone on. The whole had ended with the German army in danger of annihilation. Allenby, with his British, Sepoy, Arab, and French forces had overcome the Turk in the Holy Lands. Bulgaria had also collapsed. The Italians had defeated the Austrians. "Lying placards" had failed to stem the tide of resentment of the German people at home that was directed toward the war and its makers. The wretched Kaiser had fled to Holland to escape the "mob." The "War Lords" were in hiding, desperately penning frenzied "excuses," "explanations" and "denials." The final attempt at a peaceful settlement, without having to pay for crimes committed, had failed. A still great nation, groaned in agony as it struggled to free itself from unbreakable shackles bound about itself, by itself. The field fighting was done— but the recovery bid fair to be more painful than the worst pessimist could imagine. So much for Fritz. His self invited punishment could not repay the rest of the world, particularly Belgium and France, for damage suffered because of the "Kaiser's War."

Three months of the New Year, 1919, were spent on the Continent. During that time, the war was all but forgotten, and the troops made the most of the many privileges granted to them. Several leaves to Bruxelles, one of which included visits to Louvaine and Antwerp, an "official" first long leave (and a hurried unauthorized second) to Paris, a trip (AWOL, again!) to the German Rhine, and many short passes to districts within the Mons sector, were my lucky allotment. Something of those trips follows.

Brussels is often called "Little Paris," and the name is well deserved. Just as the Frenchman glories in his beloved "Gai Paree," does the Belgian admit no peer to his wondrous Brussels. On January 6th I received the first of several leaves to this truly great city, and within a few hours was with the "leave party" on board a lorry bouncing over the "King's Highway" to the capitol city. The lorry was overcrowded, and the evil smelling exhaust was blown into our faces along with the dirt of the road, but no happier sounding lot of boys ever trod on one another's feet.

From a point of vantage on the tailboard, I could get an occasional breath of fresh air, and could also keep the less lucky members of the party posted as to our progress. The distance from Mons to Brussels is about thirty-five miles. At every town thru which we passed—Soigines, Hal, Uccle, and others—I checked the mileage and reported. At St. Gilles I shouted, "Here we are, boys!" but found that there were yet many minutes of riding to come before we reached our destination. There were frequent cries of, "What do ya say! How much more we gotta go? Can'tcha get a little life out o' this old tub?" At last, with our patience sorely tried, the lorry came to a halt. "Here ye are, Canadians! All out!" shouted the driver, as we tumbled into the busy "Marche de la Grande Place," often in other days, the scene of many hard fought battles and "friendly" jousts of old nobility. Surrounding the Place are many famous old buildings, among them the Hotel de Ville (1410) with its tower (1454) reaching up 360 feet above us, and opposite, the Maison du Roi (1443-1877) standing where several of its predecessors were destroyed by fires of peace and war, and the Maisons des Corporations, with its many figures far above the street dedicated to the various establishments of commerce. The atmosphere of these quaint buildings was charged with romance, strengthened by the many venders as they scurried around advertising their wares, which included a little of everything from cabbages to lace.

(Note on spelling: BRUSSELS–English; BRUSSEL–Belgian; BRUXELLES–French. CJC)

Leaving the square thru a narrow lane, we came upon a fine statue erected in honor of the brave English nurse, Edith Cavell, shot down by a German firing squad October 12, 1915. Miss Cavell, a professional nurse when the Hun took Brussels, had remained to nurse impartially all nationalities, including German. Arrested by Fritz, she confessed to having assisted certain Allied soldiers to escape thru the German lines, was secretly tried, condemned, and executed, in spite of the efforts of the American legation to bring her case before the highest German authorities. Certainly her record of fair service to all demanded finer consideration.

Nearby was the office of the Canadian Paymaster. To him we went, before looking up the mansion at #84 Avenue Brugman, which had been turned over to Canadians on leave. Here we found a private dwelling full of interest, most particularly the beautiful ballroom. From there, we went to the Canadian "Y" in a former German department store on Rue Neuve at the corner of Rue du Pont Neuf, where the leave party was disbanded and turned loose to "see" Brussels according to each man's idea of "seeing". Much of my time was spent in company with Cameron, although occasionally we became separated for various reasons, and carried on alone or with others.

At 38–40 Rue du Pont Neuf was "The Old Banjo Tavern" which its proprietor from Norwich, England, called "the home of the BLIGHTY BOYS." This congenial host, "Bill" Frosdick, had handbills all over the city which said that he would "...be pleased to give any information so as to be able to see the sights of Brussels in the shortest space of time also to amuse the boys with his Banjo, Dulcimer, and One string fiddle that he managed to make during his stay with Fritz." Also he advertised, "GOOD AIRED BEDS," and, "Specialty OLD SCOTCH-ALE, the glass 50 centimes." I have heard that many a soldier enjoyed the whole of his leave with "Bill" and his "ALE."

The home of the « BLIGHTY BOYS »

THE OLD BANJO TAVERN
38-40, rue du Pont-Neuf
(the street in front of the Y. M. C. A. Rue Neuve)

Speciality OLD SCOTCH-ALE the Glass 50 centimes

Mʳ WILLIAM FROSDICK, the Proprietor (from Norwich)

Will be pleased to give any information so as to be able to see the sights of Brussels in the shortest space of time also amuse the boys with his Banjo, Dulcimer And One string fiddle that he managed to make during his stay with Fritz.

GOOD AIRED BEDS

Another interesting place on Rue du Pont Neuf was the brilliant Cabaret Madrid. Here was night life enough for any trooper, with all of its glamour and alluring "entertainers". There was good music and fine dancing exhibitions, all of which could be watched or participated in, provided you kept some purchase before you on the table. If the purchase happened to be liquid, as it was expected to be, it had better be left on the table if one desired to "watch" very long, for the Madrid's liquors were potent. Cash was the big word, and woe unto the gallant of the lower ranks if some bewhiskered, rheumatic old officer at another table advertised more freely, his pile of francs, to the younger gallant's companion of the night. The rule worked both ways as well, but the reverse order seldom made an appearance. On the one exception I noted, two of the younger, and therefore truly pretty girls left their two officers several tables away, and came to the table at which Cameron and I were seated. For some time we carried on famously, but after Cam and I had purchased and consumed much of everything in the place that was drinkable, the girls were still sober, whereas two noble 12th gunners were about to go "under the table." When the two companions suggested that it was time we left, Cameron collared me and we did leave followed by our two companions. Just how and perhaps "why" the ever faithful "Cam" disconnected us from those two dangerous though attractive ma'mselles is more than I can remember. I awoke later in an armchair in the "Y", with a "head" that was never my own! Cameron sat on the floor about five feet away grunting and massaging his head, and he too insisted that the head he so carefully stroked was not his own. (But this is not "The Confessions of a Canadian Gunner.")

There were other cabarets, which we visited for a few moments only, for they were NOT at all conducive to good health. A day of sightseeing at a speed that was dazzling followed. Over the broad boulevards, thru narrow, winding alleys and lanes, into parks—and out, then to enter splendid buildings that were surely examples of architectural and constructional expertise seldom surpassed. Going from the most modern, to the dusty and musty ancient, by a simple "turning of a corner." The Palais de Justice, at the end of Rue Royale, one of the finest "piles of stone" in the city, overlooking a variety of roofs of houses so old that the oldest inhabitant has forgotten the stories he heard as a child about their original owners—La Bibliotheque, with miles of printed volumes and priceless manuscripts, and its statues and paintings—La Bourse, in the business section—La Poste Centrale, which, after all, did not seem so different from our own old Central Post Office in Boston—l'Eglise Ste. Gudule, its massive towers looking out over the quaint old roofs and the more modern structures (a sort of giant guardian of them all, which in truth it is), and inside, the wondrous sculptured figures and woodcarvings, the paintings, the marvelous stained glass windows, and the pulpit.

There were also La Chaire de Verite, which held me entranced as I studied the story carved upon it of Adam and being driven out of the garden of Eden—and then the squares, Place Rogier, and many others—the monuments which fill nearly every available space throughout the city. Colonne du Congress in Place des Martyrs (the latter, which is dedicated to the Belgians killed in battle with the Dutch in 1830)—the former, a monument to the founders of the realm, that reaches skyward for one hundred-fifty feet, crowned at the top with a Belgian hero-statue of old, and displaying on each of the corners that form its base, figures representing the essential liberties: Worship, Press, Asociation, and Education. Anspach Monument, the Statue des Comtes d'Egmont et de Hornes—all to be "seen" in just a few days. Such a whirl of interest! L'Eglise Ste. Gudule, and its Verbruggen masterpiece, that was built in 1220—L'Eglise Notre Dame des Victories, built to commemorate the battle of Woeringen in 1304—La Chapelle, dating back to 1210. Then there was the Ecole Militaire, and the Palais du Roi, in use at the time as a hospital.

THEATRE
DE LA GAITE

Duquesnoy's famous child-fountain, loaded down with countless legends, was a source of much amusement and some speculation by the troops.

Cameron and I toured together the Porte de Hal, and the last of the Palais des Netherlands, which was destroyed by fire in 1731 and was now a part of the new palace grounds—and Waterloo, where the British finally brought Napoleon to terms. All this, and much more that I have forgotten, was crowded into the all too few days I had in Brussels. I could have enjoyed three months without tiring of that city where dwells the brave King Albert and his loyal Queen Elizabeth. What a continuous round of pleasures and interests—to be followed by an evening at the Theatre de la Gaite—followed in turn by the cabarets. Sleep!?! What time for that?

We made a hurried run to Louvain, once the capitol of Belgium (14th Century), and visited the University and its noted library, the ruins of an ancient castle, the famous church of St. Pierre (15th Century), and the Hotel de Ville (1448–63), with towers and statues that rivaled in beauty the Hotel de Ville in Brussels. Here by a little stream once camped Julius Caesar with his conquering army.

Accompanied by Williams of the Light Field Artillery, I visited Antwerp on the river Scheldt. On this day the weather was "not so good," but we splashed around the cathedral over 600 years old, went to L'Eglise St. James, and into the museum, and the art gallery. This city boasts of miles of docks, and is one of the greatest commercial centers of Europe, and yet it "keeps clean." If I had had the time, a grandmotherly old lady said she would show me how to make lace, but I compromised and made a small purchase instead. In a warm and dry cafe Williams and I wasted too much time with two pleasant companions, with the result that our visit had to be cut suddenly short for a race to the train. Then back I journeyed to the city of Brooksele that was once a mere crossover for the Senne. Here in spite of my scurrying about, I enjoyed the hospitality of the widow of a Belgian officer, met on my first day in the city, for my last six hours in Brussels. Our talk was not of the war, but of Belgium and America, and the greatness of both, in art and in commerce. The 10th of January found me bidding goodbye to a city, whose charm I can never forget.

Back in St. Symphorien I did not feel the same oppressiveness I had known before. There was something to talk about. A friendly family living a few kilos up the road from our billets made our visits pleasant. The long walk under the stars, coming back after a well spent evening helped to keep us in condition. (The "us" being Cameron and myself) Then also, there were the parades for casual inspection, and for the volunteering for duty with the Army of Occupation and the upcoming Siberian Expedition. Not many of the 12th cared to extend their term of service beyond the "duration of war and six months after" period.

On February 4th, returning from a short stay with my friends, Jean and his family at Boussu-bois, I learned that my Paris leave had "come thru." Over a month before I had entered my request for this leave in the approved army fashion.

St. Symphorien, Belgique

From: Gnr. C.J.Cate, #536636
To: O.C., 12th Canadian Siege Bat.

Sir: I have the honor to request permission to be absent from my quarters for seven (7) days, for the purpose of proceeding to Paris, by train. My last leave was from May 4 to 9, 1918.

My address while on leave will be "Hotel Paris-Nice, 38 Rue du Fauberg, Montmartre.

I have the honor to be, Sir–
Your obedient servant

Gnr. C.J.Cate, January 2, 1919

(Note: There is a difference in leaves. Although I had enjoyed many days away from quarters since the 9th of May, they were not considered officially as "full leaves," and as I had requested no "hospital leave" (although entitled to one), my good friend Sgt. Cropper advised me to write as above. At any rate, it worked. CJC)

Once more Cameron was to be with me on a great trip. Together we hurried thru the necessary rites of preparation. At the battery office we went for our orders and drew desired clothing from the quartermaster. The medical officer passed us as physically fit to withstand the rigors of the "Battle of Paris," and though the paymaster shook his head when he looked into our pay books he did some needed "doctoring" (for unless we could show a certain balance we could not go). Then the baths at Havre, a quick "pick up and pack up," and we were ready to go. After a rushed lunch a lorry carried us to Mons, leaving us at the railroad station about five o'clock in the afternoon. Then the usual wait for a train long overdue. From somewhere in the recesses of my memory come the following lines, having to do with Mons—composed evidently, as the Hun drove us out in 1914, and dedicated to the day when we should return:

> But where the wave hath ebbed–
> the flood shall roar.
> And we await the tides' returning feet.

I wonder if there IS a "beyond"? I wonder IF those boys whose bodies rested in the soil about Mons could feel the rumble of the "tides returning feet"? I wonder...but enough of wondering!

We were in the station at Mons, waiting for the train that should carry us further along on our journey to "Gai Paree." All about were others also waiting. Mostly soldiers, there were a few civilians, who watched those of us in uniform as we performed foolish antics and "killed" time in various ways— watched us, with puzzled expressions on their faces. I saw one 14-year-old girl that I had seen before in one of the 12th's billets in St. Symphorien early in December. I saw also that she was very soon to become a mother. She was not, at first, glad to see me and be recognized, but after a few moments she grew friendly, and we talked for an hour or more. She did not intend to commit suicide—that "was a sin" she told me, but she prayed that she might die when the baby came. I tried to make her see my way, to live and take care of the child, and then I found that the baby was to be a FRITZ. After telling me that, she buried her face in her hands, and her sobbing was not pleasant to hear. In a little while she looked up—a "dead tired" child herself—and seemed surprised that I still sat on the packing case beside her. Could I still talk to her after that? Did I not hate her for admitting that she had "liked" a certain Fritz? And, we talked on...perhaps, she saw my way after all.

Some of the others waiting in the station that afternoon were: a 1st Brigade man whom I had met in hospital, bound for Chateau Roi and his own wedding, a rheumatic sergeant bound for Canada, a 9th C.F.A. man some 31 days A.W.O.L., hunting for his unit, and a sous-officer of Belgium's army, also Paris bound. At 8:15 there was a great stirring about and much shuttling as the train wheezed in. Cameron, the Belgian, and I crowded into a shabby remnant of a once first class compartment car. The floor boarding was loose and worn, the ceiling was so battered that had the night been clear we could have seen the stars. Instead, we saw—and felt—the rain as it oozed thru. All the glass in the doors and windows was gone, and newspapers in many languages made poor work of checking the raw draft. The train buckled, jolted, rattled, screeched, and wasted many minutes with seemingly unnecessary halts, and yet somehow, it eventually got us into Amiens (whether on the next day, or on the second day, I do not know). At any rate, it was about nine o'clock in the morning when red capped MPs ordered us out of the station until 2:15 PM.

We roamed about Amiens marveling at the speed with which war damage was being repaired. There seemed to be no place in particular that soldiers were not permitted, and yet most everywhere Cameron and I went, we found MPs who asked all manner of questions and then growled, "Get going." I suppose they were doing their duty, but I hope that by the next war, civilization will be far enough advanced, so that all the MPs of the last war can be sent "over the top" first, and then I hope we will be able to do without them for the rest of the argument. We sneaked quietly into the Canadian "Y", found a quiet corner, and slept until two o'clock. On returning to the railroad we found that the Paris train was there, and nearly ready to leave. As we started to climb aboard more MPs ordered us to see the RTO (Royal Transport Officer). This we did, and for 2f25 (about fifty cents) received a ticket to Paris, marked "Militaire–Troisieme Classe." One incident just before the train left, took our minds away from thoughts of just which death would be most painful to all MPs. An unusually attractive girl was struggling up the platform, weighted down with a heavy marine engine block. Beside her walked, none too steadily, a Canadian private who was endeavoring to offer his assistance. She seemed to think herself capable of handling the load herself, but was friendly with her refusals. Just as two MPs approached to "nab" the private, she handed her load over to him and kept back the "red caps" while he put up a great battle against booze and extra weight. Then the train moved out of Amiens, with all the smoothness of the finest American train, and we all shared in the joy of "having put one over" on the much despised MPs.

Never would my father have guessed that years later, during yet another war, his own son was to join the ranks of those much despised "soldier cops." CCC

The Amiens-Paris express was a rare treat after the other modes of transportation to which we had never become accustomed: mules, gun carriages, box- and flatcars, ancient compartment-passenger coaches, and lorries. Amiens is seventy miles from the metropolis. As the train sped over the rails, I watched flashing glimpses of little villages pass by, some neat and some not so neat, isolated farm houses, fields waiting for the spring sun, pretty groves, long straight double rows of trees which marked a highway between their trunks, and many suggestions of the earlier bombardments. But one cannot "see" a country from the windows of a speeding train, so I turned my attention to the other occupants of the compartment.

There were six of us. Cameron, the Belgian officer met in Mons, and myself, you can easily picture. Opposite me squatted an oversized elderly Frenchman whose face was behind heavy spectacles and an "ol' Bill" mustache. His cap and a heavy bag rested under the firm grip of fat fists in his lap, and his monstrous cane seemed ever ready to slide in my direction—an incident which I hoped in vain would occur. Beside him sat a vest-pocket edition Charlie Chaplin in French. These two were doing their utmost to outtalk each other with rapid fire French that was beyond my ken. As referee I should have given the decision to the little fellow, although the big man's inability to assist his talk with hands and arms undoubtedly was a tremendous handicap. The sixth passenger was a woman—tall, slender, and probably forty-five years of age. She carried no luggage other than a tiny silk bag. Every time I looked in her direction, I found her staring at me with weary eyes. Her face was very drawn and wrinkled, and her brow was marked by a deep frown which indicated a puzzled, even dazed, mental condition. Her perpetual gaze disturbed me greatly as the time passed, so I tried to melt the frown with the most pleasant smile I could muster. It failed. For a few moments she transferred her attention to Cameron, but it was soon back to me. From time to time my two soldier companions and I would talk a little, but their attention was focused for most of the trip on a newspaper divided between them. The train slipped into a more thickly settled section. There were spires, tall buildings, and then—the Gare du Nord in Paris.

Paris! The Mecca of all "leave hounds." At first sight a confusing, dazzling, and yet pleasing swirl of activity. No war ever touches Paris for very long—that is—on the OUTSIDE. It was about four o'clock in the afternoon when the sous-officer led Cameron and me thru the busy section before the Gare du Nord to a cafe in the vicinity, where we enjoyed a light lunch and champagne. This, by the way, at one of the many tables under a canvass awning out on what in America would be the sidewalk. Incidentally, it is a pleasant and neighborly custom, even in February. As we talked, I watched the people passing by—young folks—old folks—children—uniformed men and women of many nations—well dressed—poorly dressed—all intent on going somewhere about something. One can "grasp" Brussels, but Paris...!

Our Belgian friend left us at the cafe, and Cameron and I hunted around until we came upon the British Army and Navy League Club in Place de la Republic. Here we gathered needed information and enjoyed a "clean up." The evening was spent at a nearby cinema, after which we slept at the Hotel du Bon Giene. In the morning we located the Canadian "Y" headquarters at the Hotel D'Iena, on the avenue by the same name, and made arrangements for a room and breakfast at five francs per. This fine hotel became our headquarters for the rest of our stay in the city.

Leaving Cameron at the hotel I walked to the Arc de Triomphe, the hub or terminal for many fine boulevards. From this vicinity I rode in the tram to the Caserne de la Pepiniere, in response to the order issued to every man on leave to Paris. Here I received the customary advice regarding conduct, physical and otherwise. The order had been: "Every W.O., N.C.O., and man, whether on leave or duty, who stays in Paris for one night or more, is required to report himself at Police Headquarters, Caserne de la Pepiniere, Place St. Augustin (near Gare St. Lazare), immediately on arrival. (Sd.) MAURICE V. BRETT, Lt.-Col., Commandant, Paris." With this formality attended to, I was free to see the sights of Paris.

At the old caserne I met Corporal Bleasdale of the 42nd Canadian Scots (Black Watch), who told me such interesting stories of the place that I accompanied him on a preliminary survey of the city. Our ramblings led us into the Tuilleries, where I saw folks "holding down" benches, just as they do on Boston Common, and other parks—the Luxembourg, where rest the bodies of Hugo, Voltaire, Mirabeau, and others—to a part of the old wall—the Place de la Concorde, where the executions of Louis XVI and Marie Antoinette took place—and the Place de la Bastille, with its memories of a dread prison. Then, over several bridges crossing and re-crossing the Seine. From these bridges, as from a choice theater seat could be watched, with ever increasing interest and admiration, the "Capitol of Europe" in action as a most wondrous play is watched. My friend guided me also to the Palais de Justice, the Pantheon, the Bibliotheque Nationale, L'Ecole Militaire overlooking Champ de Mars, and lastly, when dusk was gathering, to the Place de l'Opera, the square before one of the great opera houses of Europe, where we were met by two girls. To one of these girls, Helene, the corporal was to be married. The other, Sussette, or "Suzy" as her chum called her, became my companion for much of the remainder of my stay in Paris. The evening

was divided between a movie at the Omnia on Boulevard Montmartre and a cabaret which made the Madrid at Brussels look like a "pocket edition."

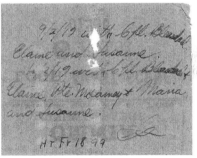

Omnia ticket (Front & Back)

Shortly before daybreak I returned to the D'Iena to find Cameron still awake and ready to agree that Paris was a "home," and that we needed to re-stock our pockets with the paper francs so necessary to proper enjoyment of our leave. Four hours later the chambermaid routed us out of our slumbers. We breakfasted and hurried to the paymaster, who deliberately (I cannot believe accidentally) overpaid our paybook balance. To the English and Colonial "Ys," the American Red Cross, and a French LOC canteen, I owe a deep gratitude, for it was their low-priced meals that permitted us to conserve on funds when Cameron and I happened to eat alone. The American "Y" was the poorest joke in France, insofar as it was of any help to us, in Paris, or anywhere else. Yes, you could find shelter for the night—if you had the price—and if you would come back later when the German-accented secretary had decided that there would be no more Americans coming in. You could also purchase sweets and smokes—at a price. You seemed to sense the "for Americans only" in the secretary's, "What's the matter with your own 'Y'?" And yet, a glance in any of our "Ys" at any time, would make you wonder if the Americans even had a "Y." I mentioned the fact to several doughboy friends, and got, "Aw, our "Y" is just a joke! And a damn poor one at that!" Perhaps I happened to hit just one particular trend of thought. I hope so, for I knew then that in MY home town in America, the folks were "digging deep" to keep up the "good work of the Y".

I cannot, in detail, describe the days that followed. They were filled with events, but I took little time for the retrospection that might have resulted in accurate notes of interest. In the pleasures of the moment I forgot the "years to come" when such notes would have been a source of great pleasure. Cameron and I traveled together much of the time but also enjoyed rambling about the various sections of the city by ourselves, selecting temporary companions here and there from among civilians. I made the acquaintance of avowed criminals, cripples, an old priest, big husky draymen, and folks both old and young. I met many who were very wealthy, to all appearances, and others who were unquestionably in dire need of better things. The uniform was my passport giving admission to cafes of dangerous repute, and to refined homes, alike. Wherever I went I found an atmosphere of welcome, which led me to believe that the French considered a Canadian something of a relative, regardless of Britain's grip on the country.

There was seldom any talk of the war. The conversation very easily drifted into channels pregnant with the interests of the speakers' personal lives, as is the way all over the world. The message wanted from me was nearly always the same—whether it be on the street, in the cafe, or in the home. "Tell us something of America, and of Canada. Are those United States as wonderful as they are pictured?" How did this thing, and that, in France, compare with things of like nature in my country? Never did I intentionally give the impression to those who almost believed it true, that here in America, money is free. Often I discovered that my descriptions did not agree with those of some of the Americans they had met. The intelligent Frenchman readily sorted the false from the true, but there were many who pictured America as a land of free money, gained without effort, and thought that practically everyone in the country was a millionaire. There were very many who looked forward to coming to the States to live. At first I tried to show them that although my country could offer them many opportunities, they would find the going rough for a long time to come. Eventually I learned that my best move was silence, for those who intended to come were sure of themselves on that score. I was not at all flattered at remarks made to me about Yankees, and though I never denied that I was one, it was seldom that I volunteered the information until I had met the person more than once. Often amusing incidents were the result of my "confession."

I met many girls while in and around Paris. Of those who left a lasting impression, there were Sussette, Jeanne of Versailles, Germaine of Suresnes, Elaine of the Louvre, and Georgia, prettiest of all, who taught me to know better than to keep her waiting for an appointment. An "affaire du coeur" was very easily acquired, and misunderstandings prevented by a frankness of speech unknown to me in America. "No" meant just that, and if the contrary condition existed, there was no question about it. Parisian girls KNOW how to dress "chic." No doubt they made the best wives in the world—for Frenchmen. As soon as the department stores closed, the troops were out in force to meet their working companions of a previous night, or to annex new ones. Often after a choice had been made, if the chosen one failed to reciprocate—well, there were always others to choose from. Compromising mix-ups often occurred, for though all girls to us were new and welcome acquaintances, sometimes the girls we saw in the evenings felt we belonged to them, with the result

that our "affairs" of the daytime, if found out thru chance meetings of daytime and evening companions, often led to temporary estrangements. My impression soon became fixed, that though the "steady" said little to me on discovery of a laxity on my part in "being true", she did all but murder the "other woman." Paris! Wine—women—song! It was well that the lack of cash curbed our ambitions.

Suzy knew her city well, and our visits to the great Louvre, Eiffel Tower, l'Opera, and countless other places of interest were usually made on foot, so that she could point out other points of note en route. It was at her suggestion that Cameron, Corporal West and I visited l'Hotel des Invalides.

Though the weather was not of the best, my fair companion and I hiked many miles over fine boulevards, thru long famous parks, into the Bois de Boulogne, and wherever our fancies chose. There were hikes during the evenings too, when we did not go to the Casino, the Gaiety, the Omnia, the Opera or stay at home. My friend was an accomplished musician on many stringed instruments, including the violin.

One week after our arrival in Paris, Cameron and I spent a day at Versailles, a twelve mile ride from the city. Leaving the station we walked along the broad Avenue St. Cloud to its end and the Place d'Armes, thru the great iron gate and across the first court to the Cour de Marbre. Here, surrounded by three walls of the Chateau, we sensed a little of the spirit of the place, and imagined, according to our individual memories of French history, that we were living in the days of Marie Antoinette and the last Louis. For a long time we roamed thru the famous halls and galleries, salons and chambers, within the Chateau. In the Chapel we met Jeanne, who suggested a walk thru the park. The lakes were covered with ice, the many fountains dry, the gardens and groves were in winter garb, but they were there, and imagination filled in the gaps. Jeanne led us thru the two Trianons and on to the lake farthest from the Chateau. Here there was skating and sliding. From a little fellow we hired two pairs of miserably dull skates, after Jeanne left us, and proceeded to enjoy a little exercise.

Cameron, an excellent skater, attracted the admiring attention of many on the ice. As I was tightening the strap which had become loose on one skate a voice said, "Pardon, m'sieur. But will you please teach me to skate?" The speaker was dressed in a costume of pink, with cheeks to match, and was undeniably pretty. She was not expecting the answer I made, and showed it when I said, "Certainly. But really, my chum is a much better teacher than I am—I'll call him." Cam came quickly and accepted the post of instructor with pleasure. After a few moments of fooling, the "girl in pink" demonstrated the fact that her knowledge of skating was well advanced. She and Cameron were well matched and made a pretty fine picture as they flashed over the ice, arm in arm.

There had been a reason for my thoughtfulness toward my mate, and that reason was Jeanne, who soon returned to the lake. We joined Cameron and his companion to enjoy ourselves until sundown. That the "girl in pink" would accept Cam's invitation to spend the evening together I did not doubt, but when we left the ice, she bade us all a friendly "au revoir" and, entering a motor-car on the boulevard was driven away.

On the 14th Cameron and I visited the Chateau de la Malmaison, and paid a franc to see the "Exposition Napolionienne de 1918, au benefice Des Oeuvres de Guerre." The name was impressive — the exhibition more so. For all the years that had come and gone since Napoleon and Josephine had enjoyed their pleasures and suffered their disappointments, the touch of both was there at Malmaison. In the Salon La Bibliotheque, the Salle du Conseil, Le Salon de Musique, Josephine's Chamber, and all about the inside and the outside of this famous old establishment, were the unmistakable influences of the Imperial Family. It was easy to picture the little great man, in counsel with his generals at the council table. What scenes of heart breaking sorrows suffered by the loyal Josephine, had those mirrors witnessed, as they peeked out from behind their red plush draperies, in her private chamber. How much had

those two great people planned together in their music room, with its rich gold and black trimmings. France has long been a republic, but the little corporal is still remembered. Out in the coach house we found the family's one time coach-of-state, still in excellent condition. Then...the city once more.

Hotel Beaumarchals, Paris

Corporal West of the 12th, was with Cameron and me, when we visited the Hotel des Invalides. Founded in the time of Louis XIV, by that monarch, as an asylum for old and disabled soldiers, the place has become a true "Musee de l'Armee", about which hover the spirits of countless war legions of all periods since the 13th–14th centuries. The many courts, corridors, and galleries are crowded to the limit of their capacity, with thousands of figures, specimens, equipment, artillery pieces, rifles, guns, blunderbusses, pistols, revolvers, targets, swords, sabers, lances, pikes, shields, armour, battle-axes, crossbows and bolts, bombs, grenades, saddles, harnesses, uniforms, and trophies gathered from every part of the world thru all the years since France was France. Many masterpieces of art are there. On pedestals and in niches are statues of every description. Mural decorations and paintings large and small cover the walls, depicting scenes of many natures, particularly those of battle. Portraits of famous men and women are crowded in with the other wall coverings. Thousands of battle flags and pennants are draped about, preserved in glass cases, and gathered into groups.

In the soldiers' Church of St. Louis, where countless troops of other days had come to worship, we found a sort of peace, in strong contrast to the battle array just looked at, and meditated there on many things. Then on thru the portico into the Royal Chapel where, under the great dome, rests the crypt which holds the remains of the "petit Emperor"—"le grand Napolienne." Near the crypt rests the heart of Vauban, the busts of Turenne, Duroc, and Bertraud, who accompanied the emperor to St. Helena, and the marshals of the palace. Not far away are many of Napoleon's personal possessions, and also, the mounted hide of his famous white charger. The French have placed Napoleon in the place of his choice. Above all a soldier when alive, he is now surrounded by battle trophies, which if he were alive, would seem (many at least) familiar. What a host of nations are represented in this great array: France, Belgium. Holland, Prussia, Austria, Hungary, Germany, Russia, Poland, Caucasus, Norway, Sweden, Italy, Greece, Spain, Switzerland, Bavaria, Balkans, England, United States, Mexico, Turkey, Persia, Muselman, Saracen, Egypt, Crimea, China, Cochinchina, Tonkin, Annam, Japan, Malaisia, India, Indochina, Algeria, Morocco, Congo, Tchad, Sahara, Madagascar, Morea—and more! L'Hotel de Invalides proved an interesting place. It was some moments after we had passed out onto the boulevard before my mind was back to the present.

Two Sundays, with their services at St. Madelene's Church, were gone, — had passed since Cameron and I had come to Paris. Our leave had expired before we realized it, in the whirl of interests. Cameron was ever a better soldier than Cate. He "obeyed" orders. "Rules and regulations, were made for a purpose," he said, as I bid him a fond goodbye at the Gare St. Lazare. "I am going back to the Battery but a few days late, and as usual, will try to pacify the SM when he learns that again you are overstaying your leave." For ten more days I remained in Paris and vicinity, enjoying every moment. What were a few Rules and Regulations to me. I was not a soldier. I was just a civilian, over there to fight when there was fighting to be done. Now the war was over. Probably I should never see Europe again. Therefore, why not make the most of an opportunity that was mine? So I reasoned with my conscienceæ...and I do not regret it.

Gaiety Theatre.

—

Balcony Stalls

No. 8813

day of 2 19 19

The day of parting came. It was easy to say good-bye to Bleasdale, Helene, and the many friends I had made, because a trip to Germany was yet to come. But, I learned with surprise that leaving "ma petite camarade de Paris"— Sussette—was not as easy as expected. She could not accompany me to the station, which was probably well, for there I had to think fast and move faster to duck two red-caps. In her home the night before we had said all the necessary things that were to be said, so that when I saw her for a moment just before leaving, a simple, "Bon Voyage," was all that was needed. The usual light heart was missing as I settled down into the upholstery of a compartment, on board the train bound "up the line."

At the battery the wise old Sergeant-Major's long, steady, calculating gaze, was my only chastisement. The unspoken rebuke, but it was sufficient. Cameron said simply, "Gunner's luck, Old Pal!' At St. Symphorien I found the Khaki College of Canada in full swing. There was another name in use among some of the officers— "Universitaire' de St. Symphorien"—and yet *another* one in use by certain of the troops. Most of us found it a help in "ducking" fatigues about town, and a very few even gained something of value from a little diligent study.

Whether driven by boredom or a desire to learn, CJC availed himself of the "Khaki College", studying Spanish and Stenography—when fatigues and leave time allowed. See letter of February 28, 1919, in Chapter X. CCC

On March 10th, at Nimy, a little distance out of Mons, the 22nd Corps held a horse racing meet. The weather for the day consisted of rain, and more rain, but the races went on, and were well attended. A few of the affairs were interesting; one or two were exciting. Betting was heavy among those who had money but I was still carrying a "dead" paybook. The most notable riding of the day was done by a jockey wearing yellow and blue colors, who, finishing six out of eight starts, ended well up in the money.

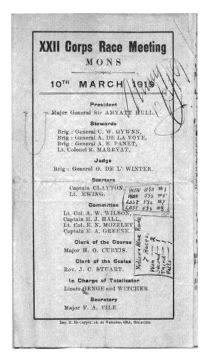

XXII Corps racing form, Mons, Belgium

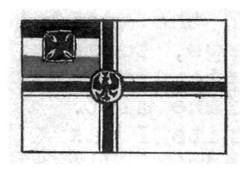

A
VISIT
TO
GERMANY

March was not half over when I learned that the 12th would remain in St. Symphorien until April—at least. The monotony of the sleepy little village was making the boys irritable, and trips to homes in surrounding towns, failed to give relief. There was but one thing for me to do, and that, was to go away for a few days. My objective was, of course, the Rhine, but from the few mates to whom I mentioned my plans, I learned that leaves to Germany were not being granted.... What to do?

With a forty-eight hour pass to Boussu in my pocket, I climbed into a lorry late one night, headed for the border. Thru Chalroi, Namur, and Liege I rode, and then when about ninety miles from St. Symphorien, I found myself on foot. On to Aachen I hiked, arriving soaked thru with rain and mud from cap to boots, and in trouble with two MPs. The splendid efforts of several French soldiers extricated me from that difficulty. I went on. A dirty well-worn French greatcoat covering the Khaki, and a shabby French trench cap where the Canadian cap should have been helped. Twelve hours were needed to cover the forty miles between Aachen and Cologne. As I approached the ancient German city, the buildings, towers, Rhine, etc., formed a picturesque setting, softened by a fine mist. Once inside the city limits I was disappointed, for the narrow, dirty streets, and the dull old houses, were not what I had expected to find. The meeting with a 4th Division Canadian Infantryman resulted in a somewhat renewed interest. Together we visited several places of interest, chief of which was the old cathedral built sometime in the 13th century. My new acquaintance's chief delight, however, was beer—when he could not get brandy—so my time was well filled with "both." The civilians I discovered were actually more friendly than many of the dwellers of St. Symphorien. This was a help. Perhaps rules against "mixing" would have helped in St.

Symphorien too.

On the following day, the man from the 4th and I visited Bonn, a place more to my liking than Cologne. Here more rules were broken, for my friend was well acquainted with a German family who made us welcome. Bonn proved to be a University town, and boasted (before the war) that the Kaiser had once been a student there. There were several interesting churches, among them the Muenster and Krensberg, which we thoroughly "inspected." The banks of the Rhine are dotted with many comfortable homes, and in summertime must present a pretty picture. It was then March—rainy and dreary. A cold, developing overnight, grew worse thru the morning. I started back toward Belgium, and before long was suffering from a well developed case of grippe. From Cologne to Mons is about 140 miles, and at the time I made the trip, everything was rain-soaked and muddy. Considering my physical and mental condition as I slowly covered the distance by foot, wagon, lorry, and train, I have since wondered many times how I ever reached my battery. For once, St. Symphorien looked good to me. Only the perfect care of an understanding Cameron, brought my temperature back to normal, thus keeping me out of hospital. I had seen the Rhine—but it was no more than worth the price.

On March 29th came a long looked for order. After a last "good bye and good luck" to many good friends in the vicinity, the 3rd Brigade entrained at Mons for Le Havre. This was our last, long, weary ride in the famous "40 HOMMES OU 8 CHEVAUX" boxcars. As we rolled slowly "DOWN the line", we passed many familiar places, and saw the civilians and soldiers making great strides in repairing the damage wrought by many battles. At night we kept warm with braziers, and when the gas and smoke grew too thick, we climbed to the roofs of the cars for fresh air.

The last day of March found us back in Le Havre where the 12th had landed a year ago. (Throughout the description of this last ride down the line I have said "we" and "us;" but now comes the confession of a last breaking of

Rules and Regulations.) I did not reach Le Havre with the battery, though I was there soon after. All letters from Sussette of Paris had carried a postscript which read, "Si vous passez Place de l'Opera a 7 heures moins 10 minutes, je passerai sans faute, tous les soirs", and it was my great pleasure to test the quality of that promise by getting into

Paris, "by hook or by crook", while the battery went on to Le Harve and made its first preparations for the departure from France. The memory of that last stolen trip to Paris has since made many discouraging hours much easier. The 12th that went thru the various processes of preparing for departure was not the same 12th that had been in those tents a year before. There were many different faces, and all the familiar faces wore a different expression....

At 6 P.M. on April 2nd, we marched off from French soil, and on to a Channel transport. The ship soon slipped quietly out of the mouth of the Seine and headed for Southampton across the channel. France was behind us, and so were the trenches, days and nights of hell, comrades whose faint "goodbyes" we really could not hear, St. Symphorien, a few real friends, Brussels, Paris, and—"ma petite camarade de Paris." Before us was a NEW world, but we did not realize it then. My whole being thrilled with the thought of "going home," and yet there was a little heaviness in my heart. Pal Cameron was beside me as we took a last look before hunting for a warm place to sleep.

"It wasn't such a bad old war, Cate," he said. "It gave us a few good 'homes'. Wouldn't you like to feel that you were coming back some time?"

"You're right, as usual, old-timer," I answered.

* * * * * * * * * * *

No "Notes" would be considered complete without mention of the world-famous "cootie". This little pet was ever true to its master, never deserting except after death. I had 'em, the "Big 4" had 'em, the 12th had 'em, the Allies had 'em, the Hun had 'em, the "civies" had 'em—in fact, EVERYBODY had 'em. It was part of the game, and for many, the worst part . At the "delousing plant" (ugly term), we filed in one door with our clothes and personal kit. As we moved along in single file, our outfits were taken by attendants, checked and sent to be baked in steam and sulfur until free from every form of germ and "cootie". Then into a big cement chamber we marched, and when more attendants were ready (Oh! What evil grins their faces bore!) we were shut in—naked. For a few seconds nothing happened. We stood staring stupidly at one another, with perspiration oozing from every pore. Then, faintly at first, but gradually increasing to a roar, came the hissing of steam. Clouds of it filled the chamber. Then water—hot, and growing hotter! For a while the place was thick with soapsuds as the boys scrubbed. We had "got the idea". Then the atmosphere within that vault grew unbearable. There was coughing, choking, spitting, shrieking, cursing, and here and there a man collapsed. Then the water became warm...cool...cold...I C Y ! Those attendants were there to KILL COOTIES, and THAT THEY DID, regardless of other possibilities. After what seemed hours, a door opened, and we dashed out of that "Hell's kitchen" and ran down a corridor to another room. Here we found seats, with numbers to correspond with those on the discs hung about our necks. Less evil attendants handed us towels, bathrobes, and smokes—and in one or two cases assisted in the rubdown. We sat down in our robes, to smoke and wait. Soon, hanging from overhead rails, came little wire cages in a long train, which stopped when the numbers upon them coincided with the numbers on our seats and discs. Here were our clothes. We made a dash for the cages, but sprang back dismayed when our fingers smelled of burning flesh. In time, even the tarnished buttons on our uniforms were cool, and we were out in the open once more. Fresh blankets were issued to us, and for the first time in many months, we were truly clean and we OUGHT to have been.

(NOTE: I was somewhat amused one day while on a visit to the Libby Museum just out of Wolfboro, New Hampshire, to find a "real" cootie from France, pinned to a card in a glass case. The legend said that the little fellow had arrived from the trenches in a letter in perfect health, although quite hungry. CJC)

CHAPTER VII

The Canadian Army
In British Isles—"After" France

The transports docked at Southampton at about one o'clock of the morning of April third, but the troops were permitted to sleep until daybreak before going off. Just before the order came to leave the boat, I was awakened by a chorus of voices shouting the old song of the line from another part of the deck:

> "I wanna go home! I wanna go home!
> I don't wanna go to the trenches no more—
> The bullets–they whistle, the cannon–they roar-r-r-r.
> Take me over the sea, Where Heinie can't get at me—
> Oh! My! I'm too young to die!
> I WANNA GO HOME!"

Long after sunrise, a troop train carried us out of the dock-shed, where for hours we had been deluged with hot coffee and cocoa, buns and Huntley and Palmer's "war-time" biscuits. We were getting something of a thrill from the sound of civilians speaking English, and from the warm friendliness of the busy girls serving out breakfasts. Although those whose work kept them near the railroad must have seen thousands of homeward bound troops come from the docks at Southampton, there were very few who did not shout a welcome to us as we rolled by. After a run of several hours we were in Milford, Surrey, marching over the same roads to the same camp, which had been our first in England over fifteen months before. Several busy days were spent at Witley Camp forming new contacts. The evenings were filled with entertainments of varied nature at the different canteens and movie halls. For demobilization purposes the personnel of the batteries were reassigned. The 12th Battery was designated as a western bound unit, and I went to the 4th, bound for St. John, New Brunswick.

(Note: I have failed to mention before that, while at St. Symphorien, a parade was held at Mons, where units were "cited," and individuals "decorated." Our Major, Colin McKay received a Military Cross, and good old Sgt. Troop, another Bar for his Military Medal. CJC)

On the 7th of April we moved to Kinmel Park camp in Rhyl (northern Wales). This shift to a camp near Conway, and that country in which I had found so much that was pleasant a year earlier, was a real pleasure. At Kinmel we found quarters in wooden huts, that were dry and easily kept clean, in spite of frequent rains. One fine afternoon as I sat on a bench outside my hut with several other mates I received a visitor who was more than welcome. Bosdet, the "Smiling Mex," stationed in another part of the great camp, had returned to his place in the "Big 4." Only Fisher was missing then.

Before I had become fully aware of the fact that a "Demobilization Leave" was to be granted, Cameron and I had left Kinmel and were rolling thru Conway on a swiftly and smoothly running train. In our possession were leaves to Ireland, dated on the 9th, and good until the 17th. At Holyhead we left the train and boarded the boat that was to take us across the Irish Sea to Dublin. Most of our fellow passengers were civilians, but we soon learned that there were several kinds of Irish civies. There were those from the north, those from the Dublin region, and those from the south. A substantially representative part from each section was aboard, and before the boat was fairly under way, we knew all the good and bad about each district. There were many invitations to many parts of the "little bit o' heaven" but we were forced to "decline with many thanks," explaining that as our time was limited we would be unable to stop in any one place more than a few hours. Of course, we knew that each part of Ireland had its wonders, and that it would take many weeks to see them all. Therefore, to see the east coast in six days, we would have to move quickly.

Dublin—or "Doo-ble-in, as it sounded to me when an Irishman said it— was just the city I had excepted to find. Too many times had I looked forward to visiting a certain place, and looking up certain things, only to be woefully disappointed. With a grizzled "old-timer" we rode, or jogged "backwards," to the Crown Hotel on Dame Street. Making this worthy hotel our headquarters we proceeded to inspect the city. Our intention was to "start right," so (although we did not purchase a clay pipe and a roll or two of black twist) we strolled into a public house and ordered "Irish" whiskey. It WAS Irish whiskey! But we were not of the breed. Like liquid fire it rolled down our throats to a point just about on a level with our third tunic buttons and there it commenced a series of revolutionary eruptions entirely beyond our ability to stop. We had seen "rough" army rum, but it had been milk compared with this particular concoction. Thus did "stout" become the official beverage for the remainder of our stay on the Emerald Isle. Out on the street again, a pretty little lady directed us to Phoenix Park. Here in this park, of which the Dublinians are justifiably proud, we met two discharged Irish Fusiliers, who to welcome us the more, dived into a pond before we could prevent the act, to capture two inquisitive swans for a welcome banquet. The sudden immersion in cold water sobered them, and we lost the swans. Later another friendly person guided us thru the breweries where Guinness Stout is made, and where visitors are expected to sample the product. We lived up to expectations but kept a clear eye for an appreciation of the many old cellars and vats. If it is "that dirty Liffey water," as many good housewives call the Stout, then may the source of that noble river up in the Wicklow region never go dry. In the course of our ramblings we visited Holy Trinity Cathedral, originally founded in 1038, St. Patrick's Church, founded in the 12th century, the University, and Dublin Castle, no longer the lively place of the 15th century. In each of these historic landmarks were relics of considerable interest.

On leaving the Gaiety Theatre after the evening's performance we were approached by a distinguished appearing gentleman of ripe age, white hair and whiskers. He suggested that he held a position of honor in a well known Irish party, and told us that our "work was not yet done, and as fighters for democracy we should enlist in Erin's cause." He walked with us for some distance, pointing out scars left on buildings and monuments by shots fired at Irish honor. Promising to consider his suggestion we parted company with him at the Round House and returned to the Crown for some sleep.

Another day of sightseeing and meeting friendly people followed a hearty breakfast. Late in the afternoon we met an English officer, who rebuked us severely for not saluting. Two MPs joined him, and when they threatened us with arrest, we fought. In three minutes a free-for-all brawl was in full swing with no less than thirty soldiers and civilians taking a very active part. There is probably no better place in the world to find backing for most any kind of a scrap than certain sections of Dublin. When Cameron and I left the "field of battle" (which happened to be a bridge over the Liffey, and a poor place for any Englisher to pick a quarrel with any Irisher) the fight was still going heartily on. At T. J. Callaghan's Dame Street store I invested six pound, fourteen in breeches, boots, puttees, hose, and rubbers. At another shop I spent a pound for a Gillette razor "made in USA." (All except the hose and rubbers are still giving good service nine years later.)

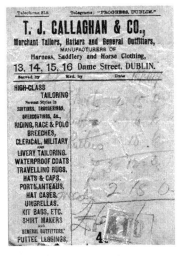

A night's riding carried us to Cork, and the 12th proved to be one of the busiest days of our period of service. The sights of this great southern Ireland city were seen from trams. Busy Queenstown was visited in the morning, and Blarney Castle in the afternoon. The day was gone before we fully realized the unlimited wealth of things interesting and sights beautiful for the visitor who cares to invest a little time in Southern Erin. Unquestionably my greatest mistake while overseas, was leaving Cork too soon. All during the ride from that city to Belfast, via Dublin—and it is a LONG ride, and for the most part a ride of ever increasing interest—my mate and I suffered from the guilty conscience which comes after a duty ill performed.

In Belfast, Robertson's Hotel become headquarters. Here we met by appointment made before leaving Wales, Bobby Robertson, Spud West, and several other 12th Battery mates. In this city I found to my surprise that the speech was very nearly the same as that of Boston. Dublin had had its accent. Cork had had a still different quirk in the speech. The rural sections had had practically all of the strong brogue. Later I learned that north of Belfast the ear hears a distinct Scottish burr. So much for the dialect—though I did hear on several occasions, the true old Irish. A party of five of us roamed about the city, visiting now and then a point of interest according to the advice of civilians. The best remembered building, from point of beauty, is the city hall. Other truly important edifices we failed to find.

Our first evening in the city was spent at the Royal Hippodrome, where we witnessed a good vaudeville bill. The second evening, as a result of being told that Ireland's finest colleens could be seen at a Prize Concert held in Ulster Hall, Cameron and I bought tickets for the front row. The concert proved to be a sort of Sunday School affair, and though we enjoyed ourselves, the participants were too young to satisfy our ideas, elastic as they were, of what a genuine Irish colleen should be. Out in the vicinity of Glengormley, Greenmony, Bellevue Gardens, and the Cave Hills, we found our ideals. THEY satisfied. One of these "ideals" was the indirect cause of my starting the seven mile hike to the city at three in the morning. Only a timely meeting with another "victim" of late hours prevented the walk. This "victim" serving in the Canadian uniform, lived nearby, and I was glad to accept his invitation to sleep at his home. Bright and early next morning I was at the home of the "ideal" of the previous night, and found that my early arrival caused a certain aloofness of the day before to melt away entirely. The new day of pleasure was scarcely begun, when an irate Cameron arrived from Belfast to tear me away from Glengormley, just in time to keep to our plan of visiting Londonderry. This trip was one of very rare beauty. The region is one from which poets and artists cannot fail to gain inspiration—unless they be of O'Henry type, and susceptible chiefly to the greater city life. (On second thought I seem to remember certain rural stories by the same O'Henry) The sea, inland streams, hills, valleys, mountains, woods, and dwellings of quaint design are here joined to form a scene more picturesque than any we had met with for many days. Days, rather than hours, would I have spent there, had not the ever cautious Cameron insisted that THIS leave be kept within the allotted time limits. Back to Belfast, and on to Larne, where we caught a boat for the sail to Stranraer. From this last mentioned Scottish town we went by train to Dumfries, and on to Carlisle (England). At Carlisle I failed in a bold attempt to sell my chum on the idea of a trip to Edinburgh to visit certain old friends. At Penrith, when the train bearing the great Cam on toward the battery slipped out of the station, I stood on the platform waving a farewell at a cloud of smoke and dust, behind which one husky Canadian was heartily cussing me—and his moment of drowsiness.

The Morning of April 17th was as fine a day's beginning as England ever had. On that morning, as Cameron sped on to complete his leave on time, I visited the enchanting Ullswater district. Here for hours (all too few) I enjoyed a degree of contentment seldom attained in company with an old native of the section. His stories of the paradise, and of folks who have been privileged to spend all the time they wished there, have been forgotten, but at the time they only added to my great pleasure.

The night found me in Burnley, where I hunted up my Blackpool friend at her home on Baker street. In a cozy living room before a comfortable open fire, I lunched and chatted with Mrs. Thompson and her nephew. A few hours of their true hospitality, and then I was forced to head for Wales, with a big bundle of postcards, camera film, and souvenirs, under my arm. These things I had sent to Mrs. Thompson to keep until my last few days on that side of the Atlantic. As I look back over those days "across," I feel a longing to see again those same kindly, hospitable friends that seemed to spring up everywhere I went. Perhaps the most valuable lesson of all the many I learned was how to enjoy a tour to the utmost. A stock of smiles. a sincere handclasp, a heart that swells with a warmth of its own making, and the habit of listening, were all that was needed to guarantee a wonderful trip no matter where I went. It is impossible to "see" a country by way of cut and dried tours. One must meet the people who live there, and who understand their country best, and then see the country with their help. (I plead guilty to an attempt at moralizing—forgive me once more.)

Upon receipt of one packet of memorabilia sent by CJC for her safekeeping, Ms Thompson replied on a postcard tucked into a parcel of her own, "Dear Friend: Your parcel received on Tuesday—hope you enjoyed cakes I sent you. Let me know if you would like more. I had a fine time at Whitsentide. Am thinking of going to Blackpool this week. Kind regards, F. Thompson." CCC

The ticket-taker at Burnley was an old, and wise, man. As he looked at my leave, which read "Belfast", thus entitling me to transportation to and from that city only, he said, "Laddie, this be the second time 'e 'ave expected me to pass 'e without right. Can 'e be thinkin' these old eyes 'ave lost their sight? Tell me noo, 'ow far 'ave 'e traveled on this leave?" Briefly, I told him of all the places I had visited during the last week, then added, "This may be the only chance I'll ever have of seeing the country from which my people came, of meeting a few new friends, saying "goodbye" to old friends. Just how much I appreciate the fact that all of my travels in your country have been made possible by the friendliness of just such folks as yourself, is more than I can tell you". Then the old man said, "'E seem honest laddie, an' I like 'e, for 'e are much like our laddies oo went over to the trenches. Get along now, to the train, and good-luck to 'e." And it WAS just such a spirit that helped me to pass countless ticket-takers "without right", to Manchester—Liverpool—across the Mersey to Birkenhead —Chester— Rhyl — and back into Kinmel Park Camp.

For two weeks Bosdet, Cameron, and I roamed about the vicinity, usually over old trails made the year before. We met many old friends who made our trips more delightful with their occasional presence. Perhaps it was at Conway, where Bosdet and I went often, that we enjoyed ourselves the most. Here it was on our first return visit that we came across our sweethearts of 1918 deeply engrossed in making love to other fellows, but what of it! At camp a varied entertainment was provided by field sports, games, the NACB Garrison Theater, a WAAC camp and picnics under their supervision, and gambling.

Money was sometimes scarce, but the "old board," poker, and craps, kept some of us in funds. Bosdet's uncanny knack of winning did not fail. The old army game of "crooked raffle" was common. Thus one day, when my luck let my last tanner (sixpence) melt away on a bad bet on the "old Kimberly" (the diamond on the infamous board) Bosdet and I resorted to the raffle. Into four foreign camps went Bosdet, selling raffle tickets on the camera which is now a prized souvenir in my possession. When the cash collected equaled a previously determined mark the drawing was held. At just this time I "happened" along, and as a "disinterested" party, was requested to draw the lucky number. Bosdet shook up the numbered stubs in his cap in a most

professional manner. Then, with the cap held high, so that I could not see what I picked in advance (and so that no one else could see where I picked it from), I reached into the lot and extracted a number. "Number 12! Who has got number 12? The lucky 12th wins!" And out of the crowd stepped a corporal, a stranger in this camp, who took the camera and marched off muttering something about, "This is the first time I ever won anything by chance." The majority of the losers would turn away and forget the incident, (unintentionally I have confessed that there WERE more than a FEW such raffles!), but there were always a few "I wonders!" from the inevitable skeptics. Then, back in Medical District #7, when the corporal had received his beer money, and I had regained possession of the camera, Bosdet and I would divide the four or five pounds of loot. With this capital, Bosdet and I usually out-gambled the gamblers, and made out a fair existence. Incidentally, the "lucky" number had been held pinched within the cap, between Bosdet's thumb and fore-finger, to eliminate as much chance of loss as possible. A simple and profitable scheme if one did not get caught. IF one was so unfortunate as to be discovered a fraud, he was sure to get plenty—even though those who served out the "plenty" were planning to try the same stunt in our camp that same day.

From the 15th there had been persistent grumbling about remaining any longer in Europe. By the 27th after several false starts for Canada had been made, the troops lost their usual good nature. Insubordination commenced, increasing in volume until whole units, and then whole camps, took active part in demonstrations in favor of leaving Wales to the Welch. On the 15th the cry was, "We wanta go home!" By the 22nd it was, "When do we go home?", louder than before, and by the 1st of May it became a spirited battle cry, "WE ARE GOING H O M E !!" The natural sequence was a series of wild riots during which some folks were hurt, and some government property was destroyed. The War Office at London heard the noise, read the reports, and sent us to Southampton on the 2nd of May. There were many high-ranking British officers who breathed a deep sigh of relief when the Royal Mail Steamer *Mauretania* sailed for Canada at 2:30 on the morning of May 4th, with a heavy boat load of "those bloomin' Canadians." There were also many who breathed deep sighs of relief on the boat.

We were headed WEST...and home! Home—relatives, friends, old familiar faces and places—one need not go 3,000 miles to war to know what that means to a Yankee. Again I heard old songs from different decks, among them one which ended with:

> "Take me over there, drop me anywhere,
> Toronto, Hull, or Montreal, I just don't care.
> Oh! Tiddle-de-iddle-de-I-ty,
> I'd rather be there than Blighty,
> Take me back to old ST. JOHN!"

* * * * * * * * * * * * *

Note: There were several unpleasant incidents (some resulting in violence, arson, and even deaths) in the camps during demobilization, mostly from impatience with the process. Part of the problem was logistics—there simply were too many men and too few ships and trains. Another was the decision by the Canadian Corps not to follow the "first in, first out" principle adopted by most armies, but instead, to return the men by units (although in some hardship cases exceptions were made). The most serious of these incidents occurred at Kinmel Park on March 4th and 5th (a month before CJC arrived there) in which a riot involving over 800 soldiers left five killed and 23 wounded. Another in mid-June, at Witley Camp, left several civilian shops and the Garrison Theatre destroyed. Fortunately, the 3rd Artillery Brigade (of which the 12 Siege Battery was a member) seems to have avoided the more serious disturbances. CCC

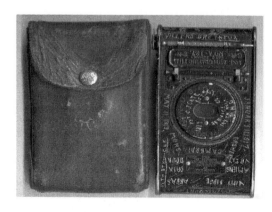

CHAPTER VIII
Canadian Army—Home Again

One of the finest vessels afloat is the Cunard liner, *Mauretania*. From stem to stern, masthead to keel, port to starboard, this wonderful boat presents that which fills the voyager with confidence in her ability to safely and surely do her work. The troops were once more normal—good natured. The guns mounted as defense against submarine attacks, though hooded, helped artillerymen to feel at home. Officers and nurses were quartered in cabins and staterooms. The rank and file was satisfied with hammocks and bunks. My bunk was the top one of a tier of three in the first class smoking-room. Meals were served in the regular dining salons, and were seldom missed, for fair weather stayed with us. For five days we crowded the decks, promenaded, read, slept, daydreamed, watched or took active part in sports and games, while the distance between the ship and Canada grew steadily less.

Mauretania meal ticket & accomodations card

So much to do, yet Bosdet and I grew restless because of the tameness of it all. We broke a dozen ship's rules, but nothing was done about it. It seemed all so unnatural to be so free from restraint. We wanted to be "bawled out" about something—anything! The freedom intoxicated us, as newfound freedom often intoxicates whole nations into losing possession of common sense——and we decided to see just "how far" we could go. We climbed high up into the ship's rigging, descended into the boiler rooms, trespassed on the bridge, invaded officers' and nurses' sections—yet, still, nothing happened. The sailors grew more friendly because they said we had the makings of riggers in us, the firemen grinned because we "went down to pay them a visit," the ship's officers even explained things in the pilothouse and about the bridge, and the returning officers were strangely unaware of our rank as they offered friendly drinks, the nurses—well, they were what nurses always have been, the best sports in the world. WHAT WAS the use of trying to be "bad" boys?

"Crown & Anchor" games on Mauretania's fantail

One morning as we strolled about looking for excitement, we saw a little window to a steward's pantry, opened about three inches. Thru the opening we studied the little room. Just inside and below the window was a deep copper sink with an outer rim about an inch in width. Around two sides of the room was a narrow shelf, and on it, opposite us, were several kinds of fruit and a closed cigar box. Apples, oranges, and bananas were a delicacy. With a long, heavy, clumsy boathook we busied ourselves taking the fruit which was quickly consumed by mates who had gathered about to watch our performance and to make critical remarks about our technique. The boathook was not suitable for spearing the cigar box and whatever it might contain, and for a few moments we were "stumped" while suggestions poured in from all sides. From the lavatory we took a mop. The end of its handle was whittled wedge-shape and a safety pin properly inserted became a hook. The slow process of coaxing the box around the shelf to the sink's rim commenced. Drawing this box over a slippery surface but one inch wide was a delicate trick. The slightest misjudgment of the ship's roll, or a bit of unsteadiness with the "coaxing," would spell disaster. Then the box was beneath the window and my left hand closed upon it. The distance from the opening to the sink's edge had meant a long reach, and when I endeavored to pull back my arm WITH the box clutched firmly in my hand, I was in exactly the same position as the small boy whose greed prevented him from removing his clenched fist thru the neck of the peanut jar. Then, two spoons fell clattering into the sink.

The door to the pantry immediately opened and I heard, "Aye Tommy. 'Ere's anuver one!" Evidently it was not a bit of luck that had left that window

opened, nor was it left
could open it no more.
must have netted its
But this time the "Big 4"
had not forgotten many
in the old days of
Bosdet's bare arm
opening. As he held the
His bent elbow joint
inches from the sill, and
matter for me to take it
as the window slammed
something said about
had any idea who the

unexplained why we
A clever trick which
inventors a lot of fun.
demonstrated that it
far worse predicaments
foraging. Instantly
flashed thru the
box I removed my arm.
brought the box a few
it was then an easy
the rest of the way just
shut! Whew! There was
the affair, but as no one
culprit or culprits might

be, Bosdet and I divided a hundred "Cunardia - Extra Fine" cigars between us. Some of them were still in my tin mess kit when I reached home, and they WERE GOOD.

Up on the "top side" were some dog kennels. One dark and cold night, when the wind blew hard, I stopped as usual at each occupied kennel, receiving a yelping, tail-wagging welcome. While petting one wire-haired pup a nurse came along to pet the same dog, and I learned that it belonged to her. For some time we petted (the pup), and then warmed ourselves with a promenade as we chatted. After that we met each night. And so, the time passed, until at 6:30 A.M. on the 9th of May, the great *Mauretania* was docked at Halifax in Nova Scotia in CANADA!

The big portals of the dock-shed were packed with expectant relatives and friends of "homecomers." As the troops poured out of the ship, Bosdet, Cameron, and I stood together in a quiet place watching them. In the excitement and confusion of getting back they were giving little thought to the separations from mates who would be more than missed later. Every little while we saw disappear a group of our own mates. Cameron perhaps, to see many of them again, but Bosdet in Mexico, and myself in Boston, far less likely to see any of them. Then the "Big 4" (what if there were but three of us in the flesh!) shook hands and parted. Except for one or two rare visits and occasional cards at Christmas our ways were separated from that moment on....

"Up town" all was confusion as meetings took place and welcoming shouts filled the air. Then gradually, came the realization that those who lived in the vicinity had gone home, that many more had simply gone off on trains to other places, and the rest of us, strangely alone, were "just waiting" in "just another town" for our own trains. As the late afternoon passed, quietly, we began to realize that friendships formed under fire of battle can become an integral part of one's existence...and that neither time nor physical separation can ever weaken that bond.

At six o'clock I entrained with the units bound for St. John and points west. All night we rode, getting some sleep while cramped into every conceivable position. Truro is the only stop that I can remember. There, although it was midnight or later, we were greeted by a band and a crowded platform. Sandwiches and hot coffee and doughnuts were served by an excited throng. Many girls were there serving chocolate bars and candy kisses—and a whole lot of kisses that were NOT candy by any means. With my souvenirs is a bunch of dried and discolored Mayflowers which I received from one sweet girl along with some other things, during that short stop at Truro.

At eight o'clock on the morning of the 10th we arrived in St. John, where we found that the government had found a quick way of turning soldiers into civilians...officially. A "welcome" speech, cut short by cries of, "Let's go!", "When do we eat!", "Cut out the guff, and do your stuff!" was followed by a good meal. Then we filed into one door of the armory as gunners, moved along from one counter or window to another, and on out another door, as misters. That was all. We had signed up for "duration of war and six months" and Canada had honored the contract. During the afternoon I met many old friends and acquaintances of 1917, who kept me occupied until 5:30 P.M. when, with a few others, I boarded the Boston bound train.

Another all-night ride followed with but one incident to interfere with sleep. At the border, several customs officials entertained the erroneous idea that we were not properly endorsed for admittance to the United States.

Then a small but mighty determined group of EX-Canadian soldiers stated their opinions, which were few, and guaranteed to back all of them against all comers. Practically every civilian in the car offered to help us "carry on." All that we had to do was "say the word." For a few moments feelings had been tense, but later as the train rolled over the border with us on board we thanked the "OTHER" civilians and went back to sleep, to awake for a few moments now and then as our party lost a man along the way.

At Dover, New Hampshire, I was greeted by several of my family in a manner that left me feeling fine for the rest of the run to North Station in Boston. At ten o'clock on the 11th I was ducking traffic before the station in an attempt to reach the subway station. An hour later I was in Belmont, hunting for more of my family, who no longer lived in the house I had left in 1917. After splashing about for a few moments in a heavy downpour, I met a little girl about seven years old. "Do you know Dotty Louise White?" I asked. "Yes," she answered, "And I know you, too. You are the big brother, Clif, who went to war." Agreeing with her I asked her to direct me to Dotty's house. This she did in a sure fashion, by taking my hand, and leading me straight to the door of her home at number eighty–nine Townsend Road. I reckon that it was a wet and muddy EX-gunner who dropped a dripping great coat and pack in the front hall to receive a warm welcome. I was "at home"—with familiar faces about me—and familiar places, and still more familiar faces not far off.

I ought to have been every bit at ease, and supremely content, but I was not. Everyone did his or her part to get the trench kinks out of my system, and to all appearances the operations were successful, but the "kinks" are still there, and there they will always remain, just as all soldiers learn to know.

CHAPTER IX
Some Historical Notes

In 1914 the small army of British "Contemptibles" took an unmerciful beating on the European mainland from the German "steamroller." Vastly outnumbered they could only fight a delaying action until the Empire's call for help could be answered.

From Canada came the C. E. F.—Canadians of English, Scottish, Irish, Welsh and French descent, and those of every other nationality and heritage of which that nation is formed. Joining them were Britishers from Mexico, Central and South America, and the United States. With them came also a sprinkling of every other nationality, including many Chinese who crossed the Pacific, the North American continent, and the Atlantic to answer the call. All welded into one useful force for the carrying out of Canada's part in the Great War. Good friends, bad enemies, independents, all ready for individual or free-for-all combat. Always reliable in action, subject to mischief at leisure, picturesque on parade if not models of the drill, they joined together to fight the common enemy. 418,052 went "over", 361,414 came back. 34,496 were killed in action, another 17,182 died of wounds, and 4,960 died of other causes.

From Australia, 6,000 miles from the fields of France, came the "Aussies." Healthy, hearty, husky Colonials with their dashing campaign hats and full tailored tunics. Not too easily made friends with, but firm allies once the ceremony of the handshakes was accomplished. From New Zealand, came the "Anzacs," tough and game like the Britishers from South Africa. From every quarter of the globe came the men to carry on the fight so ably begun by that handful of "Contemptibles." And even from that "other" nation in North America, came a smattering of Yankees whose forefathers had fought with and against the British Crown, to don the uniform of that beleaguered empire. Together, along with half the rest of the world, the combined Allies won the war, but at a cost that would have been unthinkable by any participant prior to its beginning.

1.   The war came to an end simply because the German army was hopelessly defeated on the field before November 11. The Imperial navy had been substantially defeated at the start of the war. No internal disorders caused the defeat, for it was not until the people at home realized the hopeless condition of the army, and sensed the predicament in which the fast weakening High Command found itself, that serious civil outbreaks occurred.

At the end of September the Kaiser was accepting resignations from most of his cabinet ministers, installing Prince Maximillian (of Baden) as the new chancellor over a new cabinet, and proclaiming in a new tone that, "The German people should cooperate more effectively than hitherto in deciding the fate of the Fatherland." It was at this time that Ludendorff, and thru him, Hindenburg, lost their nerve, with the resultant spread of "nerves" throughout the staff at Spa. On October 2, the spirit of the Great General Staff was expressed in the Reichstag by a messenger from Spa: "The Supreme Army Command has had to come to the extremely painful determination that according to all human calculations there no longer exists any prospect of compelling the enemy to plead for peace," and further, "The enemy has been enabled to make good his losses (in men) through the assistance of America," whereas German resources were at an end, and, "Each day brings our opponent nearer to his goal and will make him less inclined to conclude with a peace which is tolerable."

Imagine the effect produced upon the listeners in the Reichtag by this report! German messages to Washington (Pres. Wilson) brought back, in due time, answers sufficiently strong in proof of the Allied realization of military supremacy, to cause considerable consternation in Berlin. The German people's cry, "Better a dreadful end, than a horror without end," was heard at a cabinet meeting October 17, when Ludendorff asked Secretary of State Scheidermann, "Couldn't your Excellency succeed in elevating the morale of the masses?" and received for reply, "It is a question of potatoes. We have no longer any meat. We cannot deliver potatoes because we are short (of cars). We have absolutely no fats left. It is a wonder what north and east Berlin live on. It would be sheer dishonesty if we left any doubt on the question."

Following a bitter session on October 25, Ludendorff admitted to two junior officers, "There is no hope. Germany is lost." On the 26th after the Kaiser had relieved Ludendorff of his command, the former General-in-Chief bitterly exclaimed, "In a fortnight there will be no longer a Kaiser in Germany." The mutinies at Kiel, Hamburg, Bremen, Hanover, Rostock and other centers occurred after October 28. Bolshevism was creeping into the country from Russia. On November 10, the Kaiser finally saw the necessity of abdication, although he said, "I am so awfully ashamed. I cannot find it in my heart to do this. I cannot go away. If there be but one faithful battalion here, I shall remain at Spa." What was in the mind of Wilhelm II when he spoke thus? His pleas, however, fell upon deaf ears, and the EX-supreme War Lord fled the place of exile provided by the Dutch government and an old friend, Count Bentnick, at Amerongen.

Two days earlier the German armistice Commission had been presented to Foch in the forest of Compeigne. "What do you desire, gentlemen?" the marshal had asked. They were there to inquire about Allied peace proposals. "I have no terms," Foch informed them, then he added, "I will let you know the Allies' conditions when you have asked for an armistice. Do you ask for an armistice?" "Ja!" came the response.

Then the terms: The surrender of 5000 cannon, 30,000 machine guns, 2,000 aeroplanes, 5,000 locomotives, six battle cruisers, 10 battleships, six smaller craft and ALL submarines, the order to sweep all German mine fields, to evacuate all invaded countries (including Alsace-Lorraine,invaded in 1871), to abandon the Treaties of Brest-Litovsk and Bucharest (Rumania), to retire beyond the Rhine, to release all Allied prisoners immediately, and to submit to Allied occupation of German railheads, bridges, and other vital points. The Commission rushed its report to Berlin. All the world waited breathlessly for the answer. At five o'clock on the eleventh of November, the commission was signing documents as directed by Foch, and six hours later the Armistice went into effect.

2. At Versailles on June 28, 1919, the German delegates, Hermann Miller and Johannes Bell, in the presence of political rulers of France, Britain, and America, and a "vast concourse of lesser dignitaries," put their names to the most humiliating peace ever imposed on a great people. Germany was prostrate economically, diplomatically, and militarily. Other treaties have been made since that eventful June day, many of which concerned new boundaries. The German territory is still great, though Belgium has received a little slice, France the return of Alsace-Lorraine, and Poland a big slice including a wide outlet to the Baltic Sea, thus separating East Prussia from the Fatherland. Danzig has been made a "free" city and port. Lithuania has a narrow section of the former East Prussia, and Denmark (by no means an ally during the war) has pushed her southern boundary further south. Austria-Hungary, whose ultimatum to Serbia in 1914 opened the gates to the terrible slaughter that followed, has indeed been humbled. Czecho-Slovakia, had been created entirely from Austro-Hungarian "conquest" territory, and great sections have become part of Poland, Rumania, Yugoslavia, and Italy. Bulgaria no longer boasts of an Aegean Sea border. The Turks still have a foothold on Europe near Istanbul (Constantinople) but are closely watched. Out of territory once part of the Russian Empire have sprung the nations of Estonia, Latvia, Lithuania, most of the new Poland, and a part of Rumania. The Great War of 1914–1918 truly led to many geographical changes, as well as other things.

3. Germany could have prevented the war, if her leaders and people had not been "conquest hungry" and if the "1914 Crisis" had been handled with clear and clean intelligence. She probably would have won the war had she honored Belgian neutrality, thus holding Great Britain at peace for a much longer period, had she abstained from unrestricted submarine warfare thus respecting the power of the United States, and if she had not forced an "iron-gloved" peace at Brest-Litovsk when Russia cracked, thus demonstrating to the world her desire for absolute control regardless of the rights of others. Out of the ruins has arisen a new hope in an old Europe, struggling toward an objective of peaceful prosperity. If only warfare could be abolished, then those

who follow after us might realize a true Christianity, but it is doubtful if human nature will be changed by any amount of warfare for any very great length of time. War costs of all the ages will not be likely to halt blood-and-gain thirsty leaders and cloudy-brained followers of the future.

4. The Great War reminded both friend and foe that it was not wise for any nation or group of nations, to become so intoxicated with power as to make war upon other nations for the purpose of subjugating them to the rule of a few selfish men. The youngest great nation of the world became the greatest single power. The greatest army in the world was reduced to a thin shadow. New nations were made for former downtrodden peoples. "Deutschtum" failed to rule, the "pickle-haube" became a souvenir for Allied soldiers, and although Germany lost over 1,600,000 of the 8,500,000 lives sacrificed to the god of war, "Der Tag" did not come.

5. German War Losses: Approximately 2.4 million dead (25% between ages 19–22; 60% between 19–29; 800,000 civilians dead from lack of proper nourishment). Birth decrease–3.5 million. Some 1,537,000 on her pension rolls. These are but a few statistics. The losses in cash, land and materials, to say nothing of her standing in the world are beyond a mere human's understanding.

6. I will not trouble you with a mass of statistics, but will suggest just a few. More accurate and complete records will be available in later years in all libraries:

Miscellaneous War Statistics

Nation	No. 1	No. 2	No. 3	No, 4	No, 5	No. 6
	(X (1000)	(X 1000)	(X 1000)		(X 1000)	
France	5.6G	3,700	2,559	55.4	4,800	51.5
Belgium	0.4G	150		6.0		51.5
Gt. Britain		1,000	1,718	18.3	3,076	51.5
Canada			419		202	51.5
Italy	9.0G	180			1,400	51.5
Russia	115.4L	5,000				31.0
Germany	27.5L	5,000	3,562		6,485	51.5
Aust-Hung	414.8L	2,000			4,550	51.0
Turkey	2.1L	1,200				49.0
Bulgaria	3.5L					
U. S. A.			1,900	20.3		19.3

Col.1, Sq. miles area gained (G) or lost (L), Col.2,Original mobilization, Col.3,War strength at armistice, Col.4.Percent of line held Nov. 11, 1918, Col.5,Loss in killed, wounded, etc., Col.6,Months at war (These figures are from various early accounts and probably approximate only).

7. War costs run high. Uncle Sam loaned to fighting nations as a result of war's expense much in cash and in supplies. For instance: Italy–$1,648,034,051, France–over $3.25B, Belgium–over$375M, Russia–over $192M, United Kingdom–$4.277B, and strange as it may seem, Austria drew over $24M, Hungary–over $1.5M, and to other smaller nations–a total of over $400M. And since the war, according to some, Germany has been treated right royally—in spite of some contrary remarks from certain of her natives.

Some more war costs: commodity prices of the present (April 9, 1927) are greater than those of the year before the war—greater in United States by 47%, France–527%, Canada–51%, Germany–31%, United Kingdom–46%, Italy–581%, Japan–201%, Australia–58% and Belgium–759%, according to an article in the "Dearborn Independent" of above date.

8. War Loans Issued in the United States

First	$ 1,989,455,550 @ 3.5%	1932 - 1947*
Second	3,807,865,050 @ 4.00%	1927 - 1942
Third	4,175,650,050 @ 4.25%	1928
Fourth	6,964,581,000 @ 4.25%	1933 - 1938
Fifth	4,495,373,000 @ 4.25%	1922 - 1923
Total	$ 21,432,924,700	* Maturity

War debt per capita–$202, Gross debt per capita (1920)–$240. War debts paid to June 30, 1925–$4.969B. (Proof that American purses back up America—as they naturally should, but what expensive "fireworks"!)

9. Our Revolution cost in killed, 4,044 and in wounded, 6,004. The War with Germany cost (Allies & Entente) over 8,500,000 killed alone! We are progressing.

10. Napoleon was a big general in his day, but he never knew what a big battle looked like. In the latter half of 1918 there occurred some "real" battles. Whereas at Gettysburg in our own Civil War the Union batteries fired 33,000 rounds in three days, during a single day of the final British drive from Etaing/ Cagnicourt thru Cambrai, Valenciennes and the Hindenburg Line to Mons in Belgium (September 2 to Armistice) allied artillery under Currie and Haig fired 943,857 shells. Under General Pershing at St Mihiel, French and American batteries supporting the advance of over half a million soldiers fired a million rounds in four hours! The 47-day offensive in the Argonne Forest (October–

November) also under Pershing drew 1,200,000 American troops into the line against 40 German divisions under Von der Marwitz. Despite an order which read "The safety of the Fatherland is in your hands," the German forces crumbled in this greatest battle ever fought by Americans although at a cost to the latter measured by a casualty list of 120,000 Yanks. The Northern Italy/ Piave River campaign, from the Alps to the Adriatic in October, resulting in the collapse of Austria on November 4th yielded 300,000 prisoners and 7000 guns. In May of 1918 Ludendorff had 207 divisions in the line and 36 in reserve. On September 1st, the Germans numbered 1,339.000 riflemen with no replacements, while Allies numbered 1,682,000 riflemen with many thousands to draw upon if necessary. September 15th found the Germans with 185 divisions in the line and but nineteen in reserve—as for what happened in November, see the terms of the Armistice. Such was the scale upon which 1918's battles were fought.

11. Contracting nations to the peace treaty were: United States of America, United Kingdom of Great Britain and Ireland, Canada, Australia, South Africa, New Zealand, India, France, Italy, Japan, Belgium, Bolivia, Brazil, China, Cuba, Ecuador, Hellennes, Guatemala, Haiti, Hedjas, Honduras, Liberia, Nicaragua, Panama, Peru, Poland, Portugal, Rumania, Serbia (including Croats & Slovenes), Siam, Czecho-Slovakia, Uruguay, and Germany and her Allies. Indeed, it was a great "World" war.

12. Norway, Sweden, Denmark, Holland, Switzerland, Spain, Argentina, Chile, and Mexico maintained diplomatic relations with belligerents on both sides.

13. The League of Nations includes (1925) 55 nations as result of the "Treaty of Versailles," effective January 10, 1920. Their purpose: to settle all international disputes by arbitration at meetings held at Geneva, Switzerland, thus ending forever the specter of global wars.

14. Germany's "Big Bertha" guns (there were two) which shelled Paris in 1918 were adapted from naval guns provided with new bores. Preparations took six to nine months. Caliber–8.25 inches. Shell–300 pounds. Charge (propellant)–300 pounds. Angle of firing–65 degrees elevation. Culminating point of trajectory (highest point shell reaches as it roars on to target)–22 miles. Range–up to about 75 miles. Aim was calculated without actual registration. Guns were mounted with carriages on flanged wheels on rails—therefore, somewhat mobile.

15. The Lusitania was sunk 2:15 p.m., May 7, 1915 by the U–20, with loss of 1152 lives out of the 1916 souls aboard (Elbert & Alice Hubbard of Roycroft among those lost). The unwritten law of the sea: "In time of war belligerents have right to capture enemy merchantmen, also to sink their prizes—but only

after challenging each ship and then allowing all on board to get away in life-boats," recognized by all nations (Germany included) was thus violated by the German Submarine Commander Schwieger, who ordered the torpedoes fired that caused the Lusitania to sink in twenty minutes. Schwieger, "moved with mixed feelings," wrote in the log of the U-20: "3:10. Torpedo shot at distance of 700 meters, going 3 meters below surface. Hits steering center behind bridge. In addition to torpedo, a second explosion must have taken place (Boiler, coal, or powder?) Bridge and part of ship where torpedo hit are torn apart, and fire follows." The following notice had appeared in certain American papers on May 1, 1915:

"Notice! TRAVELERS intending to embark on the Atlantic voyage are reminded that a state of war exists between Germany and her allies and Great Britain and her allies; that the zone of war includes the waters adjacent to the British Isles; that, in accordance with formal notice given by the Imperial German Government, vessels flying the flag of Great Britain, or of any of her allies, are liable to destruction in those waters and that travelers sailing in the war zone on ships of Great Britain or her allies do so at their own risk.
    Imperial German Embassy.
    Washington, D.C., April 22, 1915"

Regarding the fact or fancy that the great liner (sister ship to the Mauretania that brought me back from Europe) carried munitions, "The proof is absolute that she (Lusitania) was not and never had been armed, nor did she carry any explosives,"–Judge Julius Mayer, August 18, 1916.

Among other "duties" of the U-20 was the sinking of the Cymric and the Hesperian, and accompanying Sir Roger Casement to the Irish Coast. The submarine was abandoned in October, 1916, fast aground near the Danish coast. About a year later (Sept. (?) 1917, the U-20's old commander Schwieger was lost (so the report says) with his crew and the U-88 in the North Channel.

16. Variety in cigarettes' names did not necessarily mean variety in taste, but here are some brands common to us of the British Armies: Player's Navy Cut, Player's Haversack, Red Hussar, Ruby Queen, Honey Bee, Lydd's Best, Goldflake, The Flag, Kingfisher, Woodbine (ask the Tommy who smoked), Tucket's Arna, Gainsbourough, T & B, Burlington, Sovereign, Sweet Caporal, Bees Wing, Badmanton, Arfa Mo, and the American's old standby, "Bull Durham" which was and still is a "roll your own." Names—just names, but read 'em over to an old British Territorial or Colonial Soldier. (Note: I smoked a pipe by preference.)

17. A Canadian gunner's monthly rate of pay was "a dollar a day and ten cents field allowance" ($1.10). In Canada he usually drew pay monthly–$33; in

England–3/15 (3 pounds, 15 shillings); in France–40f (francs). Balance of unused pay was credited against a leave time or to cover allotments, etc. (Normally a pound is $4.80, a shilling is 24 cents, a franc, 20 cents).

For serving in the C.E.F., Gnr. Cate received $652.30. This plus his "war service gratuity" of $250.00 disbursed on separation in May 1919, netted him a grand total of $902.30 for his nineteen and one half months of active duty in the Canadian Army. CCC

18. For most soldiers on active service, the letter from home is a powerful influence for good—a tangible bit of the "old life"—an antidote to the poisons of warfare. Few of us could guess all that went on in the inner mind of mates behind the loud laugh, the jest, the torrid curse, the half-suppressed groan or sigh. Under khaki shirt were emotions and aches never mentioned. There were "blue" days—mud, wet, cold, filth, vermin, heat, unsatisfied hunger and thirst, improper clothing and equipment, seemingly unnecessary fatiguing duties, dangers seen and unseen, relaxed morals, illness, wounds, death, horrid unmentionables, and an infinite variety and number of devilish causes of weakened morale. The letter from home saved countless men from immediate or lingering death. May the Great Spirit bless all those who served those who served for them by writing those letters.

I was very fortunate—and I know it—in receiving many letters from many people at frequent intervals. The "box" helped, but it was the "written word" that WORKED WONDERS. Mother, Grandmothers, Father, Sister, Brothers, "Dutch," "Gren," and many others were the true spirits that kept my spirit up to par. I received over 200 letters, cards, and boxes while on the "other side." Of this total, over forty were from "Dutch," over thirty from Mother, third place was taken by "Gren," Grandmother Allard and "M.F.S.", and the balance came from myriad others. The first letter to reach me overseas was from Mother, the next from "Dutch" and the third from "Gren." The final letter to reach me in England was from "Dutch." In France the first to reach me was Mrs. Thompson, a good friend in England, and close behind came Mother and "Dutch". The last to arrive in France was from Corp. Bleasdale, in Paris. The first letter to reach me after entering into the service was from Mother, and the final word, once again, from "Dutch." Take it from one who knows—the above record should stand forever as a service of inestimable value.

19. In the 3rd Artillery Brigade were four batteries, of which the 12th, containing 6 howitzers, was one. Divided into three 2-gun sections plus a Staff Section, the Battery was commanded initially by Major Robinson (later, Major Colin McKay, MC). In Battery Headquarters were the executive officer, Captain Skinner, Sergeant–Major Candy, and HQ Staff. Each section was commanded by a Lieutenant (Right Section–Lt. Palmer, Center Section–Lt. Bacon, Left Section–Lt. McNeal, Staff Section–Lt. Walford). A Sergeant com-

manded each subsection, and each of the two crews making up the "sub" was led by a Corporal. Lest we forget—the busiest man in the battery was the Sergeant–Major (called a First Sergeant in U.S.A.) in direct contact with every duty of the unit.

The 12th Siege Battery was one of fourteen Siege and Heavy Batteries supporting the C.E.F. in France at the signing of the Armistice. Seven of the batteries were commanded by men of St. John, N.B., the home of the 3rd Field Artillery Regiment (known as The Loyal Company), which had the distinction of being the oldest artillery unit in Canada, and the third oldest in the British Commonwealth. CCC (From their website, www.saintjohn.nbcc.ca-Heritage/3far/index.)

20. Roster "A" Gun–12th Battery: (**June 1, 1918**)—Sgt. Troop, Corporal Henry, Bombardiers Byers and McCrae, Gunners Brown, Bosdet, Cameron, Cate, Clarke, Fisher, Mason, McConnell, McNutt, and Tulippe. (These men formed the two crews for the battery's No.1 Gun.); (**January 5, 1919**)—Sgt. Troop (MM), Bdrs. Byers, *Cameron*, and Stratton, Gnrs. Cate, Gilchrist, Hall, Hanson, Kirk, McNutt, Marston, Mounce, Moore, Pollock, Raph, Tait, Toungue, Wilde, and Wade. (Five of the originals were still in the crew. Those underlined represent members wounded or gassed that returned from hospital. Only one, Cameron [italics], never left the battery.) Snapshots of most of these men are in my album thanks to "VPK" (the camera that stuck with me––see Chapter X)—and much luck.

21. As the '18 Somme drive was about to start (August 8, 1918) the roster of the two "sister" guns, "A" and "B" which formed "Right Section" of the 12th Battery seems to have been: ("A" sub-section)–Sgt Troop, Corporal Henry, Bombardiers Budd, Cameron, McCrae, Gunners Allen, Andrews, Bosdet, Byers, Cate, Colwell, Fisher, Gilchrist, Kleisher, McNutt, Hugh McKenzie, R.C. McConnell, Paynter, and Tulippe, plus Anti-aircraft Lewis Gunner Mason and Medical Orderly Brown; ("B" sub-section)–Sgt Cropper, Corp. "Spud" West, Bdrs. McCann, Vincent, Barnwell, Gnrs. Agafonof, Barber, Beveridge, Duncan, Fairclough, Fitzpatrick, Graham, Horncastle, Jenkins, Kay, Kent, Lloyd, K.P. McKenzie, Ross, Sparrow, Spinney, Stratton, Tregitt, Trethaway. Officer in Charge: Lieutenant (Leftenant) Palmer. Each subsection was divided into two crews each serving in turn twenty-four–hour stretches. #1 Crew of "A" sub sect. consisted of: Bdr. Cameron (#1–in charge of crew), Bdr. Budd (gun-layer or sighter), Gnr. Cate (#2–responsible for breech-handling and firing of gun), Gnrs. Andrews, Colwell, Fisher, McNutt, McConnell, & Paynter. Five men were needed to man the gun in action; the others kept busy supplying ammunition, etc.

22. Call to Action!. Out of warm blankets and the semi-safety of a dugout my (six inch howitzer) crew would rush in answer to, "Right Section—ACTION!" A sequence of orders would follow, something like this: "Number

One gun: Amatol, Fuze one-oh-six, N-C-Tok, Size Sixteen, Charge Four——,"
varied according to various types of shell, fuze, charge, etc., to be used. Then
would come the "switch" followed by the "elevation," and "Load-Up and report when ready." Often we fired on "receipt of elevation" or without other
orders than "S.O.S. Number——." In the latter case with a previously arranged
shell and load at a pre-arranged target. Orders varied, but the activities about
the gun were much the same for all.

Our howitzer differed from a gun in many ways. It was of shorter barrel,
its projectile traveled higher and dropped more directly upon the target. Generally, it was the most accurate gun in the service. Its extreme range was about
9 kilos at extreme elevation of 44.5°, with charge #5 or #6. If I remember
correctly, its barrel weighed some 3800 pounds. It could provide an elastic
barrage of no mean proportions, destroy a trench system or level a town, and
not infrequently was it used for "sniping."

Our shell measured 6 inches in diameter and weighed 100 pounds. It was
loaded with "HE" (high explosive) or one of the several forms of gas. The
latter was held in liquid form in a small glass bottle in the heart of the shell.
When the shell came to us, a ringed plug was screwed into its nose. This we
removed when preparing for firing, inserting a silk bag containing a detonator
or "booster charge" of TNT (Trinitrotoluene) into a little well (about the depth
and size of the average man's index finger), after which we screwed home the
fuze in place of the plug. Several types of fuzes were used, usually the two
known as 1-0-1-E or 1-0-6, both of percussion type (detonated upon striking
target).

Charges or propellants were TNT or cordyte (or cordite)—a smokeless
powder composed of nitroglycerin, guncotton, and mineral jelly of dull wax
color in the form of macaroni-minus-the-hole-like strings. The TNT was of
dull wax color in the form similar to split peas and about the same size. These
charges were delivered to us in silk bags, each bag representing a single charge–
–hence "charge four" for four bags or "six" for six bags. The first charge or bag
had a red patch sewed to its base in which was black powder. Charges were
tied together before insertion into the breech behind the shell.

With shell and charge in place the breech was closed, a "tube" (.303 cal.
cartridge) slipped into the rifle breech fitted to the gun breech, and when all
was ready—gun sighted and elevated to firing position—a quick pull on a short
cord jerked the pin to which it was attached from the rifle breech causing the
firing pin to detonate the fulminate cap in the base of the "tube," igniting the
"cordite" in the "tube" which, expanding as it burned, forced its way thru the
vent in the gun breech, igniting the powder in the red patch fitted to the base
of the charge, igniting in turn the main charge of TNT or cordite, and our
"calling card" was on its way to our German friends howling a warning to them

as it went (a warning rarely heard by those near our target in time to save themselves).

I ought to mention, after going this far, that before the shell was rammed "home" in the breech, a "safety pin" had been pulled from the fuze. If we had forgotten this little matter our shell would have been a well known "dud." The rate of fire varied from "rapid"—about 2 per minute (if we could keep it up)— to "harassing", which was varied slow fire when we simply dropped shells "here and there" over a chosen area to harass the enemy.

23. Some Continental towns and locations the 12th will not forget: FRANCE early 1918—Le Havre, Rouen, St. Pol, Aubigny, Mt. St. Eloi, Vimy and the *Ridge, Nine Elmes, Plank Road*, Thelus and the *Wood*; July, 1918— Blavincourt, Belfort, Beaufort, Avant-le-Comte, Tinques, Harbarque, Dainville, Arras, *Daisy-O-Pip*; August, 1918—Rheubempre, Amiens, Villers Bretonneux, Wiencourt, Caix, Vrely, Rosieres-en-Santerre, Meharicourt, Longeau, *Vineyards*; September, 1918—Villers, Cagnicourt, *Arras-Cambrai Road, Douai-Cambrai Road, Bourlon Wood*; October, 1918—*Haynecourt Plains*, Haynecourt, Epinoy, Sancourt, Bleycourt, Douai, Cambrai, Eswars, *Canal du Nord*, Queant, Villers-en-Couchy (?), Abscon (?), Le Sentinel, Valenciennes. November 1918—St. Saulve, Rhombles. BELGIUM—Boussu, Bossu-Bois, Hornu, Jemappes, Mons, Havre, St. Symphorien, Ghlin; Post Armistice—Bruxelles, Hal, Antwerp, Louvain, St. Denis, Chalroi, Namur, Liege; FRANCE (again)—Paris, Suresnes, Versailles, Malmaison, Fontainbleau; GERMANY 1919—Aachen, Cologne, Bonn. (italicized names locations, not towns)

24. GAS!—and the following journey: Battery 1st Aid Station, Field Dressing Station, Field Ambulance Station, Field Hospital Station, #22 Canadian Clearing Station, #4 General Hospital at Camieres, #6 Convalescent Camp at Etaples, #12 Convalescent at Wimereux, #7 Ration Depot at Artillery General Base at Bologne, C.C.R.C. 4th Division Wing at Marenla, C.C.R.C. 2nd Division at Aubin St. Vasst,:and so on.

25. Paperwork on demobilization: Dispersal Sheets, Service Records, Profession Reports, Pay Books Balanced, Where desirous of spending 30-day leave in Canada (attended to in St. Symphorien, Belgium in Jan., Feb., & March, 1919), "Deloused"-1st, Embarkation Cards, Quartermaster Reports, Medical Board (Le Havre, France in April), Clothing Reports, Gratuities Sheet, Dental Inspection, "Deloused"–2nd, QMS&ICS Sheets, Pay-Master ($5), Clothing Issue, Kit Issue (Witley Camp, England in April), Surplus C&K Return, Medical Board (again), Pay-Master (ditto), Transportation arrangements, Passports, Discharges (St. John, N.B., Canada–May, 1919). This is by no means complete, but it gives many steps taken.

26. Music for the 12th by Service Bands. Canada–236th Battalion (Kilties);

At sea on the Grampion–Foresters, Scotts; England (Witley)–104th Battalion, (Deepcut)–1st London Rifles Regiment; (Lydd)–Royal Marine Light Infantry; (Codford)–Australian; France: (Vimy)–Highlanders; (Arras)–Canadian; (Reubembre)–317th Infantry, American Expeditionary Forces; (Le Havre)–Imperial Guards; (Rouen)–Scotts Guards; (Arras)–50th Battalion, Cherissey Scotts; Belgium: (Boussu and other towns)–1st Army Corps Band.

27. The message that ended the war on the American fronts as transmitted by Major Beaumont shortly after 7 A.M. on the morning of November 11, 1918:

> SIGNAL CORPS UNITED STATES ARMY
> Telegram
> Nov. 11, 1918.

> To Commanding Generals, First, Third, Sixth and Colonial Corps: Number 357, Section GS PERIOD Armistice with Germany has been signed PERIOD All hostilities cease at eleven hours this date, the eleventh instant PERIOD Instructions contained in telegram No. TWO FOUR SEVEN Section GS those Headquarters will be complied with PERIOD Acknowledge receipt PERIOD.
> DRUM

> Official: Copies to:

> Edward C. McGuire   Chief, Air Service,
> Major Cavalry,   Chief, Artillery,
> Sec. Gen. Staff.   Chief of Staff Dpts.

28. This chapter started out to be a small collection of miscellaneous notes and is growing into a "grab bag" volume by itself...I'll end it with a sampling of the spirit of war as reflected by fight-inspired brains that poured onto paper from the pens of many writers.

ENGLAND:

TO THE TROUBLER OF THE WORLD

> "At last we know you, War-Lord. You, that flung
>> The gauntlet down, down the mask you wore,
>> Publish your heart, and let its pent hate pour,
> You that had God forever on your tongue.
> We are old in war, and if in guile we are young,
>> Young also is the spirit that evermore
>> Burns in our bosom even as heretofore.

Nor are these thews unbraced, these nerves unstrung.
We do not with God's name make wanton play:
        We are not on such easy terms with Heaven:
But, in Earth's hearing we can verily say,
        'Our hands are pure; for peace, for peace we have striven;
        And not by earth shall soon he be forgiven,
Who lit the fire accursed that flames to-day!'"
        (*Wm. Watson, London Times, August 6, 1914*)

FRANCE:

"Ils ne passseront pas!" [Battle cry, Verdun, 1916, expressing the spirit of the "line"]
        (*"...They will never pass", was the concluding sentence of French General Nivelle's defiant 'Order of the Day' delivered July 12, 1916, at the defense of Fort Souville during the exhausting battle of Verdun. CCC*)

        Mon corps a' la Terre,
        Mon ame a' Dieu,
        Mon coeur a' France.
        (*Expressing the spirit of the individual soldier—scribbling found on a shell casing in Verdun, 1916.*)

SOUTH SLAV:

"SONG OF WARNING"

Bosnia lives; she is not dead,
Vain it is that you have buried her body!
Fire still glows within the fettered captive;
Nor yet is the time for singing her dirge -
        ...Emperor! Dost thou not hear when
        the revolvers dart flame?...
The leaden balls hiss against thy very throne! (*Ref. Unknown*)

HUN:

Thor stood at the midnight end of the world,
        His battle-mace flew from his hand:
"So far as my clangorous hammer I've hurled,
        Mine are the sea and the land!"
And onward hurtled the mighty sledge
        O'er the wide, wide earth to fall
At last on the Southland's furthest edge,
        In token that HIS was all.

Since then 'tis joyous German right
    With the hammer lands to win.
We mean to inherit world-wide might
    As the Hammer-God's kith and kin.
        (Felix Dahn, German poet-historian)

Traumt Ihr den Friedenstag?
Traume wer traumen mag!
Krieg ist das Losungswort!
Sieg, und so kling es fort.
(Goethe's "Euphorion")

"Gott Strafe England"
(Teutonic public sentiment, 1914)

We will never forgo our hate,
Hate by water and hate by land,
Hate of the head and hate of the hand.
Hate of the hammer and hate of the crown,
Hate of the seventy millions choking down.
We love as one, we hate as one,
We have but one foe alone:
England!
(Hymn of Hate, from The Barvarian Lisauer, 1914)

    (Chanted by the German Navy and much talked of at one time during the war, which is now, I hope, merely a matter of forgotten record)

U.S.A.:

Wake from the sloth of night
And drain life's precious bowl!
The hour has come to smite —
Or lose a people's soul!
    (Robert Underwood Johnson's Summons to Americans)

Oh, it is wickedness to clothe
Yon hideous, grinning thing that stalks
Hidden in music like a queen
That in a garden of glory walks,
'Til good men love the thing they loathe;

Art, thou hast many infamies,
But not an infamy like this.
Oh, snap the fife and still the drum,
And show the monster as she is.
                    (from the pen of Richard LeGallienne, on WAR)

All these I hate—war and its panoply,
The lie that hides its ghastly mockery,
That makes its glories out of women's tears,
The toil of peasant thru burdened years,
The legacy of long disease that preys
On bone and body in the after-days.
        God's curses pour,
Until it shrivel with its votaries
And die away in its own fiery seas,
        That nevermore
Its dreadful call of murder may be heard;
A thing accursed in every deed and word
        From blood-drenched shore to shore!
                    (from Joseph Miller's "Hymn of Hate")

* * * * * * * * * * * * * * *

That wise "old timer" Sophocles said, so it is written, "War does not of choice destroy bad men, but good ever."

...and a great old German warrior, General Von Moltke, who certainly ought to know wrote, "Every war is a national calamity whether victorious or not."

"War is the concentration of all human crimes...It turns man into a beast of prey...that he may become the destroyer of his race...(*Probably William Henry Channing*)

"There never was a good war or a bad peace...(*Ben Franklin*)

"As long as nations meet on the fields of war—as long as they sustain the relations of savages to each other—as long as they put the laurel and the oak on the brows of those who kill—just so long will citizens resort to violence, and quarrels be settled by dagger and revolver." (*Robert Ingersoll in an address entitled, "Crimes Against Criminals"*)

"...and all this madness, all this rage, all this flaming death of our civilization and our hopes, has been brought about because a set of official gentlemen, living luxurious lives, mostly stupid, and all without imagination or heart, have chosen that it should occur rather than that any one of them should suffer some infinitesimal rebuff to his country's pride..." (*Bertrand Russell, 1914*)

"...whilst terror and bloodshed reign in the land - there can be no process of thought..." (*Richard Cobden*)

Who of us, cannot agree with so many of these thoughts? We KNOW that war is all wrong, but strike up the bands, bring forth your silver-tongued orators with their crying of "war for democracy and (what-have-you)," speed up the presses with their stories of violated "rights," unfurl your banners, march up and down our streets with your uniformed men—and watch the "flower of a nation" rush to the "colors"—and glorious deal—"glorious?" The spirit that burns inside the breasts of the youth who flock to the "call of their land" is the "glorious" part of it—all else is mockery—cheap, terrible, tragic mockery!

Even so, at all times, "BE PREPARED!"

* * * * * * * *

(Note added in 1929: I thought nothing more needed to be added to the thoughts expressed above. Sadly, it appears that some of the lessons learned from those years of 1914 to 1918 have lost their punch. We'll take a peek at a few of the telegrams the ex-Kaiser of Germany is receiving on his 70th birthday at Doorn, Holland, January 27, 1929. CJC)

"Program for the 70th birthday of the all highest—his majesty the Kaiser and King." (*Monarchists' meetings in many German cities*).

"...in grateful remembrance of the services which the house of Hohenzollern rendered to Prussia and to Germany and of how your majesty's work was ever governed by the principle that the king is the first servant of his country." (*Nationalist League*).

"...deepest gratitude to the Kaiser who convened the 1st international conference for workingmen's protection and introduced social insurance." (*German National Labour League*).

"...demand the return of his majesty to the fatherland, deeming that the right of every German to reside in the fatherland cannot be denied." (*Nationalist League at Hamburg*).

"To the supreme war lord of unvanquished forces—sincere congratulations and most respectful greetings on your 70th birthday from hundreds of thousands of former German soldiers." (*The Stahhelm [German War Veterans Organization*)

It was this same German Kaiser Wilhelm II who said to recruits in 1891, "It may come to pass that you will have to shoot down and stab your own relations and brothers." And in 1913, "I look upon the People and the Nation, as handed on to me as an responsibility conferred on me by God, and I believe, as it is written in the Bible, that it is my duty to increase this heritage for which one day I shall be called upon to give an account. Whoever tries to interfere with my task, I shall crush."

(...happy thoughts!)

(Note: Scattered throughout, I have used dates, conversations, and the bulk of important general historical information taken from: <u>Europe Since Waterloo</u>, by William Stearns Davis, The Century Company, New York, 1926.. CJC)

CHAPTER X
Souvenir Notes

Although never a true "souvenir hunter" I have always appreciated the value of some specimen or token of foreign lands to those who stay at home. Among my few souvenirs are several which are of interest to any who may

chance to see them and hear their story, but the real interest in each souvenir is, naturally, in the mind of the original owner. He alone knows the full story. In his mind only will the souvenir start a series of reminiscences carrying him back over the years to live over again...the past. It has been said, "Let the past stay buried, live for today and for the future," and perhaps that is not a bad thought, but most of us enjoy mental repetition of certain past experiences.

The following index and notes merely record the existence of what is left of a once full bag of tricks— greatly reduced now by friendly invasion and pillage.

Cover of the "Kit Bag" scrapbook

<u>Acorns–Twin:</u> from near Witley Camp in memory of a certain event in which Bosdet & Cate played a major role.

<u>Ash Tray:</u> from Danzig, Germany, a gift from an "ex-gob," Ray Cate, carrying the inscription, "Salem Aleikum".

<u>A.V. of C.E.F.:</u> American Volunteers of the Canadian Expeditionary forces; Charter Membership Card No. 1137. At Witley camp, Milford, Surrey, England in April, 1919, a meeting of Americans serving in the C.E.F. was held at which the purposes of this organization were discussed and many "Yankees" paid the first dues of a half-crown and became charter members. At this time Ed-

ward J. Donnelly was chief promoter and later he became General Secretary and Treasurer. James J. Graves of Chicago was to be president. On returning to Boston after demobilization I learned that Mr. "D" (of Chelsea) had disappeared with the association's funds. Captured later, he was given a sentence which he served in due time. The organization lived thru the strain and is still going strong with a number of posts scattered throughout the U. S. Boston's most prominent post (1924) is "Vimy Post #1 at Dudley Street. On the occasion of Plymouth's 300th birthday celebration the Post turned out in full to join the very colorful parade held in that Cape town on "President's Day" when former Pres. Warren G. Harding was in office.

Automatic Pistol, Holster, Shoulder Thong (braided leather): received from German officer prisoner near Cagnicourt along the Arras–Cambrai Road. (Nothing now is left except photos made before they were stolen from my car parked on Charles Street, Boston.

Badges: Canadian Army issue "For Service at the Front, #179255, Class A", as shown here; regular issue Canadian Service Badge; United States Army issue with star as shown here. (See also "Medals") *[See end of Chapter VIII]*

Buttons: See "Uniform"

Black-Jack: Lead-filled leather case with leather thong (wrist grip), which first was introduced to the Cate family by a civilian in London—Ray Cate being the receiver during a "gob-civilian scrap."

Billfolds: Black leather case purchased in Canada in September, 1917 which served well throughout the balance of the war. Green leather case bought in the British Army & Navy League Club in Paris, France in February, 1919.

Books, booklets, pamphlets: (Black notebook)–miscellaneous assortment of notes made overseas; (Blue notebook)–as above. Both were bought in French shops; British Museum visitor's information; "Canada & Her Soldiers" pamphlet; "Canadian Soldier's Song Book" issued by Canadian YMCA; "Conway & Deganwy" informational literature about two beautiful towns of northern Wales; Dictionary (English-French) bought in France and used to great advantage daily; "Final Blow of the 1st Army–1918"; "First Aid", a Red Cross issue; "Hotel des Invalides et Mus'ee de l'Armee" visitor's guide; "Land Settlement"–a gov't issue; "Mauretania–Royal Mail Steamer"–a description of that great craft; "New Testament" from the Canadian Bible Society; "Plas-Mawr"–description of an historic house in Conway, Wales, in which Queen Elisabeth once held forth; "Returned Soldier's Handbook of Information"–gov't issue; "Spanish"–3 small volumes as issued to those of us in St. Symphorien who attended Spanish classes at the "Khaki Kollege," known also as the University of St. Symphorien; "Versailles"–another guide book for visitors; and a few miscellaneous pieces of no particular importance, except to me.

Camera: Vest Pocket Kodak #14406–was purchased from Robey-French in Boston (May 1917) and presented to me by "Dutch". It became my most-treasured companion, recording many events in U.S.Army in Massachusetts, and Canadian Army in Canada, British Isles and France. It was destroyed by shell fire near Cagnicourt; Camera of same type (#97518) was purchased by Bosdet in London for 2 pounds–six, and after the loss of #14406 it was given to me as a replacement. This latter camera is the famous "crooked-raffle" camera of Kenmel Park Camp, North Wales (mentioned in Chapter 8). On its surface is scratched the names of many places in which it served me. Cameras were "taboo" to unofficial photographers for very good reason, but the wealth of war time pictures all over the world testify to the fact that they were "in action." My compact friend fitted nicely into the 1st Aid dressing pocket of my tunic. Cameras were often lost—including my own, but the vigilance of comrades, particularly Cameron of the "Big 4" resulted in its return. Film, at a premium, was supplied by men returning from hospital or leave, and now and then by mail. Of hundreds of exposures made the majority were lost. Thieves, shellfire, gas and a host of other agents served to reduce the total to finally result in prints for my small album. Here again am I indebted to Cameron and Bosdet, particularly to Bosdet—(December 25, 1926, V.P.K.#97518 though some-what the worse for its service at the front and elsewhere, still serves me faith-fully—More power to Eastman Kodak Company of Rochester, New York—Again, still serving as of May 12, 1931.) *[See end of Chapter VII]*

Cap: German Trench–picked up from the "Haynecourt Field" position during the final drive toward Cambrai.

Cartridges: American, English, French and German–rifle and pistol, picked up here and there; A French copper bullet hammered into a paper cutter; A flattened bullet.

Cards: French play-ing–used by the "Big 4" and others in many games.

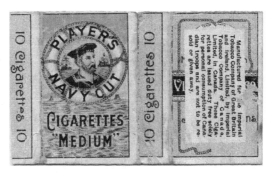

Cigarettes: Package of Player's Navy Cut, issued by the Canadian YMCA for consumption by troops only.

Cigarette Case: Of brown leather, with the "Palais de Justice of Bruxelles" stamped on face. A gift from a friend met in Bruxelles in January, 1919.

Cigarette Holder: A treasured momento given to me by an old Belgian friend near St. Symphorien in March, 1919. Figures of two horses, tree stump and leaves carved on fine ivory bowl. Stem and mouthpiece of amber.

Cigarette Holder Case: Plush-lined case with leather covering.

Currency: A Canadian cent (1893) handed to me by a comrade with, "I'm happier when I'm broke so take my last cent and do me a favor." Also British, French, Belgian and German paper currency of uncertain value.

Decorations: (See "Medals" & "Ribbons.")

Dog Tags: (See Identification Discs) *[See Chapter IV]*

Equipment: (Such as I have left of Canadian Army Issues in France) Artillery haversack with strap; Bayonet–short, smooth, artillery; Bandoleer–leather, 5-pocket, for 50 rounds ammunition (rifle-emergency) issued at Blavincourt; Belts–wide web with brass finish; Clasp knife, with cord; Comb & odd toilet issues; 1st Aid Dressing–pads, bandages, pins and iodine, carried in pocket sewed inside front right lower tunic flap (unless replaced by V.P.K.); Housewife–sewing repair kit; Identification Discs (dog tags)–2 on cord to wear about neck, stamped with name, number, rank, branch and religion. In case of death, one to be buried with man and one to be forwarded to War Office; Infantry Pack–picked up on field near Caix to replace my own; Kit-Bag–white denim; Knife, fork & spoon–regular issue; Mess Tin–2 piece, regular issue; Ration Bag–white cotton; Revolver–damaged .38 cal, 6-shot cylinder removed from shell-wrecked British tank *(See sketch made from photo, p.51.)* near Waincourt; Shaving outfit–brush and razor; Steel Helmet–my 4th issue; Water bottle–blue enameled steel with camel hair case, and straps.

Flags: United States–small cotton, in my kit or about my person throughout my term of service. It flew above our gun positions many times and places, and rested over many "A" gun dug outs; Small Silk–carried in New Testament from the day "Dutch" gave it to me in May, 1917 until January, 1927, when it was transferred to my old Sunday School Bible; Canadian - small silk, presented to me by a friend in Nova Scotia a short time before sailing "over"; English–small silk, from "Gren" in September, 1917; French–small silk, from Suzy, a petit camarade of Paris, in February, 1919; Belgian–small cotton (I'll be honest–this one I purchased February, 1919 in Bruxelles).

Furloughs: (See Leaves)

Fuze: brass, time or percussion, fired from an English gun. Set at "0" for percussion—can be set to detonate from o to 22 seconds after firing.

<u>Frieze:</u> Two sections (rose buds)of carved wooden ornaments "removed" from the wall of 2nd class dining salon of the "RMS Mauretania" in May of 1919.

<u>German letter:</u> Letter and envelope written to a German officer killed by machine gun fire in a field near Haynecourt. *[See Chapter V]*

<u>Grapevine:</u> A piece of stem from the vineyard at Longeau, France, *(the story of which may be found on pages 59-60.)*

<u>Invoices:</u> Wounded man's kit–made out for me as the "W.M." in October, 1918; From J.J. Callahan in Dublin, Ireland—for a few purchases made in April, 1919 while on leave.

<u>Insignia:</u> (See Uniform)

<u>Identification discs:</u> (See Equipment)

<u>Labels:</u> A miscellaneous assortment.

<u>Letters:</u> From relatives and friends in and out of the service (1917-1918-1919).
<u>Letters:</u> Saved by Grandmother, Susie M. Allard, Berwick, Maine.

The third letter in the series was written by CJC's mother on the event of his leaving for Frederikton, N.B., to enlist in the Canadian Army. The letter dated Feb. 26, 1919, was written by CJC to one of his younger brothers.. CCC

Sharon, Mass.
May 6, 1917

My darling Grandma:
...This war is a terrible thing, it is just what Sherman said it was. My belief is that the harder the fighting notions go at it now, the sooner the war will end, and God will put things right again—for good.
As expected, as the Bible says, altho not directly, this great country of ours did get into it. It is a case of war between Democracy and Aristocracy, rule without military forces, and rule with military forces. The result will be as the Bible says, a genuine Democracy, a real rule without military forces and thence without war. Therefore the quickest way for this long looked for rule to come, is for every American, in fact every ally of the democratic powers, to go into this thing, however terrible [*sic*] it sounds and is, and do his or her part by joining one of the three armies:

147

I   The one in khaki, who gives his life,
II   The one in overalls, who gives his labor,
III   And the one in silks, who gives his money.

In my honest opinion and belief the one to join the first is the man from eighteen (18) to thirty-five (35) who is physically fit for army life, and he should join the department where his former experiences can help him, where he is more at home.

The man for the second is every man, woman, and child who can not be a wonderful businessman, and who can do some work, in gardening, or in factory or in shipping, even tho physically they may not be O.K.

The man for the third is the businessman, and the rich man, whose money will help run the other two armies. Not one of these three armies can exist without the other, neither can this nation exist without them all, right now, and until God takes a hand.

Every home in the country will bear a share of the sorrows, but every true American will take his or her sorrow, as it comes, and not object forcibly no matter how hard it is and no matter how much it hurts, for the country's sake, their own sake, and for God's sake.

So believing all this, I joined the Marines two weeks ago, but have got transferred to the 1st Massachusetts Ambulance Corps, and will probably be called in about three or four weeks.

Hoping to see you all soon.
                                    Love to all, Clif.

Sharon, Mass
May 20, 1917

My Darling Grandma,

Undoubtedly you have been expecting to see your grandson walk in on you any time during the past week. The two reasons why you didn't were because I have neither time nor money. One thing you can count on tho is that you will see me before my Company is sent to France, which may be in a month, or even two months tho if the truth be told no one, and least of all the officers, know when we shall go.

Saturday I planted fifteen (15) eighty-five (85) foot rows of corn, two (2) rows of spinach, five (5) of pole beans, four (4) of bush beans, one(1) of peas, four (4) beds of cucumbers, two (2) of squash and one (1) of lettuce. I have some lettuce over an inch high, and some peas about four (4) inches high. We have been using our asparagus for two weeks, and our rhubarb for nearly three. And on top of it all we have some of the poorest, rockiest, graveliest land there ever was. Our garden is scarcely more than a detestable sand bank, and yet with proper care and fertalizer [sic] we can raise a good crop. What are you folks doing for a garden this year?

There was a bad forest fire on the shores of Lake Massapoag to-day. One of the nurses here—and she's got red hair at that—and I were walking around the lake when the fire was at its worst. Of course I am just as much of a "fire fiend" as ever, and so I rushed away from nursie and went fighting fire. I emptied two extinguishers and held my end of the line clear of fire, until the hose and chemical wagons came. I had my best—and only—suit on, my nice new Six Dollar ($6) shoes were just being "broke in", and after the fire all the damage done to me was a black face and two black hands, each scorched a little, while my shoes were badly dampened from the mixture which one of the men accidentally spilled on them. Miss Dodge, the nurse, sat quietly on the stone wall and looked innocent enough, but many seemed to believe that her hair was the cause of the fire. The worst feature of the fire was the briers which formed a nasty barrier when one got caught in them. During the whole fight my two brothers, Richard and Raymond stuck beside me, both doing considerable towards putting it out.

Wow! Its 10:30 P.M. Good Night.

Love – Clifton

(Letter from CJC's mother to her mother (Susie M. Allard)

Belmont, Mass
84 Payson Rd.
July 26, 1917

Dear Mother,

Clifton has just left. He did not know where he was going after he reached the Armory as the Captain thought it best not to tell them.

He had his chum here to dinner and he stayed all night with him. They are going to try and keep together. Oh this awful war. It is an awful sight to see the thousands of boys going to the front. All Boston is one big mass of soldiers preparing for the front, it was pretty tough to see my dear big boy start for that awful field of hell this morning but I do thank God I had this pretty home for him to come to and bring his friend—the last of his being in Mass. has been happy as much so as the thought of war could let it be. He was mighty glad of it too. In that much God was good.

He felt very bad to have Peg sneak off the way she did just before time for him to go. If she had only been here this last week they would have been together. I had a big dinner for them last night. Of course we all felt bad not to have her with us. Her fits and moods certainly have kept us all in hot water. I hope to be able to see you in Oct. I have got a beautiful garden. All I can think of is Clifton just now so I guess I will close until I am in a sweeter frame of mind.

R. and R. send heaps of love and want to know if you want them to come and see you before school.

Love, Mae

THE ARMY AND NAVY
YOUNG MEN'S CHRISTIAN ASSOCIATION

Framingham, Mass.
July 29, 1917

My darling Grandma:

Just a word in regards to what moves I have made since last writing. On the 25th, we were mobilized at the Armory. Wednesday, Thursday, and Friday I spent there. Saturday I was one of a detachment of eighteen to leave the Armory for training or rather preparatory, temporary camp in Framingham. To-day there are five more details coming which will total about 5 auto-trucks, sixteen ambulances and two escorts, and thirty more men. To-morrow the full company is to come and then will begin the real work.

Last night was my night for guard duty. I had two watches with a fellow named Cohen The first watch was from ten P.M. to twelve P.M. My next from 4 A.M. to 6 A.M. I had the quartermaster's department for my post. Nothing of importance happened. The cold and heavy eyelids were my worst troubles.

The field here is a good one for the work which is done on it. Very large and level, with two brooks running thru it, all along which, are five springs of excellent water. I will send you pictures as we expect to stay here for about two weeks.

Love, Clif

P.S. I do not know whether Sis is with you or Dad. If she is with you tell her to write—also that shall hear from me soon. Regards to the Shoreys.

C

Return address: Clifton J. Cate, Framingham, Mass, Mass. Amb. Co. #1

In tent at Framingham, Mass.
August 10, 1917

My Darling Grandmother:–

After two days of rain which falls on camp in a manner which says that it is trying to make up for two weeks of sweltering heat, the whole company is pretty well drenched. Water stands in the company street, and in some of the tents, from one to four inches deep. Every little while we have to turn out to answer some bugle call. Each time on the recall we loosen our guy ropes. Should they fail they would either break or pull out the stakes and down would come the soaked tent on our heads. Once the cook tent collapsed, and believe me we worked hard for a few minutes. Next the Quartermaster's tent went in, and more work in the rain. One thing we do gain however, is time to write and mend. There is no stretcher drill, but we have to turn out for fatigue duty, guard duty, lecture, roll call, and hike just as if the sun was shining. But on the whole, in spite of the fact that some are grumbling, I am having it easier than I have had at times in the past, and I like it.

Many object to the food. I do occasionally, but on the level it is very good, except perhaps the coffee and that is usually—rotten—pardon the expression.

We leave from 6:30 to 9:45 P.M. in which to go up to town, or to enjoy ourselves anyway we can. At ten all is dark and silent. At 5:30 A.M. we turn out and there is never any sleeping over. Visitors, mail, and raisin ginger bread if packed good is always welcome, as are molasses or sugar cookies. But these must be well packed.

One of my school mates from Sharon and I were very careful in selecting our tent mates. The result is a tent full (8) of very good-natured, jolly, well-to-do, clean, honest fellows. We have a victrola, song books, and other things to make our serious business a happy one. Every day someone or more get a bundle containing good things to eat. But nothing equals a good lot of raisin ginger bread or molasses cookies.

A short time ago I got a letter from Mildred which I shall answer the next spare time I have. I was certainly glad to hear from her.

> Love to folks.
> Clifton
> Private, 1st Mass Amb.
> under Capt C. F. Ma___

YMCA stationery. Return: Private C.J. Cate, 1st Mass. Amb., Framingham, Mass.

EASTERN STEAMSHIP LINES, INC.

Steamship Gov. Dingley (On touching at Eastport, Me. en route to St. John, N.B. via Boston, Portland & Lubec
Sept. 13, 1917

My darling Grandmother:
Just a word to tell you that I am off on the first lap of my journey to France. Am being sent with five others to Fredreckston [sic], N.B. to fill up a company there. We expect to ship at once from some nearby port direct to Liverpool, England.

The trip from Boston to St. John has so far been more than fine. The weather could not have been better, the sky clear as a bell, temperature just right, and with the ship rolling just enough to make one sleepy.

We left Boston at 9:15 A.M. yesterday, touched Portland at 4:30 P.M., Eastport at 6 a.m. Will touch Lubec at about 10 a.m. and expect to reach St. John by 4 P.M. This is certainly a wonderful excursion trip in good weather costing a fellow only about fifteen dollars (perhaps even less) for a round trip ticket and taking four days and three nights for the full trip. Personally, I am feeling as well , if not better, than I ever did.

Mother was married on the seventh. Gertrude Narroway acted as bridesmaid & I acted as best man. Gertrude got a lovely pendant and yours truly an excellent wrist watch. Miss Narroway took my watch in town with her and illuminated the numerals and hands with the radium mixture which allows me to tell time just as well in absolute darkness as in the daylight. The raw material costs ($1000.00) One Thousand Dollars an ounce—think of it— one sixteenth (1/16th) of a pound of anything costing $1,000.00!

Must run now to mail this before we leave U.S.A. for the Dominion of Canada. Love to all,

Clifton

Eastern Steamship Lines stationery, no return address.

Y.M.C.A.
WITH HIS MAJESTY'S
CANADIAN FORCES ON ACTIVE SERVICE

Note this change in address:
The 8th Field Amb. Depot, C.E.F.,
West St. John, New Brunswick
September 18, 1917

Dearest Grandmother:–
Just a line to let you know that after traveling around quite a bit I am at last settled on an address—for now anyway. Should I move before you write the letter would be forwarded to me from here. So please write soon. Everything here is perfectly comfortable, the food excellent, and your boy never felt better in his life.

We may leave at any moment for England—but at the first word you shall hear from me.

I am afraid I've cheated you this time with so short a letter, but even tho it be short, it carries with it a lot of love for you and Aunt Mary.

'—I suppose I ought to include Aunties' hens, too.
Hope all is as well with you as it is with me.

Love, Clifton

(Remember every word from
home makes a bright day
brighter, and a dark day bright.)

YMCA Stationery. No return on envelope.

The 9th Overseas C.G.A.
Partridge Island
St. John, N.B.
15th Nov., 1917

Dearest Grandmother:–
    Don't forget to make the difference when you write in my address.
Also please do your best to translate this writing, for I happened to have
my fingers on my right hand between two rocks when those rocks came
uncomfortably close to one another. And altho my hand was not really
hurt, my fingers won't wiggle just as I would have them. As usual I am
feeling very well. As for my drill and the regular routine, it goes on as
usual, altho it is getting to be easier or else I am getting pretty well acquainted with it. Occasionally we have a good hard day's work to do, such
as today, so I am somewhat more ready for bed than usual.
    Two weeks ago fifty men from my old unit were sent to Halifax, N.S.
for special duty about the city. As for myself, I was transferred to the 9th
Over-Seas C.G.A. on Partridge Island, in St. John Harbor.
    As usual we are expecting to sail for England at anytime. But also as
usual we still await the word. It does look as tho we would be here all
winter yet we may leave before Thanksgiving. It is the waiting that gets
on one's nerves, but one gets used to all that.
    Snow has covered the island and the surrounding hills for several days.
The weather as a rule is cloudy, but the air itself clear and crispy. To-day
old Bay of Fundy is quite rough due to a heavy wind, and the waves pound
over the rocks just outside the barracks in great style.
    How goes things in Berwick? Is there no news at all? You can easily
realize what little there is for me to write about. Especially since I cannot
find much that would interest you and Aunt Mary in this life.
    Will say Good-Bye for now.
    Love to you and Aunt Mary,
        Clifton

CANADIAN YMCA

Reg. #536636
C.A.R., Milford,
Surrey, England   (Get it all on)
"Witley Camp",
#9 Siege Battery
January 4th, 1918

My darling Grandmother:–
You are wondering how things are in that little white cottage in Berwick. A lot of moves have been made since I last wrote. The main ones being, from Partridge Island to St. John, quarters—on board our transport and the trip across—and lastly, in these quarters in England,—some ways from home

We came over on one of Britain's best troop-ships, and altho we were greatly crowded the majority enjoyed the trip. For my part things were good enough—why not? We had very little hard work to do and there was always plenty of amusement. Concerts, contests, reading and sleeping in the sun occupied the most of our time.

The weather man realized that he must give us a goodly assortment of weather to kill the monotony—he sure did. Rainy weather, windy and sunny, also he handed us some very rough weather for several days during which the walking became difficult, and things took to sliding around in general. For instance, on Xmas day noon, while eating a fine Xmas dinner several tables, dishes, food, men and all, slid into heaps. We would be walking along and, first thing we knew we found ourselves against the side of the boat, and if we didn't grab something quick, we slid to the other side when the boat tipped back—it was sport indeed—but give me solid earth even if I have not yet been sea-sick!

I saw a very little of Ireland, enough of Scotland to make me call that part of her the neatest, cleanest and most thrifty piece of ground I've ever seen, and enough of England to make me ache to see more.

Our camp here is not as luxuriously equipped as our own home—but it is comfortable enough—and above all clean and sanitary. It sure does satisfy the most of us. We are held in quarantine for a few days before being let out to explore the camp and adjacent grounds—but at the end of that time we expect to get a pass, during which I hope to have several days in Edinburgh, Scotland and London, England.

Naturally I find a lot of new things here. The trains, houses, wagons, electrics, and most things in general are different from those at home in a more or less important way. I can tell you more about it later—it is easy enough to say that I shall like it even more than I thought.

That is all for the present since the mail-man is here watching.
Love to you and Aunt Mary.
(Regards to all the Shoreys).

Clifton
(Use this address if you ever lose my regular one—or if you should get no word in answer to letters—after a reasonable time—say a good month at least). (Gnr. C.J. Cate, #536636, C.G.A., Army Post Office, London, England)

No envelope

Reg. #536636 (Must have my number)
#12 Canadian Siege Battery
South Minden Camp
Deepcut, Hauts, Eng.

My dear Grandmother (& Aunt Mary)
Since my last letter I have done quite a bit of moving around in so far as is possible during the little time I have.

For a week after writing we remained in quarantine—then came a week's pass. The battery marched to the station at Milford in a body and proceeded from there to reach every part of Gt. Britain and Ireland according to their passes. Mine was made out to Edinburgh, Scotland.

I spent a busy six hours in London while waiting for my train. Visited as many notable places as I could in that time, including Westminster Abbey, London Tower, St. Paul's Cathedral, etc. Made some purchases along the Strand, and ended up by taking a bus which dropped me off near an Underground Station where I traveled in London's tubes to King's Cross Sta.

My first move upon arriving in Edinburgh after about ten hours of travel was to eat; second to hunt up a room. The latter being a hard job since the city was full of Canadians, Australians, Anzacs, and Highland soldiers who had already filled up the hotels. I had left Witley camp with £4, and had received another few $ from a friend at Waterloo Sta. in London making £5 or, roughly $24.50. After paying up all debts, for debts must occur in the Army, I had about $23.00. About a pound went away in London and so when I finally took count of stock my first day in Scotland I found that I was safe to spend about 16 shillings ($3.84) or so a day in seeing that particular part of Scotland.

The first day I visited Edinburgh Castle, old John Knox's home, Holy Rood Palace, Whitehorse Inn and spent the evening at a pantomime. You may believe after so many days of being tied down (from our leaving Canada to our finish of segregation at Witley) with practically no money it was great to be free with plenty of cash providing we were careful.

The next day was Sunday, so I attended morning services at a fine old church, St. Giles Cathedral—where old John Knox used to preach. After services I visited the King's Chapel and in the afternoon rode out to the Firth of Forth bridge. That was all I did Sunday—but I certainly enjoyed what I did do, or rather what I did not do—other than rest.

Monday was a busy day for many of the places I visited would have taken days to see them right, in particular the National Art Galleries, Museums, and Royal High School. Among other places the same day was the prison and Arthur's Seat. I also enjoyed another pantomime at King's Theatre.

Tuesday was travel day—I took the train to *(illegible)*, not finding anything in particular here, went on to Dundee. From here I went to Broughty Ferry with one of my mates and enjoyed several hours of real hospitality in a genuine Scotch home. Got back to Edinburgh in time to climb to the top of a great monument to Sir Walter Scott. Went to bed this time in good season.

Wednesday I returned to London, after having satisfied myself that Scotland is a great country. Already I had become so satisfied with England from what little bit I had seen. After a few hours in the latter country's metropolis I returned to Milford and thence to camp, reaching there about 2:30 in the morning.

We had much more freedom than before, so visited many of the towns near camp. But we soon left camp coming to this camp in Hauts county and were not long in learning that we had found the better camp of the two.

Since coming here we have been quite busy but <u>by no means</u> have we found any <u>too hard work</u> in spite of some folks' talk at home who would have us believe that here we would find it hard. No maam—not a bit of it– –just enough to keep us in trim as you shall see for yourself when I return.

We have several hours each day as well as most Saturday and Sunday PMs in which to roam over the nearby country, and you may be sure that opportunity is not overlooked. Aldershot, Cam_?_, and Farnsbouough are three nearby and busy places. Firmley Green is a still nearer little circle of shops and houses which we like to walk out to nights. On the whole things aren't so bad with us—yet for all these joys I shall be glad to see Fritz's question answered and get back to America and my regular work.

Love to yourself and Aunt Mary and regards to the Shoreys & all of them.

Clifton

Written on plain stationary with envelope bearing artillery logo, (Canada, Quo Fas Et Gloria Ducunt), #536636, #12-C.S.B., ENG. The envelope had been opened and resealed by CENSOR 3373. Envelope was stamped with 12th Canadian Siege Battery stamp, and postmarked, "Farnborough, 10.45.AM, 7 FE 18"

Reg. #536636
#12 Canadian S. Bty. CGA
BEF France
22nd May, 1918

My darling Grandmother:–
For once I have four full hours when I am sure of being undisturbed––just the chance for a word with you—eh?

In my letter to Mildred not long ago I told her of my fine visit leave in Northern Wales and a few English Places. She has no doubt told you all about it so I won't repeat it.

Whether I told her about getting "admonished and two day's pay stopped" or not I do not remember—this the colonel gave me as a punishment for staying away two days overtime—it was well worth the trouble to me for one can not see Wales in a a day. However since I know how anxious you are to have me keep a clean crime sheet I will say for the benefit of us both that that little extra vacation is not considered bad enough to dirty my sheet—which so far has never been touched. Further, to give you an idea of my physical condition may as well add that my name has never appeared on the hospital or sick list. Never was better—the worst thing I have had being a cold which I lost way-back in Partridge Island in Canada. And for the final—both you and Aunt Mary who so well remember what "rampings" my teeth used to give me—well say that my teeth trouble got its "finis" long before my enlistment. So much for that then.

A few days ago the several...

The remainder of this letterr is mising—lost—censored—for whatever reason.

Plain military stationary in censored (6359), resealed envelope bearing the 12th Canadian Siege Battery Orderly Room stamp, and postmarked, "Codford, St Mary, 6 P.M. 26 MY 18". Return: Reg. #536636, #12CSB, BEF France.

Reg. #536636
BEF France
16th June, 1918

My dear Grandmother:–

The most I have to write about is the lack of news. In the first place it's no news for me to be in perfect health so far as I know for I never was much better than now—plenty of exercise, hardy food, open outside life––and good weather. Just two rains in two weeks.

A few words regarding my home here, which I like rather well, will help to fill up space. Tho I have already written and rewritten about the same thing to other folks. It is situated between two mounds, dug down deep below the surface, and made to look as much like the surrounding surface as possible on the outside, with a bunk, two box seats, a fireplace, shelves, bully-beef biscuit tins under the bed for closets for things we don't want mice and roaches into and well—generally cozy if you please inside. The fellow with whom I spent my last pass, Gunner Bosdet, is my mate. Most of our work was done by moonlight, for we were busy most of the day. Why do we have one bunk you ask—that's easy. You see when I am doing my twenty-four hours duty, he is off twenty-four hours—the next day, matters are just reversed.

How is the garden acting this year—and what other happenings are there in Berwick which may interest me? Would like very much to walk into your little white cottage today—but will have to put it off for a few months.

Got two letters from home yesterday; the folks seem to be quite happy over their new home. Am sure they will all like the place, for it is two large a family for a small house.

Things are very quiet to-day—it seems a lot like Sunday—for Sunday it is—but any other day has me guessing. I have hard work to keep in mind the day and date, time goes so fast.

So much for this time.
Regards to the Shoreys,
Love to you and Aunt Mary,

Clifton
No envelope.

B.E.F. France . 10th July, '18

Dearest Grandmother:–

Yours of 13th June arrived lately, and must mention the fact that so long and nice a letter sure did make things more rosy and spoke well for yourself. Such a big fat letter from U.S.A. just fits the pocket and heart fine. Just do it some more when time and news permits. Quite true, Mildred's letters are always bright and newsy—and go to the right spot—but don't let that keep your own back.

Am glad the garden has got a decent start—that ought to please Aunt Mary—but the eight chicks—I'll bet she feels like a lost sailor on a desert with only eight to worry over. Just tell her that in my travels since my battery came out of the line for a bit of rest in a real quiet town—I have found a little red brick cottage—the home of two sisters—one of whom understands English—and both of whom are very much like the two sisters on Bell St., Berwick. One is altogether interested in keeping the house shipshape—the other always fretting about outside—hunting up stray chicks, killing bugs on her vegetables and fighting a continuous war on rats and cats. Tho there are two cats about the place—and I'll say she wouldn't kill one even if she caught it. Meanwhile, they keep a room for use as an estaminet—which is simply the word for a small scale shop where wine and beer, coffee and milk as well as eggs may be bought. Of course you know that in France wine and beer are used in place of water—–or at least were before the war. The arrival of Canadians at first caused many surprises and eventually changes—for the Frenchman had yet to learn that when Americans got thirsty they drank water—not alcohol. So don't hold the fact that they sell some drinks against them, for I like both their shop and themselves—for it's a bit of home.

Never worry about the troubles I have for they are very few—[I] have learned to be happy and healthy under any circumstances. Before we know it Ill be walking up Bell St. Time goes fast and war must end eventually.

Love to Aunt Mary—Regards to Shoreys.

Clifton

Military envelope/letter combination. Passed by Censor No. 5086, Postmarked: 20 JUL. 18

B.E.F. France
September 18th, 1918

Dearest Grandma:

Yours of the middle August arrived on the 4th—as usual you were the first to remind me that I had a birthday coming in the near future with a very pretty card. My last birthday was certainly different from any previous one, but no more so than this year's 2nd October will be. In fact it seems that luck is doing its level best to make every birthday as different from the previous one as possible—and certainly has been successful for at least six years. However, you may take my word for it that 2nd October, 1919 will be more like the style of about 1909 or -10, than any other since then.

We have been working lately under a new system for this unit—results of which are to me a great deal better than ever before. Instead of all hands sticking to our positions for the duration of our stay in that spot, there are reliefs—a certain number of days are spent where all we do is eat, sleep, repair damage to our clothing, etc, get cleaned up in general and an occasional fatigue, with no sound of guns or war of any kind—a genuine rest—then we get another spell back on the job for a time twice that of our rest—and while on the job you may be sure we are busy—few chances for letter writing. When we come to the rest spot we are some tired—when we leave we are ready for anything, and today being my second one out of the noise I am sure feeling fit.

There seem to be a couple of pages missing, for the narrative continues as follows

...days for Raymond since then, and now for the vines. The fruit must look pretty good hanging from the roof and sides. Auntie sure has a fad for making her pie-fruit climb—when it isn't dwellings, hen-yard fences or wood-sheds, it is "police stations." Wow! But this fighting for Democracy is all right since it seems we must do it—but it would be much more so if we could get home in time for the using up of the afore-mentioned pie-fruit. I have eaten French pies—but oh us Yanks and Cannucks can show them something! Even the Army issue pies on certain occasions, but tho they are better than the ordinary run of such articles, they can be beaten. Enough of pies then—just what makes me want pie and talk pie so much to-day for is more than I know—unless this be the pie season of the year, & my letter is to the two champion pie makers of the world.

While I was out on my rest the last time, I sat in this same little cozy hole in the wall of the trench and wrote home—while writing a kitten walking across the wire jumped into the trench and we two speedily became acquainted. I was just thinking of her and where she went when I had to go back up the line—and behold—ye kitten's mind must have been thinking of me for here she is—returned to my hole now that I am back—guess she is hungry and my stomach says time for lunch too—so goodbye & love to you both. Clifton

No envelope. Letter on Canadian YMCA stationary.

CHURCH ARMY RECREATION UNIT
OR TENT

No. 4 General Hospital, B.E.F. France, October 16, 1918

Dearest Grandma—

Above all do not be frightened because my heading includes a hospital. True I did not come here by choice, but since I am here, and am out of bed again and running around as usual in my hospital suit of blue, am getting the best rest I have had for months. Reason for my winding up at the base is due to a very light touch of ga—one of Fritz's weapons of war which without breaking any bones sure breaks a fellow's heart for awhile. However under care of the finest of Briton's doctors and nurses a fellow is soon out of bed and ready for business. And speaking of beds—can you imagine the comfort of a soft, clean, white bed after months of hard, dirty and scarcely white bunks found "up the line"? No madam, instead of worrying about my state of health—just assure yourself that the comforts derived from being here are almost worth the discomfort endured at first..

The country about here is very different from any I have met with in France since en route to our first position. The hospital is pretty well surrounded with big hills—have not climbed them yet, but if they keep me here a day or two longer I'll know what is on the other side by seeing it from the top. As is my walks have been only along the different walks and roads near my own ward,—from the top of any of these hills I should be able to get a fine view.

Yesterday while finishing a letter to Mother one of my mates who came down the line with me but who got separated at the C.C.G., walked up and I learned that we have been in the same ward all the time. Our luck is poor there tho—for mate goes off to Blighty while I remain (so far as I know) at the Base.

Speaking of meeting mates—old timers—yesterday was my big day. During a walk to the Church Army Hut I met a fellow in Yankee uniform who looked natur—he seemed to think I looked familiar as well—and before we had spoken we knew each other. He was a member of the 1st Mass. Amb. Corps in Boston—and we were side numbers on the same ambulance at Framingham. A good chat resulted.

All manner of British troops are in this war—thus plenty of life and humor to pass away the time. Furthermore, breakfast is up and my appetite is as lively as ever—both you and Aunt May know the meaning of that.

So love to the both of you and regards to folks interested.
Write soon,

Clifton

Statinary provided by "Church ARMY". Envelope opened/passed by Censor No. 8207. Postmarked: "[unreadable] 17 OC 18"

S company, #12 Convalescent Camp
B.E.F. France. 8/11/18

Dearest Grandma:

Have not heard from Berwick for a long time—is everyone well as usual? Even Mildred has deserted me or else has not received my letters of Sept 15th and October 17th. However I can forgive her all if you will just drop a few lines now.

The weather here has been of the dampest—plenty of mud and other accessories to weeks of rain. Today however dawned with a frost covering everything in the open—our tent flap crackled and snapped in fine style when we hopped out of our warm blankets at reveille. The sun got to work early and all bids fair to be dry and fine by night. It is so clear now that we can see for miles out on the Atlantic from our camp on a coast hill. The smacks and steamers seem to forget that there is a war on—they with the calm manner which the few farmers about here are hauling in their turnips or preparing the ground for next spring produce such a peaceful appearance that the spirit of the troops is high. Not only that but the chalk cliffs of Dover—across the channel are very plain today—hundreds of lads whose homes are in Blighty are cheered by that sight—tho the camp spirit here is of the best—all the rain in France can't quench their feeling.

The proper amount of physical training and the afternoon hikes are making us more fit for the line than we were when we came down. Good food and plenty of sleep are also great factors in the freshness of our health. These things with regular passes to town and the numerous manners of recreation are making me feel better than ever—so much so that the doctor will soon decide that my wounds are completely healed and away on the job I'll go, and ready for anything too since a better rest and change I have not had for months.

Naturally in the hospital I made acquaintances which came in handy when we reached our convalescent camp—now all of them have returned to duty but me—however I have the companionship of several other Canadians so we are well away.

Wish I could spend this Thanksgiving with you—however next year either that or Xmas day will be spent at #16 Bell St.

Since this letter will be the nearest to Xmas of any, accept my love and best wishes for a Merry one now. *(runing out of ink, he continues in pencil)* (Ink gone!) Of course this includes Aunt Mary—her hens and your kittens!!

Regards to Shoreys and other friends interested.

Love, Clifton

Plain Military starionary, passed by Censor No. _935[?]. No postmark.

Reg. #536636 C.G.A.
B.E.F. France
11th December, '18

Dearest Grandma—

Address to my battery as usual. After a short search I arrived back to my unit last Saturday—finding them quartered very comfortably in a convent. Parades are not at all hard so that much of the time is our own. Getting acquainted with the towns about here especially the larger ones, mixing with the civilians more than we have for some time, concerts, plenty to read—and always letters to write—well you see, time does not hang too heavily on our hands. Under all the other feelings tho is the one big desire—no matter how fine the Belgians or French treat us—home is what we are looking forward to now in the near future.

In Valenciennes a week ago I met a lad from Somersworth by some chance—tho we had never known each other we were not long in learning that each knew many of the same families at home so naturally we enjoyed the hour we had together. On Sunday last I was in Mons which by the way is quite a town. I hope soon to get to Brussels which all the fellows tell me is a very interesting city. Antwerp too—according to a mate of mine is also worth taking in—but I have a very poor chance of seeing the interesting points of all Europe or even Belgium or France since our time in each town is usually limited.

Have not had my usual mail since going down the line but hope now that I am back to get it all soon.

Weather here is very moderate—tho a bit too rainy—how about Berwick? How are you and Aunt Mary feeling this Xmas—how goes things in general? Has Mildred been around lately—how is she—and her folks? How about those of your particular little circle? Please write and tell Mildred that if she does not hear from me 'tis not because I do not write—she should not wait for a letter before writing.

Jolliest of Xmases & best of New Year to you all.

Love, Clifton

Plain Military Stationary. Envelope passed by Censor No. 6599, Postmarked: "Army Opst Office, 15 DE 18"

Reg #536636 C.G.A.
B.E.F. France
X'mas Day

Dearest Grandma:

The Christmas that we all expected to be so unlike X'mas has so far proved out to be somewhat like X'mas after all. The first snow of the year in this part of Belgium fell during the night—and this morning dawned unusually bright and snappy, with patches of snow here and there over the houses and fields. And even now at mid-afternoon there is some snow left. After breakfast my section met in one of the billets and received cigars, tobacco and candy from our section commander, and his wife in Canada. Of course there are no parades to-day—and in spite of any reason there may be for our not enjoying X'mas as usual—that reason is being brushed aside for the spirit of Christmas has invaded the place in a most earnest way. A mate and I had made arrangements to spent the afternoon and evening with some civilian friends in Hornu—but as it happened my mate was hit for guard duty. As a result I have taken his place since it is quite important that he should keep his engagement whereas it makes little difference to me. This evening our battery will have its X'mas dinner in a very good hall in town - and it is to be some dinner too. Roast turkey and all the fixings, vegetables of all the necessary kinds, puddings, good things to drink—we shall be well off indeed. There won't be any pumpkin pie such as I used to get, and hope to get yet before very long at #16 Bell St.—but there are numerous substitutes. One of the best things of all is the fact that the War is over!—and that we know, in so far as it is possible, where our next X'mas is to be spent.

We are no longer quartered at Boussu, but have changed for billets which are more quiet and which are not uncomfortable. Our particular hostess is very kind - forever trying to make us more comfortable. Much of our washing she does for the sake of the help it is to us. Last night she cooked some ruffles —n other words queer looking things tasting much like our own griddle cakes—those with syrup which we made ourselves went very well indeed. On the whole we are quite well off.

My turn for the beat comes in about five minutes so will finish up with love for you and Aunt Mary, and regards for the Shoreys and others who may ask for me. We may well feel thankful that there is such a short while between now and the time when I shall give you my love in person. Write soon.

Clifton

Letter written on plain, lined paper. No envelope.

Reg. #536636 C.G.A.
St. Symphorien, Belgium
26 Feb., 1919

Dearest Grandma:–

Am absolutely out of paper of the proper sort for writing but I am sure it matters not to you what I use. Returned to my battery a few days ago after a fifteen day absence to Paris. While there made side trips to Versailles, Malmaison, Suresnes, and Fountainbleau and came home by way of Rouen, Etaples, Arras, Valenciennes and Mons—a fine trip in every way. Got back hungry, tired, dirty and "broke"—but happy (SATISFIED AT LEAST), not because of leaving Paris but because of what I had seen. I hardly believed it likely that Paris would give me a better time than Bruxelles—Belgium's capitol—never-the-less she did. From my first day there, when I met an old Canadian Scottish friend and thru him made numerous other acquaintances. Until the day I came away—your most loving son was as busy a lad as any in that city.

As far as was possible I made all my visits explorations, with all the necessary etc's, by foot. As a result I think I have seen the place as thoroughly as is possible for a Canadian soldier to see in the time. It would take a book to tell you of all the places that filled in my time—on one day it would be the museums, Louvre or Luxemburg for instance, another time churches, Madeline for example, and all the time taking in monuments— Eiffel Tower, Les Invalides and Napoleon's resting place (the former holds the most complete set of War Trophies from the present back to ages so dusty they are all but forgotten), the Pantheon, Bastille prison, Chamber of Deputies, Observatory, Palais Rolyale, Hotel de Ville—oh I cannot begin to name them all—and it would only tire you if I did. Enjoyed a very beautiful trip on the rivers Seine and Marne by launch. At Versailles after finishing with the Palace and Peace Conference, my mate and I worked in three hours of excellent skating on the King's Lake. While at Malmaison looking over old Napoleon's chateau—and just beginning to realize what "imperial beauty" of his day was like—I met an old friend who was with me for a while in Scotland and later in north Wales. That evening we enjoyed the Opera—the music and general run of the dramas enacted— tho I confess the language was beyond me. Many other theatres came in my programme too, of course, from a light musical comedy to the deepest kind of drama old Paris produces. Oh it was all very fine, I would not have missed it for a year's pay—but now that I have seen it—am more anxious than ever to tread on good old New England soil once more. The Bois du Boulogne produced a find district for an afternoon hike when I grew a bit tired of the city. Of course I visited the business district among the first because the main stores of all cities attract me very much—in this case Printemps and Galleries du Lafayette seem to be Paris' most grande. It was good to get back to something like civil conveniences for a while—the noise, bustle and confusion of the streets have done me a lot of good—it was fine to be able to step onto a tram or take the Metro (subway) to any point you wanted to reach—and better still were the baths, meal service, and beds in my hotel.

The different soldiers' institutions reached about their highest success in Paris too. My quarters were for the most part at Hotel d' Sena— now managed by our Canadian Y.M.C.A., formerly one of the finest hotels there—is yet of course. But all the other clubs and organizations for troops are on a like scale—the British Army and Navy League Club is the finest thing of its kind I have found—it is at Hotel Morden. The American Red Cross Canteens (for Yankees only—but I felt that I had the right to use them) were another great asset to my purse.

And after all my three pages of chatter I must come tumbling back to little old St. Symphorien, about the most pitiful specimen of a town this side of the water—but we are leaving March 6th for France, where we wait until the 12th, and off to Weymouth, England. There we get eight days leave—go thru all kinds of demobilization stunts and sail for Canada about the middle of April. Now then Susan Allard and Mary Banfil, expect this boy of yours to come traveling in any time after FIRST OR middle May.

Have not talked about the gardens and chicks this time but of course you're expected to. Love to you & Auntie.

Regards to Shoreys,

Clifton

(G. Please tell Mildred her letter is on its way to her—will leave tomorrow..)

Plain Military stationary. Envelope Passed by Censor No.. 6599, and postmarked: ARMY POST OFFICE 27 FE 19.

The following letter was written to CJC's younger brother, Raymond. CCC

St. Symphorien, Belgium
28th February, 1919

Dear Ray:–

What in the name of commonsense are you doing in Somersworth, N.H., at work, when you should be in Waverly, Mass., in school? Come old sport, out with it—what happened? Have we ceased to be partners? There must be some mighty good reason why you would drop your studies in this manner—and it is not complimentary to me when you do it and won't even let a fellow know it. As soon as I return from Europe it is back to the books for me for awhile—and surely if I am going on as usual you are not the pal to desert me. You do not intend to make your life's work whatever it will grow to from the position you now have—the idea in this game is to make yourself capable of drawing down the best possible salary—isn't it? And it is a cinch that if a chap quits the studies at High School the day will soon come when he has reached the position where his limit of responsibility lies—that means that from then on he draws the same pay until he begins to go down instead of up. A fine outlook that— I don't think—and neither do you. If you want to work until next Fall— c'est bien, but start in again with me then. How about it old-timer—have I your promise to "carry on" with me—to stick to the studies until we are qualified to tackle a job proper—until our brains are developed to a degree that will help to hold down a responsible position? Think it over hard—and let me know in your next letter which I hope won't be too long in coming...

...Our branch of the Khaki-College of Canada, known as the University of St. Symphorien, helps to pass away quite a bit of time for members of the 2nd Brigade, C.G.A. (my brigade). My studies—Spanish and Stenography—one hour of each per day. Of course guard-duties, leaves, and odds and ends of things are continually interrupting the class-work, however, it does serve to get the brain back into a fairly smooth running condition.

We are leaving Belgium for Le Havre, France, on the sixth of March. Leave Le Havre on the twelfth for Weymouth, England. While there, demobilization commences and by the 1st of May (we leave "Blighty" for Canada the middle of April). I shall be pretty nearly ready to go home. While in England we get eight days leave—most of which I shall spend in Ireland, the remainder in Cornwall and Devonshire. The latter is the section of England that Gertrude recommends—and being British, she ought to know.

Now then Ray it is 11 P.M., and I am as sleepy as the town I am in—so after going out and dropping a few bully-beef tins in the general vicinity of a home-sick cat just outside I am going to roll up in my blankets and get the full benefit of some sleep.

Think over my first paragraph, and then write—but don't be too long in thinking about it—I want a letter—and besides there can only be one answer for us sport.

As ever

Your brother and pal. Clif

Reg. #536636 Gnr. C.J. Cate
3rd Bde., C.G.A., 12th Bty.
B.E.F.., France

St, Symphorien, Belgium
27th March, 1919

Dearest Grandmother:–
This is certainly to be a very short letter but it contains—what is to the writer—good news. To-morrow at this time I shall (my whole brigade for that matter) be en route to Le Havre, France. From there to Southhampton, England is only a step. From England to Canada a mere matter of—circumstances as produced by the future. At any rate after my leave—during which I hope to visit Ireland and the Cornwall-Devonshire district of England—we will be well under-way towards the finish of our stay on the wrong side of the Atlantic.

Life in St. Symphorien goes on unaltered—the usual sports, parades (the word as we use it means—falling in for roll-call and inspection), the usual hikes over the usual ground. Occasionally a long one to Mons, or perhaps a pass to N_?_ or Challroi.

As far as my health is concerned—am O.K. As far as what I want most to see now is concerned—it is home and the old faces. I am not the only lad in this Canadian Expeditionary Force whose tears on parting will be other than tears of sorrow.

Good weather should be well under-way by the time I cross the Canadian-United States border. Here at present it is just as common to have snow, rain, sun, cold or heat—anything at all seems to be the style.

We have received our last continental mail—but that does not mean "stop writing"—one never knows how long we may be in "Blighty" or in Canada. When I walk in on you some time in May or June—then you may say—"guess Clifton isn't looking forward to a letter for a few days at any rate."

Now then this queer scribble has hardly taken on the appearance of a letter—was not supposed to—but just before I turned around (dog-fashion) to find some soft spot of my tile-floor-bed—I wanted to show you that as usual—from my first day here until to-day, my last—Mildred Shorey, Aunt Susan and my Aunt Mary are occupying a place in my mind and heart.

Love to you both, and regards to the Shoreys.

Clifton.

Plain Military Stationery. Enveloped passed by Censor No. 6___, postmarked:

Army Post Office 28 MR 19.

(Fragment of a letter written in Ireland)

Robinson's Temperance Hotel
82, Donegall Street
Belfast.
14th April 1919

Dearest Grandma:–
Just a word from old Ireland that you may know that...

(Envelopes without letters)

1. On YMCA stationery stamped, "Orderly Room, 12th Canadian Siege Battery",. Postmarked, "Farnborough, 1.45 PM, 4 MR, 18". Return: #536636, #12 C.S.Bn., Deepcut, Hants.

2. Plain envelope Censored (3373) and resealed. Envelope stamped with 12th Canadian Siege Battery stamp, and postmarked, [unreadable], 19 AP 18. Return: Reg #536636, #12 CSB, A.P.O. Eng.

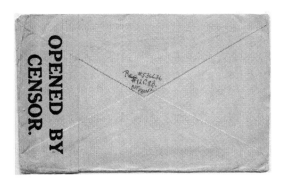

Leaves: (Canadian Service)–naming the following destinations (which had little to do with where one actually went): Edinborough, Conway, Boussu, Bruxelles, Paris, Belfast and others in Scotland, Wales, Belgium, France and Ireland—Properly called Pass.

Maps: City of Paris; 40 Miles about Bettws-y-coed; British Isles; War fronts and areas.

Match case: From the "Old Banjo Tavern", #38–40 rue du Pont-Neuf, Brussels, Belgium. Here, Bill Frosdick, (from Norwich) made a "Specialty OLD SCOTCH–ALE the Glass 50 centimes, also amuse the boys with his Banjo, Dulcimer and One string fiddle that he managed to make during his stay with Fritz." and, "GOOD AIRED BEDS."

Mauretania: (See Books, Ribbons, Photo Album, Post Card Album, and Frieze.)

May flowers: The bunch mentioned on page 122, from Truro, N.S., May 1919.

Medals: Canadian Victory; British General Service; American Victory; and one presented by the town of Sharon, Massachusetts to those who went overseas from that town.

Mirror & Case: Carried thru much of my active service without a crack. Purchased in France in early 1918.

Mug: Miniature beer mug from Germany.

Note: From one artillery man to another which I was never able to deliver for certain definite reasons.

Notebooks: (See Books)

Papers: Dropped to us from airplanes, as: "KEEP YOUR MOUTH SHUT! The success of any operation we carry out depends chiefly on surprise. DO NOT TALK–When you know that your Unit is making preparations for an attack, don't talk about them to men in other Units or to strangers, and keep your mouth shut, especially in public places. Do not be inquisitive about what other Units are doing; if you hear or see anything, keep it to yourself. If you hear anyone else talking about operations, stop him at once. The success of the operations and the lives of your comrades depend upon your SILENCE. If you ever should have the misfortune to be taken prisoner, don't give the enemy any information beyond your rank and name. In answer to all other questions you need only say, "I cannot answer." He cannot compel you to give any other information. He may use threats. He will respect you if your courage, patriotism, and self-control do not fail. Every word you say may cause the death of one of your comrades. Either after or before you are openly examined, Germans, disguised as British Officers or men, will be sent among you or will await you in the cages or quarters or hospital to which you are taken. Germans will be placed where they can overhear what you say without being seen by you. DO NOT BE TAKEN IN BY ANY OF THESE TRICKS" [See *scan. Chapter V]*; Dental Exam; Discharge–USA; Discharge–C.E.F.; Dispersal Certificate; Facts About the War; Caucasus Campaigne of Russia; Paris Chamber of Commerce–March 1916; Form of Will; Gratuity Notices; Inventory Wounded Man's Effects; Medal Notice; Seal of Gt. Britain–"His Majesty the King has been graciously pleased to authorize the issue of the enclosed medal, which I am directed by the Honourable the Minister of Militia and Defense to convey to you herewith," signed by the Adj. Gen., Canadian Militia—etc; Permit to Proceed to U.S. ordcr.; Soldier's Will; War Service Badge Certificate; Also, such forms as were supplied by government and private parties for registered letters and soldier's postal-cards, telegrams, cables.

Pipes: Chinese pipe –a swap aboard the Grampian.

Pen: Waterman Fountain - carried throughout service in both armies.

Pencil Portrait of U.S. Sailor: By Ray Cate November 11, 1918.

Photo (Aerial): Showing town and trench system under fire, 9/28/17. Location 36c–N4acd–10ab.

Photographs: See Album for prints of Chinese Labor Corps for report of one sick member who tried smoking the pipe I gave him in exchange); German–large bowl, long stem, brought back to me by Ray Cate from Danzig, Germany.

Pipers Lead the March: Print of Highlanders "going in" with the bags squealing out a march.

Plane: Piece of airplane wing from the wreckage of the first plane witnessed by me to crash, in which loss of life resulted. *(See Chapter IV)*

Post Cards: See album for cards.

Post card envelopes: Jackets of cards purchased in many places.

Programs: Banjo Tavern; Cabaret Madrid; Casino de Paris; Gaiety (Dublin); Gaite (Brussels); Garrison Theatre (NACB at Rhyl, Wales); L'Alhambra (Mons); Race (22nd Army Corps at Nimy, Belgium); Royal Hippodrome (Belfast); Ulster Hall (Belfast); YMCA Sightseeing Trip; etc.

Patrique Robichaud: In which Lieut. Walker of the 9th Battery puts words into a French-Canadian's mouth in poetic fashion, describing his enlistment in the 4th Battery of Home Defense. Pat's story follows:

My name is Patrique Aime Isidore Robichaud;

I libe la bas in Kent County till seven mount' ago -
In summer work my fader's place - milk cow an' mak de hay -
An' all de winter chop on wood for two tree dollar day.

I got one frien' to me also call Jadus Arsenault
Dat's always lookin' out for troub' an'always on de go;
An' so I'm not so moche surprise to hear dat feller say
He mak voyage to Richebucto — she's fifteen mile away.

De ver' nex' Monday afternoon Jadus come back encore;
I see him passin' up de road 'bout half pas' two tree four.
He's holler out, "Mon cher Patrique, you lak come off wit' me
Be soger on some Ile Partridge on Comical Batterie?"

When Jadus spik lak dat I tink he mus' be gone crazee,
But when he's tole me all his news, dat job look good to me —
One dollar ten for every day an' plantee grub to eat
Wit' fine new uniform to wear — I make my min' trees vite.

Jadus arrange de whole bizness. He's put himself en route
An' spik some man on telephone is officer of recruit.
Nex' day we pass us on de train — don'have to pay no fare;
King George is settlin' all de bill; for money he don' care.

Nex' morning on Saint Jean we walk long tam to fin' some bridge
For pass us on dat soger place dey call de Ile Partridge.
But someone tole us after while de only ting do do
Is go on board of big steamboat dat's call de Sissiboo.

We fin' de boat all right, but when we mak' de embarquer,
We don' feel too moch satisfy — no money lef' for pay.
But some big general on deck - McCollom he is call -
Is tole us not to scare ourse'f; King George arrange for all.

When de capitaine get front end in front an' back end at the back,
He fin' tree little fishin' boats is takin' all de track.
He rng some bell to stop de ship till all dem boat go by;
But all de swear word he is spik soun' lak, "My my, my my."

[*The following passage comes from Chapter III.*]

De Sissiboo is ver' nice ship when she is by the shore
But near dat Isle Partridge she roll, an' den she roll some more.
You 'member how dose voyageurs go sick lak little pup . . .
An' every tam de ship go down, de inside she go up?

Well jus' lak dat an' mebbe worse de inside she is go,
On me an' on my frien' also, dis Jadus Arsenault.

There are 3 blank pages in the original manuscript indicating that the saga of Mr Robichaud is only partly represented. To date, I have been unnable to unearth the origin of this delightful ballad. CCC

Receipts: Of a varied nature.

Registration: Police form for hotel in Dublin.

Ribbons: Military Cross–part of ribbon similar to that with which our Major (Colon McKay) was decorated at Mons in 1919; American and Canadian Victory; British General Service; Sharon Medal; R.M.S. Mauretania; Belgian shoulder strap ribbon.

Rose of Meharicourt: Petals from the rose referred to in the text and poem *(See Chapter V)*.

Souvenir: Of the "Poker Battle of Rhyl" won by Bosdet.

Swagger Stick: Bamboo cane with leather wrist strap and tassel, a gift from Suzy de Paris in February, 1919.

Telegrams: Several—one in particular informing Mother that "private Clifton Joseph Cate transferred to No. 5 Rest Camp" shortly after she had received information that he had been killed in action. (Not that time!)

Testimonials: Regarding service in War–from U.S.A., Massachusetts, and the Town of Sharon (Mass.).

Tickets (Transportation): Amiens to Paris; Mailot to Suresnes & Malmaison; Ferry across St. John River; Halifax to Glasgow on the SS Grampian; Southampton to Halifax on the Mauretania (the last two include berth and meals); Halifax to St. John (C.N.R.); Royal Transport Officer out of Rhyl, Etaples and Mons; Paris trams - also trams in Etaples, Suresnes, Porte Maillot, Mons, & Boussu; Subway tickets from Paris Metro, Poissonniere, Madeleine, Etoille, Maillot, St. Lazarre, Boissiere, Dauphine, Le Peletiere, Paris Nord-Sud, Montparnasse, Solferino, and others.

Tickets (Theatre): L'Alhambra (Mons); Casino de Paris (Paris); English Cinema (Lydd); Gaite (Brussels); Gaiety (Dublin); Hippodrome (Belfast & Sheerness); Cinema (Jemappes); Malmaison & Exposition Napoleonienne; Moderne & Palais (Brussels); Omnia (Paris); Palais du Trocadero (Paris); Societe Les Amis Reunis (St. Symphorien); Garrison (Rhyl); and many others.

Tickets (Meal & Lodging): Mauretania; Grampian; LeHavre; (Breakfast, dinner, tea, supper at various camps); Hotel D'I'ena (Paris - Canadian Y.M.C.A.); 100 gram bread and 25 gram sugar (as issued with leaves to Paris, etc.)

Tickets & Cards (Identification, hotels, misc.): Kinmel Park Camp; British Army & Navy League (Paris); other Paris lodgings; D'Ostend; Empire; Florida; Paris Army; Salvation Army; Church Army; Soldiers' Hostel; Windsor and others (some of these may have been outside Paris); Message cards from YMCA and Crown Hotel in Dublin; Welcome Card issued by K.C. of Canada, Church Army Huts; Farewell cards from Chaplains of Abergele, Wales on our departure for Canada, etc.

Uniform A: (U.S. Army issue) - Complete "O.D." woolen outfit, ditto in cottons; Cords from all branches of service; (Canadian Army issue) - Field Artillery great coat; Imperial roll-collar tunic; soft trench cap; bedford-cord breeches (purchased T.J.Calaghan, Dublin); roll puttees (Fox's); Boots (dress & issue); and misc. articles.

Uniform B: Insignia and Markings (Buttons); "CANADA"–for shoulder straps; "12"; "9"; "C.G.A."; "C.F.A."; "C.A.M.C."; the maple leaf in copper; brass with and without artillery markings; cap ornaments (the artillery gun with its "Quo Fas et Gloria Ducunt" and "Ubique"—("Everywhere"—locations to which the 3rd Artillery Brigade might be expected to be found in the case of need); the bursting grenade for the fusilier, etc.); service chevrons of blue silk, "wound stripes" of gold silk thread and of brass; 3rd Brigade Artillery markings buttons; brass and black eagle; brass Imperial and Canadian Artillery; dull leather for line service; German gray Crown and "Gott Mit Uns"; etc.

Watch: Just before leaving for Canada Dad White presented me with an Ingersoll wrist watch. "Gren" painted the figures and hands with radium paint. Twice during the following two years the watch mysteriously disappeared and twice it was less mysteriously returned. It served me more than well—timing the firing of "A" gun and thus on many occasions the whole battery of six guns. In fair and foul weather, under hottest fire and during the calms, in action, on leave and in hospital this little friend stood by me, ticking lustily away and ever reliable as a time piece. At all times—especially during the mean, cold, dreary and dark night hours when "on watch"—it was a tangible bit of "HOME". Its glowing hands and figures supplied warmth to a tired spirit—it was indeed a friend. Then I came "home" and someone (probably the meanest man or woman in the world) caused it to disappear a third and last time. The loss of a friend is a tragedy!!!

(See the Kit Bag, a scrapbook of souvenirs; the Photo Album, a collection of war time "snaps"; the Post Card Album, a collection of post cards from many places; and the Gold Box which holds a few more souvenirs.   CJC)

* * * * * * * * * * * *

Note: The Gold Box has quite vanished, but the Kit Bag, and both Photo Albums were still in existence, along with several remaining articles of equipment when I undertook the task of resurrecting my father's Memoir in the spring of 2001. The goal was to bring to light as much as possible the remarkable journey and reminiscences of a father who rarely said anything at all about these happenings to a son who, sadly, felt it too intrusive, perhaps, to ask. I did the work partly in order to share its contents with the other children of Gnr. Cate, and their children to follow, that they all be gifted with this unique window to the (our) past. But more especially I did it for me, because what was an undefinable sense of irretrievable loss, was partially allayed by a mystical sense of sharing as my young father and I finally got to travel those times together. CCC

12th Battery, 3rd Artillery Brigade, CGA, St. Symphorein, Belgium, 1919

Canadian Artillerymen of the 12ᵗʰ Battery, 3ʳᵈ Brigade, C.E.F. (Left to right). <u>Sitting</u>: Ferney, Henderson, Leverman, White, ?, ?, Hoag, *McCraie, Stratton, Mason, Rich, Walker, **May. <u>2ⁿᵈ Row</u>: Holmes, Byers, Philips, Hutchinson, Brown, Dawson, Landry, ?, **QMSgt Bailey, **Allaby, Lt. Agnew, **Sgt.Mjr .Candy, *West, McCollem, Richey, *Thompson, Graham, *Bachman, ***Simmons (front), Turner (rear), ***Robertson, Fraser. <u>3ʳᵈ Row</u>: Fennamore, McCloud, Joyce, Malley, Trethaway, Jacques, Jeffries, English, McIlvity, ***Smith, ?, Sharpe, Wyllie, *Puddington, Sills, ***Triggett, **Lee, Lambert, Mawhinney, Sharpe, **Troop. <u>4ᵗʰ Row</u>: Snowball, Stacey, Ryan, Murphy, Gonzalles, Foley, Cunningham, McInnis, ***Grey, Bullock, ***Emm, ***Smith,?, ***Yates, McNutt, Cameron (the only man present of the "Big-4"–Bosdet, Fisher, and Cate were in hospital).

(* Corporal, ** Sergeant, *** Signalman. All others, except Lt Agnew, were Bombardiers or Gunners.)

177

ISBN 1-41205355-2

Made in the USA
Lexington, KY
18 November 2012